THE
ACCIDENTAL
SPY

SEAN O'DRISCOLL

m
B
MIRROR BOOKS

First published by Mirror Books in 2019

Mirror Books is part of Reach plc
10 Lower Thames Street
London EC3R 6EN
England

www.mirrorbooks.co.uk

ISBN 978-1-912624-34-8

1 3 5 7 9 10 8 6 4 2

For Sarah Hale, without whom
this book simply could not have been written.

For my parents, PJ and Enda, for Yvette Moya Angeler,
Michael Gallagher and for the people of Omagh.

INTRODUCTION

The first time I saw David Rupert was on the front page of a Sunday newspaper.

It was a picture of a smiling, heavy-set American man at an Irish republican fundraising event in Chicago. I picked up the newspaper at a Spar shop in the centre of Dublin. Other people were picking up the same newspaper, one after another, reading the headlines and looking at the photo.

The headline screamed that the FBI and MI5 had planted a spy inside the army council of the Real IRA and that its leader, Mickey McKevitt, and a dozen others, had been arrested.

This mysterious trucker turned FBI informant immediately became the object of a media obsession and endless rumours in Ireland. Who was he and where did he come from? Was he an FBI agent posing as a trucker, or a trucker who joined the FBI?

One tabloid newspaper reported that he was from Madrid, Spain. Others quickly corrected it – he was born in Madrid in upstate New York. Every major UK newspaper sent reporters there to discover who he really was. His sister, the local school secretary, received a call from a journalist claiming to be his sister and explaining that the family needed his school photo. When his real sister explained who she was, the woman hung up.

In the centre of Madrid, reporters were dressing up in waders and redneck T-shirts, trying to blend in with what they thought rural America looked like, as they roamed around town searching for answers.

They discovered that he had since moved to the American Midwest. A British reporter called the beauty salon in his new home town to find out if his wife was a customer and if they sold butt implants.

The *Sunday Times* and the *Boston Globe* had reporters parked outside his house, waiting for him for days.

Reporter after reporter tried to interview his family and friends, his former workmates and his three ex-wives. Book deals were offered through his lawyer – there have been four journalists before me who have tried to tell his story, but each time he walked away.

After the journalists came a wave of Irish republicans and private detectives, driving into town looking for anything to discredit Rupert. His brother drove one Real IRA supporter away with a handgun.

All that time, Rupert and his wife, Maureen, were touring America in an FBI-hired car, staying out of Irish bars and anywhere the press were likely to gather.

"I was good at that because I'm never one for talking to strangers," he said.

His reticence is what impressed Real IRA leader McKevitt in the first place. A large, stoic, unmoved American was also perfect as a spy for the FBI and MI5.

It is this reticence that has kept Rupert an enigma for so long. 17 years later, as I was writing this book, the BBC sent two reporters back to Madrid after they heard he was talking to a journalist. After begging Rupert to talk, they, like many before them, went home without a story.

My contact with Ireland's most elusive spy came through Facebook. I spent 20 years writing about the Real IRA and other republican groups and I had become good friends with Michael Gallagher, the head of the support group for the Omagh bomb victims. I saw that Rupert was also Mr Gallagher's Facebook friend. I first wrote to him seeking a quote for the *Times* after the European Court of Justice praised his evidence against McKevitt as reliable and consistent.

I was surprised when he replied to my query. He would co-operate with my article on one condition – I should try to get an article published in the local newspaper in Madrid so that his sister and friends could read it.

It was so heartwarmingly parochial a request that I instantly liked him. He had been vilified by defence lawyers as a liar, a philanderer, an opportunist, a snitch, a terrorist and an arsonist, yet he appeared to be quite a humble man, someone concerned with the slow-moving politics of his home town and someone who disliked the drama of the international media.

As soon as I wrote the article in the *Times*, there were immediate requests from other journalists for his contact details, but he refused to say any more. Over time, in many, many hours of conversation, the complexity of his personality emerged, and the reasons for his reticence became apparent – both the obvious concerns about an IRA revenge attack and the culture of small-town America, which distrusted big-town media and the fleeting fame it offered. I hope I have done justice to his complex personality and the most extraordinary story I have come across in 20 years of journalism. I hope it answers many unanswered questions and raises some uncomfortable questions for security forces in the US, Ireland and the UK. Most of all, I hope it helps to explain the combination of injury, rage and ego that fuels international terrorism and the quiet patience it takes to bring it to an end.

CHAPTER 1

On a quiet wooded road, in a state the FBI does not want named, sits a two-storey house where leaves gather in the driveway and pine cones roll across the porch. It looks like any other house in this sloped, forested road except for the two English mastiffs that patrol the perimeter and the security cameras discreetly placed in the eaves.

A camera swivels every so often if one of the dogs barks loudly at a squirrel or a passing stranger.

The owner, in T-shirt and shorts, walks slowly to the gate.

His movement is deliberate, pushing his towering frame forward with his chin up and his arms swinging in front of his belly. He is 300 pounds with a boyish smile that makes him look like an overfed toddler dressed in adult clothes.

He extends a shovel-like hand in an upward movement of greeting. "How ya doin'?"

His left leg has a chunk missing, earned while trying to stop a dog fight when he owned six mastiffs.

His jovial greeting is tempered by a flinty addition, "You didn't bring any other visitors from Ireland with you, did ya?"

On the front door hangs a small pumpkin, and just inside the door, his wife, younger and slimmer, offers squash and pepper soup.

Her arm carries a visible scar from the 142 stitches she needed when one of the dogs bit her. They used to have a lot more ill-tempered dogs when security was tighter.

Standing arm in arm in the hallway, the couple look like an oddity from *National Geographic*: he, the leader of a lost tribe of giants and she, the smiling anthropologist who found him.

Leaning over the sofa, he offers tea. It is autumn and they have just returned from the farmers' market. The silence in the living room is filled with the sound of two mastiffs rapidly sniffing the air. They know the farmers' market bags mean there is meat, they just don't know where it's stored.

Behind him, as he speaks, there is a miniature carved harp, a gift from Irish republican prisoners. It sits like an artefact from another dimension, incongruous and disjointed in this scene of blissful Americana. I don't like it, amid the soup and the autumnal leaves and the rolling woodland, yet it's the reason I am here. It is the reason the dogs and security cameras are here and why this couple are living in the woods, and not in the big city.

Its presence is a pulsating and shrill alarm, pulling us out of mid-afternoon tea and soup and transporting us to bomb-making factories on the Irish border and the screams of a market town on a carnival Saturday.

"So," he says, wrapping his hand around a tea cup that seems to shrink to dollhouse scale, "where do ya wanna begin?"

*****

My rental car barely crests the top of the Adirondack mountains. I can feel the back wheel slip and the car jolt and hang just over a flood culvert. I move to first gear and slide across the road and over the top.

It is ink dark and the only lights are the stars, my headlamps and the fluorescent glow of a convenience store and gas station. I stop there for a glazed doughnut and an instant coffee that sticks to the top of my mouth. "If I was you, I'd turn back 'til spring," says the store clerk.

It is November and there is a radio warning not to travel unless necessary. I have to get to Madrid, more than eight hours' drive north of New York City. The temperature is already dropping and, the Weather Channel says, the roads will be covered in a thick blanket of snow in two days – four feet is expected in places.

It will continue snowing all winter, and St Lawrence County is hurrying for winter preparation, when life slows and residents wait for the gradual emergence of colour in March and April.

When I get to Madrid, I book into a motel and walk around the next morning. It is a neat, pretty little town of 1,600 people just south of the Canadian border. There is a Native American reservation nearby and, until recent integration, there was a strong French-speaking population who owed allegiance to Quebec, just over the St Lawrence River.

The town's Spanish settlers have, like the French, long since integrated, and I'm told at the motel that the town is pronounced MAD-rid, with a distinctly American emphasis on the first syllable.

The local library had, until recently, a permanent display honouring its most famous son. There were photographs of David Rupert, his mobile phone and computer, and newspaper articles from all over the world chronicling his story.

Now few young people in the town have heard of him. I have heavy frost on my breath as I ask around town. The young librarian doesn't know who he is, nor does the clerk at the local convenience store. Everyone over the age of 50 simply says, "Oh, you mean Joebe?"

David Rupert was born in July 1951, the youngest of seven children, and was raised on a farm in the remote woodlands three miles outside Madrid.

His father's family, and many others, had fled New York City to escape Washington's advancing army in the War of Independence. They were British loyalists who had fought their fellow Americans through the Hudson Valley until the cause was lost, and America was won.

Linguists link the northern St Lawrence dialect to that of the Appalachian Mountains, and Rupert was 12 years of age before he learned in school that Russia was against, and not "agin" America, and that writing "prinnear", meaning "pretty near", brought a drop in grade.

Six children came before him: Bud, Dale and three sisters, Wanda, Bonnie and Betty. The sixth, Gary, died in his cot, leaving a seven-year gap between David and the next youngest brother, Dale.

His paternal grandfather was tall, over 6ft, and hefty, and so were his maternal uncles. Those genes combined to create, in the final baby, one that set new family and hospital records.

His father, a manager at the local aluminium plant, nicknamed his rotund, two-year-old son after the Montreal labour agitator Joe Beef.

Joe Beef was condensed to Joebe and when I interview Betty and Wanda they both try to say "David" but tell me that it sounds odd, and say it's easier to refer to their brother by his nickname.

By kindergarten, Joebe was double the height and width of the two local girls in his class.

Betty recalls that he was "this big, smiling kid that we babied and made such a fuss of".

By the age of eight, he was too big for hand-me-down clothes from Bud and Dale and had to be driven into Madrid to the teenage section of the drapery store.

When he was 11, he was 6ft 1, weighed 270 pounds, and loomed awkwardly over the other children. That same year, Wanda came back from business school in nearby Watertown and locked her brother out of the house as a joke. He got worked up and kicked the lower half of the door in.

"He's 11 years old and he's kicking the door down. I got in trouble for that one. He really was a very big boy," Wanda recalls.

At 12, the boys his age shared jokes about how America could fight off Soviet nukes by putting Joebe's fat belly in their way.

His standard response to the name-calling was simply, "I'm twice as tall as you and twice as smart as you, so shut up."

His mother would hold him when he told her about the bullying and say, "Every mother's lamb is the whitest."

She had left St Lawrence County only twice in her life and urged her son to travel. "Go out into the world and make some noise," she said.

Progression through adolescence would not be easy. He had astigmatism in his left eye, leaving school texts blurry and confusing.

He compensated by slowly memorising large passages of books at home and then reading them out in class. He developed a very strong, close to photographic, memory that became his single greatest accomplishment in school.

He was a rebel, Wanda recalls, but it was largely directed and quasi-political. He organised several sits-ins at the school canteen when the food rations were sparse, a pragmatic act of defiance for a teenager who weighed twice as much as those around him.

Being so big had advantages. He looked 25 or 30 and could get served alcohol in any bar. At age 15, he lost his virginity to a much older married woman who believed his claim that he was 25. She met him in a bar while her husband was out of the country and she was looking for fun.

Being sexualised in mid-1960s America, long before his classmates, had a profound effect. Women came easy and it began a safari hunt for new female company that was to last 30 years.

His height and size also allowed him to bluff his way into work. At age 16, 6ft 7 and 300 pounds, he left school and got a job in construction, his employers believing his was at least 25.

War came in Vietnam and, aged 18, he was drafted. A military bus brought him and the teenage boys of Madrid to the induction centre in Syracuse. A doctor deemed him medically obese and he was immediately discharged, while all his friends went on to boot camp. A military bus was offered to army rejects later that day. He couldn't wait that long to leave and took a Greyhound bus back to Madrid and the crying hugs of his mother.

From there, he was expected to follow his father and sister, Wanda, into the Alcoa aluminium plant in Massena, a larger town east of Madrid.

Joebe and the other teenagers would place a flattened Zippo lighter in their hands and walk beside the magnetic cylinders where the aluminium was reduced. The Zippo, pulled by the magnetism, would stand up in their hands.

The magnetism pulled the galvanised zinc from mailboxes on the other side of the road, leaving them rusty on the plant side and shining and new on the other.

Residents complained about cancer scares but in 1960s America, it never made it past the St Lawrence County planning office.

His father died from smoking unfiltered cigarettes and, Joebe believed, the 30 years of magnetism pulling the iron in his blood.

He decided at the funeral, while shaking hands with the factory managers, that he would never work in the aluminium plant.

By St Lawrence standards, Massena was a cosmopolitan hub. Immigrants moved in their thousands from New York City to work in the ever-expanding aluminium plant. There were Cuban girls, and Mexican, and French. The family, like many in the area, were "very vaguely anti-Catholic and anti-French," he recalls. Two years before he died, his father told him to wear orange on St Patrick's Day to annoy Massena's growing community of Irish Catholics. When his sister later married a Catholic, his mother said, "Your grandfather would turn in his grave if he saw this."

Hormones have their own prejudices and Joebe found the freckles and milky skin of the Irish girls the most beautiful.

Aged 21, he started dating Tamara Buckley, an Irish American woman in Massena. She was five years his elder and he was impressed by her maturity. They married the following year.

He got a job working for his new father-in-law selling pensions and insurance with the Northwestern Mutual Life Insurance Company.

It was the first of a series of jobs that would result in other people losing money.

Joebe had developed a rebellious, outsider mentality, and it fed into how he viewed his role in society.

He discovered that he could earn insurance commissions before the insurance or pension sale was complete. If the deal fell through, brokers would have to give the money back to the company. By the time he left Northwestern two years later, he owed thousands and, in addition, a $2,000 loan from his father-in-law's boss.

That same year, he declared bankruptcy to escape repaying the money, the first of several trips to the bankruptcy courts.

He was gaining a reputation in Massena.

One former acquaintance, out walking his dog before the snow enveloped the town, recalled, "He was kinda all over the place. Not a bad guy but kinda shady, like he could smile one past you."

His two years with Northwestern were his one and only venture into white-collar office work.

He didn't feel he belonged in "their" world.

He got a job as a lumberjack and timber buyer for several years, cutting forests along the Canadian border.

It was 30 degrees below zero in the winter, so cold that they were forced to stop work when the machines froze.

Through it all, Tamara was dismayed by the financial fallout between her husband and father, who never forgave what he saw as a betrayal.

She found solace in the born-again Christian movement that was sweeping 1970s America in correction to the excesses of the 60s.

The meetings were energetic and intense. Tamara and her friends would speak in tongues and jump up and down to the sound of frenzied drum beats. Her husband, whom she called Dave, not Joebe, would stand beside her, awkwardly clapping and looking at his watch.

"It was a major, major problem in our marriage. I think I lost her to them," he recalls.

Tamara later divorced and married someone in the Christian meetings named Kenny, who had ridden the school bus with Rupert when they were kids.

It was about this time that Rupert first met Julie Smith, whose father was a vice president of Massena Savings and Loan Association and a major political force in Massena's town council. He also owned the town's meat market, where Julie worked. She soon became his second wife.

Rupert set up his own trucking company, hauling aluminium to Detroit and developing a cross-border business to Canada.

It was the infancy of modern trucking. The interstates, like the East Coast I-95, were not yet complete and truckers would have to use local roads for 20 or 30 miles.

The trucks had 220 horsepower diesel engines, half that of a modern 440 horsepower small pickup truck.

A steep hill meant dropping down to first and barely reaching the top at 10 miles an hour.

By 1980, Reagan was in power, trucking was deregulated and money started to roll in. Rupert used it to buy up as much of Massena as he could. First, there was Charlie's Bar in the centre of town, where aluminium plant engineers mixed freely with the local motorbike gang, Satan's Soldiers. Rupert called them Satin Soldiers to annoy them.

Then he bought the rundown hotel across the road, because it had a bar, and later, the Boardwalk coffee shop, which he renovated and called the Wildside Café.

Soon, he got in trouble with the Savings and Loan for a house mortgage he did not repay.

He moved the money between accounts to escape the debt and declared bankruptcy in 1984. As with Tamara before her, Julie found that her father had been burned by Rupert.

They moved down to St Petersburg, in western Florida, to escape the intractable financial mess, and Rupert ran his trucking company from there.

St Petersburg, on an island reached by bridge from Tampa, was booming in the 1980s.

The warm air, long days and bright colours were redemption from the cold air and small-town politics of St Lawrence County.

Julie was working as a masseuse and became more and more influenced by new age spirituality.

Her husband spent his time working out at a St Petersburg muscle gym called The Iron Work. "It was a bunch of guys with a lot of muscle and probably not a whole lot of brains," he says.

Its owner, Bob Hodge, was a former steroid user with a gravelly voice who had reformed and saw in Rupert an opportunity. Pantomine TV wrestling was only just beginning in the 1980s and it was hungry for the novel. He referred Rupert to a coach in Tampa who prepared fighters for TV theatrics.

At 6ft 7 and 350 pounds, Rupert was chosen to play a caped giant who could lift other wrestlers by their spangled shorts and throw them around the ring. Rupert, always hungry for the next business that would make a fortune, signed up immediately.

It was to be a painful experience. "When you are 350 pounds and you are repeatedly thrown on your back, you really feel it. I was real beat up. I did a few training sessions with this guy and had enough. I knew there must be easier ways to make money."

The following year, always searching for some unorthodox business idea, he planned to set up a gambling ship in international waters, with the help of the mafia and 38-year-old David M.R. DeValta, who lived in a high-walled Florida mansion and was a financier for General Pinochet, the dictator of Chile. At that time, Pinochet was salting off millions of dollars and hiding it in America.

For Rupert, the idea fell apart at their first meeting.

"I brought down this mobster from Syracuse named Guy A. Scalzi. He drove his big Lincoln down from New York because he's scared of flying. He went out to a steakhouse with us to hear our proposal. It was me, him and David DeValta, Pinochet's guy. Scalzi was a thug and a bad drunk. David was much more refined but also couldn't hold his drink. So Scalzi says that he'll run a red-hot poker up DeValta's ass if the deal goes wrong. DeValta goes for him and the two of them are screaming at each other in the restaurant. I couldn't have that, Pinochet's people on one side and the mob on the other, nothing good was going to come of this."

But through all his gimmicks, it was the money from trucking that kept coming in. Deregulation meant that smaller trucking companies could act as agents for larger ones, and soon he was moving freight for America's biggest haulers.

As trucking expanded in the late 80s and into the 1990s, his marriage to Julie became more and more volatile. The couple moved up and down between New York and St Petersburg but Julie longed to stay in Florida, where her massage business and new-age beliefs found greater currency than in rural New York. They formally split in 1992.

It had a devastating effect.

Like Tamara, Julie was kind, thoughtful and committed and yet, for the second time, his marriage had fallen apart.

He lost his pubs and café in New York because of time spent in Florida. Also, the trucking business was starting to fade, eaten by cheaper competition.

With DeValta, the financier, he would go drinking and womanising in the beach bars of St Petersburg.

Their usual was called Jimmy B's, which blasted 1990s rock while patrons played air-guitar and knocked back shots.

One night, he heard the sound of traditional Irish music from across the road. "I was getting tired of his horrible bar scene and suddenly I hear what sounded like bluegrass, but it's Irish fiddle and I just connected with it. I want to hear more, because it was traditional and away from everything going on in the beach bar."

He wandered over to the green-coloured Irish bar called the Harp and Thistle. Inside, a band was mixing traditional Irish music with Irish rebel songs. Many Irish Americans casually supported the Irish Republican Army terrorist group and its campaign of bombings and shootings against the British state. Some gathered to sing support for the IRA, many others just sang along with the folk songs.

"I was just curious," Rupert recalls. "I knew nothing about Ireland, but I liked this music. It seemed pure and had some meaning. So I left the beach bar and went over to the Harp and Thistle. It was the biggest decision of my life."

CHAPTER 2

He could barely hear her above the rebel songs, the cheers, the stomping of feet and the clink of glasses.

She had fiery red hair, curled to the shoulder, sallow skin and piercing eyes. She danced around his giant bulk. Her name was Linda.

Rupert had been a regular at the Harp and Thistle for several months.

The owners, Pat and Bob Packer, built the pub in defiance of the bland beach bars around them. Only Irish traditional or folk music was permitted and there were live acts five nights a week. Searching for authenticity, the Packers pulled out the cigarette machine, pool table and jukebox and the TV was only switched on Monday nights. Anyone who wandered in from the beach wearing a bikini or shorts had to cover up with an oversized Harp and Thistle T-shirt.

The main entertainment was the music and Pat herself, who liked to dress outlandishly and would drag customers out to dance. She was always in search of the exotic, the carnival, to keep the energy alive.

Michael Jones, the barman, was a former seminary student, who dressed as a monk while legally marrying people in the bar, to cheers from the crowd. Pat first met him when he and two nuns came into the bar dressed as clowns and did some impromptu juggling.

He was now a semi-professional magician and would bring Gina, his sawn-in-half lady, into the pub to entertain the crowd when they weren't performing at his revue show further down the beach. He also performed free tarot readings and illusions for the customers while serving in the bar.

In Linda, Pat found a fellow party animal. When not working, Linda was in the Harp and Thistle, dancing with Pat and her friends and occasionally going up on stage to sing.

"Pat was never in a bad mood and she loved to be at the centre of everything. Pretty soon, we had people coming from Michigan, Boston and New York just to spend St Patrick's Day with us," remembers another barman at the time, Sean Nordquist. "They wanted an Irish community in Florida and when they found it, there was an explosion of people – students, retirees, tourists, people walking by, it was a real big party."

Every four years, Pat dressed head to toe in red, white and blue for the Republican National Convention, where she loved to be interviewed by reporters about her devotion to presidents Reagan and Bush.

Children were welcome in the bar and would be given colouring books and markers in exchange for doing Irish dancing on stage. The local running group started and finished at the pub, where Pat offered them Guinness or cocoa.

At the back of the bar was a cottage occupied by a man named Pelican Joe, who walked around with a chainsaw in a shopping trolley, cutting slabs of wood into the shape of pelicans for $50 a time.

His eccentricity was too much, even for Pat. He was barred from the bar after slashing all four tyres of her Cadillac. After his death, the Packers moved the touring musicians into his house. The Guinness Duo, Rupert's favourite, were a husband-and-wife act flown in from Prince Edward Island, Canada, for six weeks at a time. One visiting Irish musician was pulled over by a Florida traffic cop, who discovered he only had an old-fashioned Irish driving licence. The cop escorted him to the pub and stayed for his session. The cop, too, became a regular.

Politics in an Irish American bar is complicated.

The Harp and Thistle sponsored pro-IRA bands when they played at festivals in Tampa, but never wanted them performing in the bar.

Bob, an ex-navy man, was adamant that the bands could play rebel songs, but there were to be no overt displays of support for the IRA and strictly no fundraising for the IRA, Sinn Féin, Irish Northern Aid or a multitude of front groups.

"There were IRA sympathisers there but there were also a lot of English, who definitely were not of that persuasion," remembers Nordquist. "You couldn't have that with so many tourists and British retirees coming in and out."

The Harp and Thistle was so successful at luring away customers that the beach bar across the road launched an embargo, refusing to allow Harp and Thistle customers to come over to buy cigarettes. The beach bar would order a tow truck if any of the weekend hordes dared to pull into its cark park. Even wearing a T-shirt from the Harp and Thistle or any other Irish bar led to eviction.

The Guinness Duo were blasting out 'Rathlin Island' when Rupert suggested that he and Linda go out to the deck to talk. It was summer. Outside, the heat of Florida mingled with the stolid sweat rushing out from the bar. Sand blew up from under the deck.

Her full name was Linda Vaughan. She was a staffer for a local state senator and she had been chairwoman of the Paul Tsongas For President campaign in Florida.

Senator Tsongas, the most liberal of the mainstream Democratic candidates, had stunned political commentators by winning the New Hampshire primary.

Linda had been busy organising fundraisers and rallies for him in Florida. If he could beat Bill Clinton here, he would likely win the nomination, and the White House. Linda might be chosen as a White House staff member as a reward.

Sometimes she was at the podium with Tsongas, other times she was at the back of the auditorium, telling reporters that the Tsongas campaign was sure he could beat Clinton and retake the party for the liberal wing. Clinton won the state but Linda had shown she could run a major campaign. Now, dancing in the Harp and Thistle, she was letting go after an exhausting political season.

The first night they talked, Rupert discovered that Linda was also a lobbyist for Irish Northern Aid, or Noraid, the American political representative of the IRA. "She was beautiful and she was smart and exciting," Rupert recalls. "She talked a lot about the cause in Ireland. I played along.

"She was done with her Paul Tsongas campaign since he was out by then and she was working on a congressional campaign for another Democrat. She was staying in a condo in Sarasota, which was a fairly long drive for someone who had been drinking. So, being a gentleman, at the end of the night I invited her home. Things developed from there. I discovered she was really liberal and really republican, in the Irish sense. So I tried to impress her with my knowledge of Ireland. I was having to learn a lot about politics."

"Linda was always out fighting for a cause," remembers her best friend, Barbara DeVane, who had campaigned with her since the 1970s. "When we weren't doing that, we were partying. Linda was an absolute party animal and she was magnetic for both men and women because she had so much energy. I often heard about the Harp and Thistle, because she loved Irish things, but there was a party going on somewhere every night of the week."

Rupert was always a Democrat but was on the periphery of the system looking in. Linda, sophisticated, wild, hedonistic and rebellious, was at its core. She asked about his views on all kinds of issues. He was intrigued by her and her politics.

"At the time, there was a battle between the progressives, like us, and the Dixiecrats, for control of the Democratic Party in the south," says Barbara. "Tallahassee, the state capital, was very progressive but all around us, in the rural counties, were Dixiecrats, who were real southern, conservative Democrats. Blue Dogs, they are also called. A lot of them defected to the Republicans in the mid-1990s Republican Revolution and Jeb Bush was elected governor. I despised them, and so did Linda, and we were trying to take the party from them."

Pat and Linda personified the two wings of Irish American life: the older conservative pro-life and low-tax self-employed and the younger, progressive wing that saw the Northern Irish problem not through lachrymose ballads and shamrock jerseys, but as a political issue that could be solved, violently if necessary.

The previous summer, Linda was guest speaker at the IRA hunger strike commemoration in Bundoran in the north-west of

Ireland, in which she spoke of Irish America's unyielding support for the IRA's armed struggle. "She was so excited about making the speech and about speaking in Ireland, she really was committed. Only those close to her could work out that she was an IRA supporter. She pretty much let me fill in the gaps to what was going on," said Barbara.

Dating her from the first night he met her, Rupert was trying to catch up with Linda's social life and her politics.

"I was impressing her with a little knowledge of Irish republicanism combined with a lot of feigned fervour. It was a winning strategy."

He invited her to the Cayman Islands on holiday.

"As usual, because of my size, I had my knee in the aisle a bit. The flight attendant came down the aisle and hit me with the cart, it split my knee open. So Linda and I spent a few days in the Cayman Islands with me not being able to bend my knee and in pain. I could drink but it hurt to have sex. That was real bad luck."

Linda introduced Rupert to Barbara DeVane over breakfast. She was excited because it looked as if she was about to succeed in her long struggle to have Tallahassee twinned with Sligo in the Irish Republic. The organising committee had a budget and she was allowed to travel to Sligo at least once a year. She invited Rupert to come. He agreed immediately.

What united them apart from physical attraction? He wasn't a dancer, and wasn't sophisticated or overtly political. He was big and protective and his blue-collar simplicity was a break from the Florida politicos, brokers, reporters and scammers who filled her answering machine, looking for dates.

She and Rupert were battling the system, as they saw it. She, with a college degree and a career in politics, was fighting against the Blue Dogs and the Republicans for the Equal Rights Amendment and tightening gun control. Rupert's battle was far more nebulous, but equally intense. It was against the system run by men in suits, who were trying to pin him down with tax and mortgages, rates and penalties. He had spent his whole life trying to find a way to escape the system, but never knowing how.

What they had in common meant that her world would become his, that the definable goals of her anti-establishment politics would seep into his innate feeling of being wronged, and that he would attach himself to one of her causes.

"We were kinda hoping he would get involved in the liberal causes here in Florida, fighting for women's rights or for the environment," says Barbara DeVane. "We hoped he would get on board with Linda's ideals about taking the Democratic party from the Blue Dogs, but it wasn't to be."

*****

"Ah hello, Linda! How are ye?"

Vincent Murray leant across the bar to give Linda a peck on the cheek and, looking up, shook hands with Rupert.

"This is David. He'll be with me here for a few days."

"Welcome to Ireland."

Murray, who was then a member of Sligo town council for Sinn Féin, the IRA's political wing, raises his hands to show me his first impression of Rupert.

"He comes into a bar and he's this huge big tall man. You think: Jesus, he'd be a great full back, you know? He was a nice, friendly big fella."

Murray's accent, once hard and Northern, has softened over the years since moving an hour south of the Irish border.

His bar in the centre of Sligo was festooned with Gaelic football and republican memorabilia. On stage in the bar was Sean Sands, brother of the IRA's greatest martyr, Bobby Sands, singing republican ballads.

Vincent Murray met Linda for the first time when Sligo hosted the Fleadh Cheoil na hÉireann, an annual traditional music festival that attracts over 100,000 people.

"I still remember her in her black Guinness top. She was really beautiful for her age, she stood out straight away and she knew so much about politics," he recalls. Linda was dating Murray's best friend within days of meeting, but that soon ended.

She took Rupert to Vincent Murray's bar to discuss the twinning of Tallahassee and Sligo, but also to talk to Murray about the Irish republican scene in Florida.

Until now, the violence in Northern Ireland was almost theoretical for Linda: it was all about ethnic solidarity and a salty addition to the bourgeois politics of Florida.

In the real world of Irish politics, the agony of sectarian conflict dragged on. When Linda and David arrived, rumours were rippling through Murray's bar about the discovery of a woman's body in Sligo five weeks previously.

She was strangled and beaten to death by three IRA members, allegedly to stop her revealing that they were working for MI5, the internal UK section of the British secret service.

As soon as her body was found, the IRA kidnapped the three men, tortured them and shot them in the back of the head. Their naked, hooded bodies were found along border roads a week later.

The IRA released a detailed statement, saying the men disgraced themselves by spying for MI5 and the police.

The violence in Northern Ireland had rolled on all year, in an increasingly futile wave of attack and counter-attack by paramilitary groups who identified as either Irish or British. In January of 1992, the IRA blew up eight Protestant construction workers who had been doing repair work on a British army base.

The following month, a policeman shot three people inside the main Belfast offices of Sinn Féin. He then committed suicide. The next day, in revenge for the killing of the construction workers, the British loyalist group, the Ulster Freedom Fighters, shot dead five Irish civilians, including a 15-year-old boy, in a bookie's shop in a nationalist area of Belfast. A week later, four IRA members were shot dead in County Tyrone in an ambush at a church car park after firing heavy machine guns at a police and British military base.

In April, the IRA unveiled a new tactic: bombing the financial centre of London to weaken the British government's resolve to stay in Northern Ireland. On 10 April, a bomb in the Baltic Exchange in the centre of London killed three people, including a 15-year-old girl. Insurance claims from the devastated financial district exceeded £800m.

There were also smaller confrontations that received almost no external coverage. In May, British parachute regiment soldiers smashed up two nationalist pubs in Coalisland, County Tyrone in revenge for a roadside bomb that blew a soldier's legs off.

Two of Vincent Murray's brothers had been jailed for bombings and he himself had been an election volunteer for Bobby Sands, the IRA hunger striker, when he won his seat in the British parliament in 1981.

His volunteering included meeting the other nationalist candidate and persuading him that it was "not a good idea" for him to run against Sands.

Vincent's brother, Marcus, was one of 38 IRA prisoners who led a mass escape from the Maze Prison in Belfast in 1983. Vincent, who was playing a football match that day, asked the referee for the time because he was waiting for his brother's escape. Marcus and another IRA man were stopped at a British army checkpoint in Northern Ireland. They claimed to be good friends but didn't know each other's surnames. They were arrested and thrown back in prison.

In jail, Marcus, like Vincent, was beginning to recognise the futility of the violence, especially when weighed against the ardent socialist beliefs of their mother.

"We were looking for a socialist all-Ireland republic and what was happening? In some cases, the IRA were killing fellow socialists," says Vincent Murray. "It was framed as you being either British or Irish, but it was working-class people who were being hurt."

Murray, a fit-looking man with tight dark hair, takes a sip of beer and corrects himself. "Actually, I'm not sure I like the phrase 'working class'. I prefer 'people with a working spirit'."

Linda and Rupert, who were staying at the Silver Swan Hotel downtown, visited Vincent's pub several times over the next few days, listening to the rebel songs. Linda loved it. It wasn't the hokey, neutered ballads of the Harp and Thistle. This was the real thing, IRA members shouting republican slogans in a pub in Ireland. "She was an extremist in every way – in politics, in partying. It was only natural that she was drawn to extreme people," says Barbara DeVane.

Rupert remembers her clapping along to the songs and hugging Vincent Murray, who was to become a lifelong friend.

After three days, the couple drove north to Bundoran, County Donegal, a seaside town just inside the Irish Republic that was steeped in the Irish rebel cause. It was raining and windy as they drove into town. Linda wanted to meet another pub owner who was also a local councillor.

Joe O'Neill greeted her with a vigorous handshake. "Linda, Lord God!" he said.

O'Neill was a member of Bundoran town council for the hardline republican breakaway group, Republican Sinn Féin. His group, and its paramilitary wing, the Continuity IRA, were as conservative, Catholic and enthusiastic about violence against the British as Murray's left-wing republicanism was socialist, internationalist and wringing with self-doubt.

In 1986, O'Neill and his comrades walked out of Sinn Féin's Ard Fheis (Annual Convention) when it agreed to take seats in the southern parliament. As far they were concerned, there could be no parliament in Ireland, even a nationalist one, until it was an all-Ireland parliament. They hated the mainstream IRA, which they felt was moving towards peace and constitutional politics.

O'Neill, like Murray, was an avid player of Gaelic football. Now in his 60s, he had several county championship medals and once broke the Irish record for the longest free kick. He had a strong voice and, in his bar and at republican commemorations, he was an accomplished singer of unsophisticated rebel ballads. 'Four Green Fields' and 'Come Out Ye Black And Tans' were his standards.

The Continuity IRA was run by old men like O'Neill and it lacked the funding, resources and sophistication of the larger mainstream IRA (commonly referred to as the Provisional IRA, or Provos).

What Republican Sinn Féin and the Continuity IRA lacked in effectiveness, they gained in romance, conservative Catholicism, republican history and their claim to embody the spirit of the first all-Ireland parliament, before the country was divided in the 1920s between the independent, majority Catholic south and the British, majority Protestant north.

O'Neill had a straggly beard and a crooked, beaten nose. He drove an old Mercedes on which he mounted a loudspeaker for announcing Republican Sinn Féin's endless list of IRA commemorations and marches.

He had a wild, untamed look, what Americans might expect the IRA to be – a devoutly Catholic, Gaelic-football-playing, charming, violent, cunning, rebel-ballad-singing pub owner.

He also ran a real estate business from nearby Ballyshannon, where he took Rupert on his first visit.

"Joe and I really hit it off," remembers Rupert. "He had a real passion for history and I was his pupil. He told me about the history of Ireland, where this battle took place and that battle took place. He was very clear – the British had no right to be in Northern Ireland, the country should be reunited. That was about as far as the argument went."

Rupert and Linda returned to Florida, after Linda had assured both the Provisional and Continuity IRA they had the full backing of Irish America.

After they returned, Linda's daily phone calls to Rupert began to slacken off to one call every three days. When she called, she was distracted and rushed, like she was readying herself to go out for the night. Rupert would have to wait in a long line of suitors. He discovered that she was seeing a married man.

"Linda was this magnet," says Barbara DeVane. "If David Rupert says he was her boyfriend, well, maybe that's a bit of an exaggeration. She dated a lot and lived a lot and I think he was just someone she was seeing for a while."

"Linda and I didn't last a whole long time," says Rupert. "I learned pretty quickly she had other boyfriends, so I wasn't exactly going to stop myself with other women in Florida. But I really liked Ireland, and Joe said he could find me a place if I wanted to come back. I was also really intrigued about the politics and the history and I wanted to know more."

In Christmas 1992, he returned to Ireland by himself. There was something about the country that filled some hidden void.

"It was like going back 40 years when I was in the west coast. The mountains, the history, I loved it all."

It was to be the most disastrous trip of his life.

"Things were going bad for the trucking company in New York and that culminated with what happened on 7 December, 1992, while I was staying at the hotel in Sligo. I got the news that a driver of mine killed three kids near Evansville, Indiana, across the river in Kentucky.

"There were three or four kids in the front of a pickup truck and they had just left church. My driver had missed his turn and was turning around to go the other way. This pickup came over the hill and smashed underneath the trailer, killing three of the kids."

Elizabeth Elliott, who was driving the pickup, was the daughter of the county prosecutor. The driver went to jail for several weeks and they tied up the truck and the trailer for months before it was returned to Rupert.

"It wasn't either side's fault but we were sued for $50m," says Rupert. "We really took a hit and we just couldn't recover. I was horribly bothered by the deaths, it was a nightmare."

In 1993 he wound up the trucking business in upstate New York, while still based in Florida.

A major freight company came down to St Petersburg to see him. They really wanted him as an agent, as he had a talent for trucking.

He agreed to move to Chicago to work as an agent in the city's largest truck depot, while consoling himself with visits to Ireland to see his friend Joe and staying for a few days in Sligo to see the Murrays.

In Vincent Murray's bar, he heard some men joking with one of their members, named Sean, about the murder of Lord Mountbatten, who was blown up while fishing in Sligo in 1979, and died along with his 14-year-old grandson, a 15-year-old local boy and the Dowager Lady Brabourne. "They were all joking with the guy like: 'Oh you wouldn't know anything about that would you, Sean?' – like they knew he was in on it. That kind of surprised me."

Vincent Murray: "I'm a republican, there were republicans coming in and out and things might be exaggerated while the pints are flying. I certainly didn't know anything about Mountbatten's death, but maybe somebody did."

Rupert visited Ireland three times in 1993, each time learning more and more about the IRA's struggle against the British.

On his last trip, O'Neill dropped him back to the hotel in his old Mercedes.

Across the road, in an unmarked car, a plain-clothes Irish policeman, or garda, was clicking a camera furiously as Joe said goodbye. Rupert and Joe smiling. Click. They shake hands. Click. Rupert enters the hotel. Click.

The photographer put down his camera, turned the car around and headed back to Sligo police station. Later, he drove back to Dublin to his bosses at Special Branch, the anti-terrorism police.

A group of Special Branch officers gathered around a table. They recognised Joe O'Neill, the conservative Catholic die-hard, immediately. But they all had one question: Who was the 6ft 7, 300-pound yank, and what was he doing here?

One of the team, now a senior Special Branch officer, remembers it well. "You would know the other people around – the Murrays and the O'Neills, but there's this huge American in the middle and there was concern because if he was funding things in Ireland, or if he was opening gun-running links from Chicago, this was going to be a problem."

He opened a file and wrote in marker: "Sligo/Donegal: Unknown American."

David Rupert, who knew almost nothing of Ireland just a year before, was now a terror suspect.

CHAPTER 3

Agent Ed Buckley pulls up at the Calumet Truck Plaza, 20 miles south of Chicago.

It is a hot summer day in late July 1994 and the warm air is heavy with the acrid smell of diesel. Calumet is the city's largest truck depot, a self-contained town with 22 fuel pumps, a diner, shops, tattoo parlour, motel and masseuse. It rests uneasily inside the old Dutch township of South Holland, which strictly prohibits Sunday trading and the sale of alcohol, and in which the truck plaza is a jarring and modern intrusion.

Buckley is holding an envelope in his hand, containing photographs from Ireland of David Rupert and Joe O'Neill.

The Irish police have contacted Interpol about the mysterious American, and Interpol have contacted the FBI. Buckley walks up the stairs to Rupert's office. Lawsuits from the fatal crash have destroyed Rupert's New York operations and he has moved to Chicago, one of America's great trucking centres.

His office shares a corridor with a tattoo artist, a masseuse and a preacher, all of whom offer redemption of some kind to the travel-weary trucker.

Inside the office, Buckley shows his FBI badge and puts the photos on the table.

"Buckley was like no other FBI agent. He was a real maverick type, hand on hip, pointing at me. His language was pretty coarse," says Rupert. "He was really trying to impress upon me the seriousness of the situation, that I was seen with Joe O'Neill and Vincent Murray, another Irish republican, and that I was in trouble. To be honest with you, with everything that was going on in Chicago trucking, I was relieved this was about Ireland."

Buckley, thick-set and frumpy, had spent a decade hunting out IRA gun-runners in Chicago's large Irish community.

"He was acting the real blowhard, trying to shake me down with some scare story about how the FBI knew I was mixed up in Irish terrorism. I said, 'Look, all trucker stories start with three things: a bar, a beer and a woman. In my case, that's the Harp and Thistle, Guinness and Linda Vaughan.'"

Rupert's attitude was deliberately guyish and light-hearted, but Buckley was not smiling. He told Rupert that if he wanted to stay out of trouble he should inform the FBI about what the IRA was doing in Chicago and in Ireland.

"I said, 'I got nothing to tell ya. I've got no problem with the people over there and I don't even know anything.'"

Buckley was known as the bulldog of the Chicago field office, the only one who would wander into a trucking depot unannounced and demand answers.

He left after 10 minutes of questions and promised that he would be back.

"I didn't think a whole lot of it at the time," says Rupert. "I had so much going on, this guy was just another problem." Rupert was, yet again, recently divorced. This time the marriage had lasted six months. It was to a woman he met online named Jacqueline Decker

– a tumultuous relationship that was to scar him for life. Even now, he finds it difficult to talk about, but it gave him a definite goal: to marry for love, and end the destructive cycle.

He had been flirting with the operations manager of the plaza, Maureen Brennan, who had rented the office to him for $300 a month.

Maureen, quick-witted, slim and petite with brown hair and a bright smile, was from an Irish American family in the adjoining Dolton area of Chicago's exurbs.

Her mother, second generation Irish, never fulfilled her lifelong dream of visiting her ancestral home.

For many Irish people scattered around the world, the death of thousands in Northern Ireland was not a backdrop to rebel ballads, but a deep and painful wound.

One day, Maureen saw her mother crying in the kitchen after the evening news. "I asked her what was wrong and she said, 'Why are the Irish killing each other?'"

Maureen was pregnant at 19 and gave birth at 20 to her daughter, Dorothy, or 'Dorie'. She married Dorothy's father, against the wishes of her family, but it ended quickly. Her second marriage also rapidly ended in divorce and, at 22, Maureen turned up at Calumet Auto Trucking, looking for a job.

"I knew I was in a man's world and so I had to work harder than anyone to prove myself. We used bleepers in those days and my bleeper was never off. There was a hundred staff and I had to solve everyone's problems. After a few years, I was running the place."

Being a pretty young woman who hosted 1,000 truckers every day was not easy. "They were always flirting, with me and every woman. They were on the road a long time and they were lonely.

They would always tell you that they had a big place back home and that they were well off. I just laughed."

Maureen and the plaza owner, Eugene Suppelsa, liked to hire young men from the evangelical churches of South Holland for the garage and shops because they could be trusted, but their Dutch Calvinist faith clashed frequently with the immoral ways of trucking.

One day, she got a call from the garage manager saying one of the local boys was refusing to fix a tyre on a truck because the truck was carrying alcohol. Another refused to pump diesel for a beer truck. "One time, I got a call from the store because one of the truckers bought a Playboy and the guy wouldn't serve him. I literally had to run from downstairs, ring it up for this embarrassed trucker and get back to work."

The plaza handled 1,000 trucks a day and pumped over one million gallons of diesel a month, and behind it all was a myriad of scams to boost profits.

It ran two sets of books, one for the government and one for Gene, the owner, who bought a new Porsche every few years and whose main passion was jazz accordion. When he wasn't playing accordion in his office, he was enjoying the scamming that was systemic in the trucking business.

"One night he called me at 11pm and told me to get $10,000 from the safe," says Maureen. "He was buying a stolen forklift worth $100,000 for 10 grand and needed the money fast. They scrapped the forklift's serial numbers and used it in the plaza for years."

Staff would steal from them just as easily. Maureen used a trucker's cab for her own surveillance after food kept disappearing from the restaurant. One of the employees could be seen smuggling the food out in the linen basket and loading it into the back of his car.

In the afternoon, pimps would bring prostitutes up to the trucking plaza six at a time and collect them at 4am.

The prostitutes, desperate and often addicts, would knock at the truckers' cabs while they slept and ask them if they wanted company. It was the height of the 1990s crack epidemic. Some truckers would park further down the road to avoid the 2am knock.

"It was a hopeless situation," says Maureen. "You would call the cops and get the hookers busted but they would bail out the next morning and be right back there that same day."

The problem reached its worst point when Maureen's immediate supervisor found one of the women inside the office building and chased her out onto the roof. "We looked up and he's holding her out over the ledge and he is shouting, 'Do you want to die? Do you want to die?' We had to go up there and talk him down from it."

In a city that was still reeling from a crime wave, the threat of violence was a regular hazard in Rupert's office. As his business expanded, more and more drivers would come from the poor neighbourhoods looking for work.

"I told one of them he'd failed a drug test and he got real mad and pulled this small knife on me. I said, 'First of all, look at me. You are not even going to penetrate my belly fat with that thing and the second you do it, I will drop-punch you to the floor.'"

Rupert's preoccupation was in proving to himself, after three divorces, that he could find love.

The same week as FBI Agent Buckley's visit, he was planning a motorbike trip with one of his truckers, John Orndorff, and Orndorff's wife, Nancy.

Maureen remembers it well. "I was passing through the diner and John asks me if I wanted to go on a bike ride with them to

Wisconsin that Sunday. I knew John was married and his wife was right there, so I figured this was Dave's way of asking me out."

That Sunday, Maureen rode hundreds of miles on the back of Rupert's oversized BMW motorcycle all the way to Wisconsin and back. By the time they made it back to South Holland, they were dating.

Within a few days, he asked her to come with him to Ireland, promising her they would stay at Ashford Castle, the country's most beautiful hotel, and tour the west coast.

Maureen accepted immediately.

She had never been outside America before, except for a disastrous honeymoon in Acapulco with her second husband. Her whole life had been lived within a five-mile radius – from her home in Dolton to the truck plaza. She drank with work mates but everything else went to college tuition for her daughter Dorie.

"Well," says Maureen., her voice quivering, "I just couldn't believe it when he asked me to go. My mom had passed away six months earlier so it was my chance to live her dream of going to Ireland."

*****

"So we arrive into Joe O'Neill's pub in Donegal and there is this dog, Rebel, sitting on the bar stool and the place is wall-to-wall IRA posters. It was all threatening stuff. And women were coming in with prams and dancing around while Joe is up on stage singing all these IRA rebel ballads. I thought, 'Jesus, what is this?'"

Maureen Brennan was meeting Rupert's new world.

"I liked Joe, he was this good old boy from the old IRA, that's how I saw it at the time," she says.

"Then we drove down to Vincent Murray's place and it's more Republicans and more rebel ballads. We had a good time, and I just got into it. I've lived my whole life in a man's world at the truck stop, so this was just an extension of that. I drank up with the rest of them. I loved Ireland, the friendliness and the beauty. We both wanted to be there."

David drove with Joe O'Neill to visit the Republican Sinn Féin headquarters in Dublin, where they picked up some arts and crafts made by prisoners – Celtic design bodhrans and miniature harps, to take back to Donegal.

On the way back, Joe said that he had to meet Ruairí Ó Brádaigh and several of the Continuity IRA army council at Ó Brádaigh's house in Roscommon. Rupert wasn't allowed to attend, so Joe dropped him off at a hotel in Roscommon town for an hour.

Rupert knew better than to argue. He sat in the lobby listening to the muzak. In his wallet, he discovered Ed Buckley's business card: "Ed Buckley. Agent. Federal Bureau of Investigation", with the FBI and Justice Department logo. It was a serious lapse – one that would have got him killed had it been discovered.

"I knew the FBI had this rule – never flush anything down a toilet unless you flush it three times because it can float back up again," said Rupert. "I was worried about doing that, so I just took the card out of my wallet and ate it. I had it chewed to pieces and swallowed by the time Joe came back to the hotel." Joe spoke excitedly about the coming Continuity IRA bombing campaign, now that the Provisional IRA was on ceasefire.

David and Maureen flew back to Chicago four days later.

Agent Ed Buckley drove to Calumet to see David. The mainstream Provisional IRA had just declared a ceasefire. President Clinton was heavily involved in brokering a potential peace deal and wanted to know if the ceasefire would hold, or if disaffected

IRA members would break away and restart the bombings.

"Buckley is all worked up," says Rupert. "He says to me, 'the FBI will pay for the trips to Ireland for you and Maureen. You just have to tell us what's happening.'

"I thought, 'Hey, if I can sucker the FBI into paying for our trips, great.' We both loved Ireland, so why not? I didn't know anything anyway, so let the government sponsor us in Ireland."

That night, he told Maureen about the FBI visits.

She was astounded. "It was like something out of this world, the FBI following our movements and wanting to pay for our trips. To be honest, after 20 years as a woman in the trucking business, nothing scared me. It was exciting and if the FBI pay for us, great. Looking back now, I had no fucking idea how deep into this thing we would go."

CHAPTER 4

At 6pm on 9 February 1996, Gerry Adams, the leader of the IRA's political wing, Sinn Féin, called the White House and asked to speak to Anthony Lake, President Clinton's national security adviser. He had disturbing news that the IRA's ceasefire was about to break, and promised to call back. He was harried and people were talking in the background.

One hour later, a 3,000-pound truck bomb exploded in the Docklands in London's financial district, killing two people and seriously injuring six others. The blast destroyed three office buildings, and severely damaged the light rail line. Bloodied office workers, with glass in their heads, ran screaming from nearby pubs.

The 18-month ceasefire broke down because the IRA refused to surrender its weapons before Sinn Féin entered peace talks with the British government. Chief among those adamant that there should be no weapon surrender was Mickey McKevitt, the IRA's quartermaster general. He controlled all of the IRA's huge quantity of weapons and explosives, mostly stored in underground bunkers in farms south of the border and, after building it up over decades, he was not going to destroy the weapons, or the power they held.

In Chicago, news that the IRA was back to violence was met with renewed FBI interest in David Rupert. He and Maureen had married after three months and had spent the year travelling back and forth to Ireland, collecting bits and pieces of information on the mainstream Provisional IRA, mostly through Vincent Murray's bar in Sligo, and the never-on-ceasefire Continuity IRA, through Joe O'Neill's bar in Bundoran. In Sligo, Rupert had learned that the IRA was sneaking its members to the US through Shannon Airport. Shannon town had accepted a large number of Irish republican refugees from the north when the violence erupted in the late 1960s. Now republican supporters were helping to spirit IRA members to US-bound flights.

"The FBI were all about that information because, at the time, US visas for IRA members was a huge issue," says Rupert. "Clinton was giving visas to Irish republicans as a reward for peace and if you had them using Shannon to get in and out of the US, then America was losing a major bargaining chip."

As Buckley had hoped, once Rupert had accepted the free holidays to Ireland, he was more amenable to revealing the secrets of IRA members living in the border region, where the IRA were strongest and where its largest bombs were manufactured, including the Docklands bomb.

For Rupert, who had tried everything from clown wrestling to mob-supported offshore gambling, being an FBI spy was another layer of excitement for a mind fascinated by the grey area between legal and illegal.

Maureen was in awe of her new husband. When they first met, he was a trucking agent. Now he was revealing himself to be a committed spy in the murky world of international terrorism. For a woman who had spent almost her entire life within a five-mile radius, it was an escape. "An escape into the IRA, that's what he offered," she says.

Over several meetings with Buckley at a restaurant near FBI headquarters in downtown Chicago, Rupert suggested that instead of bar-hopping, he and Maureen would like to set up their own bar along the border so the IRA could come to them, and so they would be in control. He wanted the FBI's clearance and funding.

Most FBI agents would have turned down foreign operations as absurd but Buckley, the free-thinking maverick, readily agreed. The FBI was under huge pressure from the White House to gather IRA intelligence and to shut down its US fundraising and arms shipments in an effort to squeeze it towards peace.

The agreement between Rupert and Buckley, worked out over lunch in Chicago, is a matter of dispute even today and it would be unwise to interfere. Rupert said he was told the FBI would help to keep the pub in operation. Buckley believes that Rupert heard "$8,500 from the FBI" and assumed that he was going to be a contract spy. He believed that the FBI could never overstep the role of the CIA, or the Irish police, in running a foreign operation.

At that time, Rupert was in the process of selling his trucking agency in Chicago so that he and Maureen could find a pub in Ireland and move there full-time. He had spent his life in trucking, it was time to move on, to be a spy, to live the life of intrigue to which he had always aspired.

In June, David and Maureen flew into Shannon and drove up to Sligo to see Vincent Murray, whose pub customers were now on an FBI list for aiding the violation of US immigration and anti-terrorism laws.

Rupert offered to pay for the lease on Murray's pub.

"He did make the offer and I suppose at the time I was interested in getting out of the business but nothing came of it," says Murray. "To be honest, I thought he was talking bullshit."

Next, they drove up to Joe O'Neill, who was running an estate agency in Ballyshannon, a few miles from his pub in Bundoran.

He showed them a few bars on the market. As they drove around, Joe spoke in code to David.

"It was kind of sexist," says Maureen. "I was either left out of conversations or Joe drove off with David by himself. I got the feeling that in Joe's world, women were for the home and for pulling pints."

He took them to the Drowes, a bar in Tullaghan, a short drive south of Bundoran, in the tiny sliver of land where County Leitrim meets the Atlantic coastline. It came with its own caravan park, where some northern IRA members spent their summers. The two-storey yellow building, on the main street going through the village, had a small shop, a two-bed apartment upstairs and fishing rights to the salmon-rich Drowes river, which met the Atlantic Ocean just to the right of the bar. On the other side of the bar, close to the caravan park, were steep cliffs where the Atlantic smashed against the rock, sending plumes of mist over the edge.

They decided to take it. They flew back to the US to make final arrangements and then, on 31 July 1996, they signed the lease and shook hands with Mick McNulty, the bar owner. The FBI, which supplied $8,500 cash for the deposit and rent, was now in the Irish pub business.

The Ruperts had a lot to do to get the place ready. They hired a cleaner and remodelled some of the bar. Rupert quickly discovered that there was more work than he initially thought. "We found used condoms, there were lots of empty beer bottles, there was a freezer full of old salmon that customers would use to pay their bar bill, it was a mess."

They put Maureen's maiden name on advertising leaflets for the reopened pub because her name sounded more Irish. Covering all bases, the leaflets gave the bar's address as being in the Republic of Ireland followed by the parenthesis (The Free State), the IRA's dismissive term for the southern state.

A local woman, Pauline McGovern, was hired to help them run the place. "Pauline showed me how to wash glasses and pull pints," says Maureen, who had never worked in a bar before. "When I put ice in a mixed drink she would say: 'No! no! No ice for that now.'"

The bar clientele was a mixture of IRA people, holiday makers, fishermen, locals and visiting ODCs (ordinary decent criminals).

"Some families were kind of half and half," said Rupert. "Like maybe one half of the family was IRA and the other half were criminals, who would be expected to steal a car or two for the cause when it was required."

Whole families would come in on rainy days and spend hours drinking and singing.

"You have to be careful with the ODCs. I had a beatbox in there playing music and people are up dancing. I turned around and it's been stolen. We had some rough customers in there. I had to physically throw some of them out of the bar at closing time."

David and Maureen learned why the bar was up for lease — it had no Guinness and its stock was old.

"When we moved in, we discovered all these leftover spirits that weren't selling," says Rupert. "There was this nasty green liqueur, Pernod. I wanted to get rid of it so I put up a sign saying one pound a shot. That was a big success. Some guys spent all day drinking shot after shot and then I would find green vomit sprayed all over the toilets."

Their best customer was Frank O'Rourke, who was dating Pauline's sister.

"Frank was supposed to paint the place for me but I discovered that he made the same offer to another bar in exchange for drink. He and a friend drank through $1,500 worth of booze in the other bar and didn't paint an inch.

"So once the cheap shots started, Maureen phoned me shouting because Frank was lying on the floor not moving. She says, 'Frank's dead.'

"I said, 'Is he on the green stuff?' She said 'yeah', so I said, 'Just drag him to the couch. If he moves, he's ok, if not, call an ambulance.'"

"I was terrified," says Maureen. "I kept saying, 'We've killed Frank, we've killed Frank'. Then Frank gets up behind me, wipes his mouth and says he wants another drink. I thought some members of my family were alcoholic, but they were just wannabees. Frank and some of our customers in the Drowes were the real thing. It was all-day drinking, every day, the same four guys propping up the bar."

Their single biggest problem was not the old liquor, but the lack of Guinness, and that was how they entered the bomb-making business.

Without Guinness, a rural bar was bound to fail and the previous bar manager had not paid the Guinness invoices, so they cut her off.

"Maureen and I both knew that without Guinness we're finished. I asked round. Turned out the IRA had a good racket smuggling Guinness across the border.

"So I learned about this bar in Sligo where I could buy the Guinness kegs out the back door for cash. It was run from the north and the big problem now was the empty kegs. We had a lot of them and even if we convinced Guinness to start supplying again, they would refuse to take these kegs, because they were obviously smuggled from somewhere in the UK because of their serial numbers. So I ended up giving the local scrapyard all the kegs just to get rid of them."

Joe O'Neill heard about the beer keg surplus and moved quickly to take them.

"They were ideal casing to pack bombs into, the IRA had been using them for decades. Best of all, the serial numbers on the kegs were untraceable because they'd come through unknown smuggling routes in the north," said Rupert.

Joe O'Neill's group, the Continuity IRA, was taking in Provisional IRA members disillusioned with the peace talks and was bombing the border area, often using the long-established IRA method of packing bombs into beer kegs.

Two weeks before the Drowes opened, the Continuity IRA exploded a 1,200lb bomb outside a hotel in Enniskillen, County Fermanagh, injuring 17 people, most of them wedding guests, as they fled the hotel.

"Joe never said bomb or explosive or gun when he came in. He never talked on the phone and he never said any incriminating word in case he was being bugged. He would simply come in and say, 'I need a few kegs.' Then he would make an explosive motion with his hands.

"So I would write down the UK serial numbers of the kegs before I would hand them over to Joe, so the FBI would know where they came from if there was a bomb."

As a close friend of O'Neill, Rupert was under tight scrutiny from local gardaí. "There was one cop, Marcus Mulligan, he didn't like me very much because I was Continuity IRA."

"I had nothing against him personally," says the now-retired Garda Mulligan. "But he was a known associate of Joe O'Neill. Rupert seemed a nice enough fella, but O'Neill was very well known to us," he said.

Mulligan, and other gardaí in the area, kept the Drowes under occasional surveillance.

For the bar patrons, and the families in the caravan park, the Ruperts were a popular novelty.

"They loved to hear Dave's stories about America," says Maureen. "One of the women from the caravan park loved to imitate his drawl. She'd say, 'If I taaalk realll slooooow, I can taaaalk likkke Daaaaviidd.'"

"Everyone called me 'the Big Yank'," said David. "We bought an old Volkswagen Jetta and we used to drive customers home for free every night so they could get tanked in the bar if they wanted. That made me popular. One night I'm dropping them home and Frank is drunk as usual. So I drive away from his place and I don't see him in the mirror and then I see that his pants were stuck in the door and I've dragged him 100 metres. If I hadn't checked the mirror, he would have been dead for sure.

"I swear to God, the show, *Father Ted*, is accurate if you ran a rural pub in those days. We had a whole family of farmers who would come to the pub clinging to one tractor. Father, mother, grandparents, grandchildren hanging off the side of this tractor.

"There were always fights. There was this local guy, he was the nicest guy in the world until he got drunk, then he would come at you with hands like shovels, and he's built like a fucking moose. Mostly, they kept me out of fights because of my size and because everyone knew I was connected to the Continuity IRA.

"All kinds of people were coming in and out – fuel smugglers, terrorists, beer-runners.

"There was even a local prostitute who used to come in now and then. She was used by local boys to get broken in.

"There were a lot of IRA people in the bar. One of the older women from the caravan park used to bounce her grandson on her knee and tell him that he would grow up to shoot policemen in the north. How do you defeat that? That always stuck with me."

The woman gave Rupert a miniature carved harp, made by her son-in-law and other IRA prisoners. "She never had money for the caravan rent so she gave me the harp. The caravan park was turning into a nightmare. There were supposed to be 20 caravans but there were 40 and nobody wanted to pay the rent. I'm chasing around after them all the time.

"Also, the caravan park closed for the winter but nobody took their caravans away. There was one family in particular. They decided they were going to stay the winter. So I shut the power off on them because I wasn't going to pay for the electricity all winter. That got a war going. One of them was already a few years behind on the rent. Some of them I would forget about, but not this guy because he was a real asshole.

"I took his caravan out and put it out by the road so he could get it. Then someone saw it and stripped the aluminium off it, so he sued me for the price of the caravan. I wrote back to his solicitor and it went away."

A member of the same family was drunk and abusive to customers one night, so Rupert ordered the staff to open the door. "Then I just ran at him and we both went flying out the door. I was about to land on him, so I put out my leg to block my fall and really damaged my knee. He kicked me and said he'd kill me, but he was in the next night, looking for free pints."

In the middle of all this aggravation, there were moments when Rupert questioned what they were doing.

"There was this guy who came in called Black Peter, the guy who said he'd paint the place for booze, along with Frank.

"One day at the weekend, Black Peter's girlfriend wanted him to go to the doctor because his stomach had ruptured from too much drink. She told me to pretend we were going to the lumberyard because he hated going to the doctor.

"Frank wants me to drop him home because he's drunk. He was crying in the bar because he thinks his sick cow is going to die. I drive to Bundoran. Black Peter realised he's being duped into going to the doctor. He won't go in, but his girlfriend runs in and gets the doctor to come to our car. The doctor comes out and examines him in the back seat while Frank is still crying about his cow. One needed a doctor, the other a vet.

"It was one of those moments of clarity because most of the time, I was too busy to stand back from it all. I'm sitting at the steering wheel listening to both men crying, thinking, 'Who am I, and what the fuck am I doing here?'

"There was always some hassle going on. There was a bunch of those tin boxes for collecting money for charities. One of them was for Catholic missions. Nobody ever put money in it except for pennies. One day I took it and emptied it because the bar was so small and I really needed the space. I wrote a note about how much I took out and put the note in the box.

"It was six months later when a priest showed up for the money and he got all furious with me about it because I had opened the collection box. I said, 'I don't have room for it. If you want a donation, I'll give you a donation.' So I gave him the amount that was in the collection box plus a 20-pound note.

"Then I'd have Joe O'Neill come in telling me to keep kegs for making bombs. It was like all human life was passing through this place."

One customer was horribly upset because a neighbour had threatened to sue if he didn't get rid of his goat. So the man brought his goat to the cliffs to fling it off the edge. With the momentum, he fell with the goat. He was badly bruised in the fall and the goat had to be put down.

Within a month, both Provisional and Continuity IRA members were coming down in big numbers from nearby Bundoran, unsure what to make of the eccentric American and eager to find out his true background.

Chief among them was Philip McCluskey, who was wanted in the US for allegedly running an IRA ring that smuggled 2,900 bomb detonators from Tucson, Arizona. McCluskey fled the US after he was indicted and was hiding out in Bundoran.

"McCluskey knew a lot about the FBI from his time in the US. He had a lot of dealings with one agent in New York who was chasing down the IRA, like Buckley was in Chicago. He'd sit at the bar counter and say, 'Do you know the guy?' and stare at me. I'd keep cleaning the bar and say, 'Never heard of the guy.' Then he'd ask me about another FBI agent, or a prosecutor, and I'd just shrug my shoulders and keep cleaning."

As time went on, Rupert became better and better friends with Declan Curneen, a Continuity IRA member from Leitrim. He was short, bearded and was a Republican Sinn Féin purist, who believed there should be no parliament in Ireland until there was a united Ireland.

In 1995, he was convicted of climbing up a flagpole outside an electronics factory, ripping down a Union Jack and tearing it to pieces. In prison for a few weeks for refusing to pay the fine, he went on hunger strike and Leitrim County Council called for his release. He and his son also had convictions for fighting with gardaí at an IRA commemoration in Limerick.

David visited his house and regaled him with stories of the US. Curneen, a close friend of Joe O'Neill, named one of his best greyhounds Rupert, in honour of their American friend. Human Rupert came out to Curneen's house to pet him and stand for a photo together. Canine Rupert was blue with dark streaks, an unusual colour for a greyhound and considered good luck. He raced in Donegal and all over the border area.

It was a sign for David that he was totally accepted in the Continuity IRA. Curneen loved to have Rupert over at the house to recount tales of gun battles with the Brits.

Curneen and O'Neill approached Rupert with a special project. They could see that he knew about computers – dial-up, broadband, websites – it was beyond their generation but they knew it was powerful. O'Neill asked Rupert to set up a Continuity IRA cyber-terrorism unit, and Curneen supplied young recruits to be the other cell members.

Rupert: "So we had our first meeting. I could see these two kids had no interest in this and barely knew how to switch on a computer. I suggested we learn how to hack, so we could get into MI5's webpage and post Continuity IRA symbols on its home page. I knew we had zero prospect of getting it off the ground, but it gave me cover. It made it look like I was doing something for the cause when I wasn't."

One rainy day, when Rupert was entertaining customers with trucking stories, he got a call on the phone upstairs from Ed Buckley, who told him to go to a meeting with the FBI's legal affairs liaison in Dublin.

"Chris Patton was the liaison in Ireland when I started and he was related to the general. So I left Maureen in charge of the pub while I drove down to Dublin."

Patton was in charge of liaising with Irish police so that they did not feel that the FBI was invading their jurisdiction with undercover work. Over a cup of tea, he explained that he wanted Rupert to meet a senior garda, so that Rupert's spying would not lead to a diplomatic crisis with the Irish government if it was ever uncovered.

Patton and Rupert discussed their families for an hour and waited for the garda. "Patton seemed nervous to me, an all-over-the-place kinda guy."

Chief Superintendent Dermot Jennings walked in. A tall, thin man with mousy hair and known for his efficiency, Jennings was attached to the crime and security unit and was leading the Republic of Ireland's fight against the IRA.

He had been part of a unit that was set up to tackle paramilitaries after a Marxist group, the Irish National Liberation Army, killed two gardaí in a bank raid. In 1990, he spent three months on placement with the FBI, learning modern surveillance and detection techniques that he was keen to bring to counter-terrorism work.

Under Standing Order 8 of the IRA's rules, its members were strictly prohibited from attacking police or army in the southern Republic of Ireland, with which it claimed a certain nationalist allegiance and with whom its northern members hoped to be one day politically united. Still, the IRA bitterly resented the gardaí, especially those in the anti-terrorism Special Branch, over which Jennings presided. In June, an IRA unit in the south killed a garda and seriously injured another during a bank raid. Two men rammed their car and then sprayed the two gardaí with automatic fire from AK-47s. The brutality and senselessness of the killing led to a national outcry: 50,000 people lined the streets of Limerick for the funeral and public anger refocused garda attention on breaking up IRA structures in the Republic. Jennings wanted Rupert on his side.

In the beginning, the two men got on well. They discussed life in the FBI, the pub, Joe O'Neill and the local atmosphere along the border now that the Provisional IRA's ceasefire had been shattered.

Rupert was hoping that the gardaí were going to pay him a salary, along with the FBI, but there was no mention of payment. Gardaí ran an entirely different operation from the FBI, the pace was slower and they generally refrained from paid agents and electronic bugging.

"I didn't know that at the time," said Rupert. "All I knew was that Jennings wanted to meet me again, so I was hopeful that we are going to reach a deal.

"Jennings wanted to meet in Donegal and I thought that was very dangerous as I'm well known there."

They agreed to meet in Boyle, Co Roscommon, in the Irish midlands, about an hour from the Drowes.

"I'm not one bit happy about it because it's too close to the border and my bar, but I go along, hoping Jennings is the key to keeping the pub open.

"Boyle made me nervous. A lot of people knew me and I stuck out because of my size. Here comes Jennings in a fucking bread van and he's a big fellow and he's well known by the IRA.

"He had two chairs set up in the back of this van and we sat down and talked. So I'm already nervous and then he tells me that I've been turned over to the gardaí.

"The pub was barely surviving. I'm hoping the gardaí can pay me $5,000 a month to keep it going. He said, 'What do you want, some travel expenses or something?'

"I said, 'No, I'm doing this for a living.'"

"You've got the pub there."

"Well, it's losing money."

"And so it became very apparent the gardai didn't have any money. They literally wanted me to put my life on the line for petrol money.

"I was in big trouble now. I'm an unpaid informer in a dangerous situation. I'm cut adrift from the FBI and the gardaí are offering nothing but mileage. I'm losing money and, in the bar, I'm literally surrounded by the IRA.

"I climbed out of the bread van and watched Jennings drive away. I knew he wasn't surviving on mileage money."

Rupert went back to the Drowes and told Maureen what happened. They heard from the FBI that Buckley would fly in to Ireland to sort everything out. This time, it would be at a hotel near Dublin Airport – Rupert, Buckley and Jennings.

Rupert continued with the bar work, breaking up fights and delivering drunk customers home. He was waiting anxiously for the meeting.

When he got to the hotel by the airport, Jennings and Buckley had already been talking. From their faces, it didn't look good.

Rupert set out his dilemma, that he gave up his business on the understanding that the FBI would finance him in Ireland, that the pub wasn't making any money, that if the IRA found out what he was doing, he and Maureen were both dead.

Buckley looked at Jennings and then at Rupert. He put down his tea cup. "That was never the deal," he said.

He laid out that the FBI were authorised only to pay the startup costs for taking over the Drowes, but that policing in Ireland was a garda matter and the FBI couldn't overstep its territory.

It was a financial disaster for Rupert.

"I don't get confrontational but God help you next time," said Rupert of his style in meetings. "I just got up and walked out. I walked to the car park and drove back to the pub. I was crushed."

"We were devastated and I was angry," says Maureen. "I was so angry that I felt we should never go back to them. We felt the FBI duped us. I didn't know what to do but I thought we'll just have to go back to nine-to-five jobs in trucking and we are both capable of making a good living."

"I don't really see it in those terms," says a now-retired FBI officer familiar with the case. "As far as I knew, the deal was to help them set up the bar and they would live on its proceeds. I don't know if the FBI was ever supposed to be organising their Guinness runs."

Angry and frustrated with the FBI, David and Maureen decided to drop out of the project and return to trucking in Chicago, while leaving a manager in charge of the Drowes.

They spent a week preparing and packing up. It was the darkest moment of their time in Ireland. They were broke and lost.

They left their car to Pauline McGovern's son and tried in vain to get money from residents in the caravan park. The drink stock alone had cost thousands and bar owner Mick McNulty agreed to reimburse them for it. It was their only hope of any financial salvation.

After hugs and a shake hands with staff, they flew from Shannon to a bitter and cold November in Chicago. They stayed for a week in a Red Top hotel near Maureen's parents in suburban south Chicago, while they looked for somewhere to live.

"It was the most humiliating time of my life," says Maureen. "We thought we were these big spies – we were nothing. I'm in my 40s and we had to borrow money from my father just for the deposit on an apartment. I cried and I was frustrated and didn't know what we could do."

Every day, David called the Drowes, desperate for some profit to keep them alive in Chicago.

"There was this local woman running the bar for us. I'd call her to see how we were doing. The bar was supposed to be open 14 hours a day and she would say we didn't do any business yesterday. I said, 'You didn't do any business? You're open 14 hours a day and you didn't sell one beer?'

"We couldn't find a way through and I felt I had been fucked by the FBI. The year before, I thought I had suckered the FBI into giving me free trips to Ireland. Turns out, I had been an unpaid informer living in middle-of-nowhere Ireland. The FBI had suckered me all along."

CHAPTER 5

Snow drifted sideways and lay in brackish pools of dirt at the edge of the motorway.

Wind sheared off the Great Lakes and whipped sheets of wet ice onto the windscreen. Nearly three inches of snow fell on O'Hare Airport on 20 November, the highest for that day since records began.

It was a bad winter in Chicago.

David Rupert, an FBI spy the previous month, was a delivery man in November 1996.

He was now working with the Land Air Transport Company, hauling packages and envelopes from O'Hare Airport to a sorting centre in Columbus, Ohio.

It was more dangerous to carry paper in winter than car parts – heavy loads keep a truck from slipping on icy roads. The heavier the load in November, the more truckers like it.

Bill Clinton was re-elected president that month, promising to complete his job of bringing about peace in Northern Ireland. Maureen and David, both Democrats, toasted his win, but Clinton's backchannels to the IRA were now far removed from their daily lives.

Using money borrowed from her father, they rented an apartment on West Superior Street in downtown Chicago. She was depressed: "I hated, hated, hated living downtown. I was a suburban girl and now I'm in the city. No space, no parking, there's congestion and noise. I was miserable and I told David over and over that we were done with the FBI and we had to restart our lives."

Maureen had a high-paying managerial job at the truck plaza before she met David. He had dazzled her with talk of his life as an international spy, and now they were left with nothing.

She took a job managing four convenience stores for a company called Tuxedo Junction, which served some of the most crime-ridden neighbourhoods in south Chicago.

"The pilfering by customers and employees was crazy, you just couldn't control it," says Maureen. "People walked out of there with shopping bags full of stolen stuff, they didn't even hide it.

"A lot of our staff were affiliated with gangs or were girlfriends of gang members. There was one kid from the projects, he had gotten in trouble with the law and had no job experience. I hired him to give him a chance and really thought we could turn this one around. He robbed us blind. I fired him and refused to give him his final paycheck for all the stuff he stole, which is illegal but I was so mad. He started threatening me and I shouted back, 'No, you just get the hell out of here.'"

The strain of daily theft was starting to show.

"It was driving me a bit crazy because you couldn't plan anything. One day one of the staff said that a woman had just walked out with a six-pack of beer. She was halfway down the block, so I got in my car and drove after her. I pulled up on the sidewalk in front of her, ran at her and grabbed the beer right off her."

"I felt scared just standing around to pick her up," says Rupert, who would come in to see her at the main store on South Western Avenue, close to Midway Airport.

Yet within a few weeks, they had repaid Maureen's father for the deposit on the apartment.

How could their marriage survive this financial ruin, when Rupert's three marriages had failed under less strain? In part because, through the pain he had experienced, David Rupert had matured. He no longer craved the next girlfriend and the one after that. Once that was an exciting game, now it left him feeling empty and soulless. In Florida, he had been a sad figure, cruising the beach bars for the next female fix. In Maureen he had found a best friend, a woman from the trucking world who laughed at his jokes and who made him laugh. Most of all, she had a deep sense of the absurd, honed from two decades at the trucking plaza. Their time with the FBI was absurd and so was their new life in Chicago.

Rupert, still burning with anger from his experience at the Drowes, asked for help in finding a lawyer. Maureen's daughter, Dorie, had graduated from college and was doing a job placement while preparing for law school. She put him in touch with a former prosecutor turned criminal lawyer named Jim Koch, who had an office near the FBI headquarters in downtown Chicago.

Rupert went to see him in early December and started to unravel the whole story – Linda and the IRA and the FBI showing up at the truck plaza and the free trips to Ireland and the pub in Leitrim.

"He didn't believe a word I said. He thought I was crazy. He said, 'Did they give you a badge and a gun?'

"He said he'd look into it and I didn't hear from him in weeks. I thought I'd never hear from him again so I stayed trucking to Columbus every day."

Then one morning just before Christmas, Koch called. He had spoken to the FBI, and they wanted to talk. He seemed even more surprised than Rupert.

He and Koch went together to the FBI building and were ushered into a conference room to meet Ed Buckley, Buckley's new assistant, Mark Lundgren, and the FBI lawyer Jim Krupowski.

Lundgren was polite and accommodating and enthusiastic. He was well dressed and polished and seemed almost the opposite of Buckley's gruff and confrontational style.

Rupert also liked Krupowski, who seemed sympathetic to his plight. When Rupert outlined what happened, Krupowski gave him a piece of advice: "If it's not in writing, don't expect to get it."

"I was used to the trucking world," says Rupert, "where you delivered on your honour and you subcontracted to truckers on the expectation that they would just show up. Krupowski sensed that about me and wanted to help."

From then on, whenever the FBI promised him something, he refused to accept it unless it was in writing.

"I don't know how many times I threw that in their face from that moment forward. Everything is defined by that one piece of advice from Krupowski."

By now, a peace deal in Northern Ireland was one of the most important foreign policy aims of the Clinton administration and it was causing major strain with FBI director Louis Freeh. He sided with the British in being implacably opposed to granting American visas to Gerry Adams and other IRA leaders. Adams was flanked by dozens of reporters when he visited the US for the first time during the IRA ceasefire. He appeared on Larry King and his arrival in the US made the cover of the *New York Post*. Once the IRA had bombed London and killed civilians, Freeh felt justified in taking a hard line on them. He felt they were murdering their way to negotiations.

Agents like Buckley, who had chased the IRA for years, were firmly of the director's view.

But the FBI needed David Rupert to figure out if the IRA would split into factions supporting and opposing the peace talks. They also needed his help to shut down its supply routes in the US.

With Buckley nodding approval, Krupowski offered a contract: up to $2,500 a month for infiltration of the IRA in both the US and Ireland.

"I had to laugh," says Rupert. "Up to $2,500 a month meant I could get a lot less. It was really nothing compared with the risk they wanted me to take. Maureen thought I was crazy to even consider it but I thought that if we got something in writing from the FBI, it might lead to something bigger."

"I did think he was crazy," says Maureen. "I was done with the FBI, we had come out the other side of all this stress with jobs and a life and I wanted to move on."

In February 1997, Rupert, with a roll of the eyes from Maureen, signed the contract with the FBI for $2,500 a month plus expenses. One clause in the contract stated that he should not carry out criminal acts unless they were expressly authorised by the FBI.

Buckley explained that they would fund a trucking office for Rupert in Chicago, which was to be a front for spying on IRA supporters in the US. The office would be bugged, and groups fundraising and gun-running for the IRA should be encouraged to hold their meetings there.

Rupert could pick the office, but it should be somewhere with its own entrance, so that IRA gun-runners could not claim they had gone to the building to visit another office.

They also told him that the FBI technical team wanted to fit a bugging device in the cabin of Rupert's truck. He should pick up IRA supporters in the truck and encourage them to talk.

The technical details would be worked out at a later date.

After signing the contract in the FBI's Chicago office, Rupert handed in his notice at the freight company. Now he was a paid FBI employee. In future, there would be no more vagueness, or suggestions, or maybes or promises.

"From here on in with the FBI," he says, "it was 'put it in writing or fuck off'."

That same week, 23-year-old Lance Bombardier Stephen Restorick was shot dead by what had become known as the "South Armagh Sniper", who had killed nine British soldiers and two police officers between 1990 and 1997. There were actually two sniper teams operating within the IRA's border heartland of South Armagh and they were its most effective units. The British were pulling out of many patrols because of the snipers, and rerouting helicopter sorties to avoid being hit. Most of the 20-plus IRA members involved were local farmers, whose roots in violent republicanism ran back generations. They used Barrett high-impact, long-range rifles, mounted on the back of hatchback cars, with a bullet-proof metal plate in the back through which the gun protruded. The snipers were under strict instructions: "one shot, one kill". The car would drive off immediately after the shot was fired and they had never been caught.

The chief sniper was Michael Caraher, whose brother, Fergal, was killed in 1990 when British soldiers riddled their car with bullets, allegedly when they tried to ram a soldier. Michael Caraher himself barely survived the shooting and lost a lung. When he got out of hospital, he helped devise the sniper teams.

FBI intelligence showed that the Barrett rifles had originated in Chicago, the first one being smuggled into Dublin in 1986 and brought to the north. A second was purchased in 1990 from a gun dealer in Ohio and smuggled piece by piece into Ireland.

The FBI were requested by the British specifically to short-circuit the Chicago arms route, which was run by Frank O'Neill, a Chicago publican, and others deeply committed to the republican cause.

On 27 February, Rupert flew back to Ireland and straight to the Drowes to sort out the financial mess.

"The bar was still there so I just took up residence upstairs. I had signed a contract saying I couldn't do anything illegal without the FBI's consent. Things would have to be a bit more formal now. No running illegal kegs from the north. So I get to the Drowes on the first day and I smell diesel. I knew it was fucking trouble."

A customer from just north of the border was running a fuel-laundering business near the back of the pub.

Diesel washing, or laundering, was Irish republicanism's single biggest financial asset. Diesel was sold at a reduced rate to farmers who needed it on their farms, and the UK and Irish government put a supposedly indelible dye into it so that customs officials could inspect petrol stations and ensure they weren't selling it. Using corrosive chemicals, the IRA ran an illegal tanker system that removed the dye. It then sold the diesel to petrol stations at a reduced rate and ran its own petrol stations along the border. Some border roads had petrol stations every few hundred metres in the 1980s and 90s. The IRA, and the smugglers who paid them a percentage, also smuggled cheaper petrol and diesel from the north and sold it in the south. If there was a fluctuation in prices and the south became cheaper, the fuel supply suddenly flowed the other way. The Provisional IRA chief of staff, Thomas "Slab" Murphy, had a two-way pump installed under his pig shed, which was built right on the border. Whichever side of the border had cheaper fuel, he would pump it under the pig shed to tankers waiting on the other side.

The Drowes sat along this vast network that stretched the length of the border. Located just a few miles inside the border right between Donegal and Leitrim, it was a good location for quick distribution. "I wasn't happy about this fuel business operating near the pub. You could smell the diesel all over. He had the tanks washing fuel, he made an awful fucking mess out the back. The place reeked of oil. The FBI had no interest in fuel smuggling in Leitrim and I didn't want to get busted for that.

"All the time, this guy running the diesel is a good customer in the bar. He'd come down to the pub to drink, and his wife would send his daughter with him to make sure he didn't drink too much and he'd get drunk and off they'd go back home.

"I had to try to convince him that putting it near the back of the pub on the main street wasn't a good idea and that it could be raided at any time.

"Then he moved it up to his house. Even then there was still enough fuel-washing equipment near the pub to bust any of us.

"I went up to his house and there were fuel lines running across the road in front of his house, cars had to drive over them. I said it wouldn't take long to find you, your house fucking smells like a truck stop. But I was just glad to move the fuel lines away from us."

David Rupert was in a very dangerous situation in the spring of 1997. For $30,000 a year, a tiny fraction of what he made in trucking, he was informing on both the Provisional and Continuity IRA, both of which would torture and kill him if they found out. Without his consent, the bar was storing equipment for the fuel laundering business, the IRA's most precious commodity.

He decided to cut his ties with the Drowes. The drink sales would never pay the rent and he didn't want to get implicated in the fuel scam.

He decided that he and Maureen would rent a house in Tullaghan and come and go from the US when they wanted. It was owned by Pauline's brother, who would stay there when he came back to Tullaghan from work in Galway. "It was far from ideal," said Rupert. "No offence to the guy, we just wanted our own space. Besides, there were Continuity IRA meetings taking place in the house behind his back and he was beginning to suspect we were up to something. The chief of staff came up from Limerick for one meeting and I'd leave them to it."

Soon after renting the house, he called over to see Joe O'Neill, who had an office above his pub in Bundoran.

"Joe liked to talk upstairs. He talked Continuity IRA stuff in the local graveyard but he also trusted the office because someone was usually in the bar downstairs and he and his family lived right behind it, so it was unlikely the cops could bug it." Upstairs, Joe was in a great mood. The Provisional IRA was in disarray. Their best people were disillusioned with the talk of peace and were starting to come over to the Continuity IRA.

The organisation was also being supplied with Semtex and other bomb-making equipment by Mickey McKevitt, the quartermaster general of the Provisional IRA, who was bitterly opposed to peace.

"I said, 'Joe, is there anything I can get in the US that would help the movement?'

"That's when Joe told me about this woman, a teacher in Donegal committed to the Continuity IRA. She had helped in the past and she would be waiting at the school to pick up whatever I sent from the States."

Joe had a verbal list of supplies for the Continuity IRA, which was escalating its attacks, mostly aimed at hotels and other businesses close to the border. He wanted three things: detonating cord, plastic explosives and detonators.

As the bomb parts would be sent to a school, Joe said that the plastic explosives should be stuffed inside teddy bears, the detonating cord should be disguised as skipping ropes and the dets could be hidden in radios, where they would look like electronic components.

"They had clearly done this before because they had this whole system set up.

"Also, I would be sending bomb parts by airmail to Ireland.

"You wonder how many times you have flown on a plane and some asshole has placed these in the storage where it could go off.

"I guess there was a bit of a change in my mindset at that moment. I looked at Joe. Here he is, this religious guy willing to use a Catholic school full of six and seven-year-olds to smuggle in explosives when everyone in Ireland is dreaming of peace.

"I shook his hand and said I would do my best, but I don't think I ever looked at him quite the same again."

This was a major jump. "Now Joe trusted me enough to share weapon routes from the US. I felt he was treating me like a full member of Continuity."

Rupert contacted the FBI almost immediately and gave them the address of the school.

"Ed Buckley was really pleased. It was a big change in my relationship with the FBI. The FBI wanted to shut down all these weapon and bomb routes from America and force the IRA into talks. Ed went to check the school address against past shipments from the US. He told me, 'You're doing good, Dave. Looks like we might need you for bigger things.' I didn't know what he meant but I sure as hell found out later."

*****

Several weeks later, Joe O'Neill was giving a speech outside the General Post Office in Dublin, once the headquarters of the Irish rebels in the 1916 uprising and a hallowed place in Irish republican lore.

A group from the Continuity IRA-supporting boy scout group, Fianna Éireann, were standing to attention as he spoke. I was starting in journalism and had been following Fianna Éireann for a year, trying to understand the Continuity IRA mindset, and frequently interviewing Fianna Éireann's leaders, Anthony and Alan Ryan, two Dublin brothers.

In his speech, O'Neill angrily denounced Sinn Féin and the Provisional IRA for preparing for talks. He referenced the bombing of the Docklands in London, which had killed two newspaper sellers and injured 40. He said the repeated bombing of the financial district in London "had the Brits on the run" and now the Provisional IRA was "running away from the fight" by allowing Sinn Féin to talk peace. "It's the same fight since 1916, it's the Continuity of the thing," he said.

It was a ruthlessly uncaring speech, one claiming authority from the dead of 1916, and not the living of 1997.

I was standing a few feet away, watching the reaction of passing shoppers. One woman, holding her shopping bags, shouted at O'Neill, "Give us peace. We want peace".

A drunk man tried to rush the microphone. He was screaming at O'Neill to go home. A garda grabbed the man and hugged him. "I know, I know," said the garda, putting his arm around him, "just let it go."

It was a tiny symbol of a changing Ireland. The economy was on its third year of the Celtic Tiger boom, boosted by huge inward investment from multinationals. Divorce was legalised the previous year and the Republic of Ireland yearned for peace in the north. The country wanted to develop into something new, and the narrow Catholic republicanism of Joe O'Neill seemed brutal and anachronistic.

While Joe was in Bundoran, and a member of the town council, he was largely shielded from life outside the border area, where anger and frustration at the IRA was visceral.

I walked over to the woman with the shopping, who was crying.

"We've had 30 years of this shite," she said. "I was just out getting a few things for my family and you have to face this. Why can't they just give us some fucking peace?"

CHAPTER 6

"Royal Avenue there, thanks mate."

The passenger climbed into the back of the taxi.

He was carrying a holdall in his right hand. Security was tight in Belfast – a police officer had been chatting with friends in a gay bar the day before when an Irish National Liberation Army member, wearing a wig, walked up behind him and shot him dead.

A British army helicopter hovered over the city, as it did most days, and there were extra soldiers on the streets.

As the taxi turned on to College Avenue, the back windows smashed with a low thud. Glass flew onto the road.

Three of the passenger's fingers were strewn around the cab, one of them stuck to the taxi door.

Blood was pouring from his hand. He was screaming as he searched for fingers. Dripping blood onto the seat, he put each finger he found into his pocket.

The sports bag was in tatters; wires and a large lump of charred yellow cake could be seen in its remains.

The driver stared at the bag and then at the passenger, who opened the taxi door with his uninjured left hand. Smoke followed him. A man walking his dog and a woman carrying her shopping stopped and stared.

They saw a man limp his way down College Avenue, leaving a trail of blood. He was trying to find a phone box three streets away and then make his way back to republican West Belfast. It was 10 May, 1997.

Within minutes, a car pulled up at the phone box.

Gerard "Hucker" Moyna, barely conscious, was put in the back of a car.

Hucker had already served 10 years for possession of weapons and would do life in prison if he was caught in the north. He was driven two hours west, over the border to Donegal.

As with every Saturday, Joe O'Neill was on stage at his pub in Bundoran, singing rebel ballads with Peggy, a local woman who sang and played the accordion.

"Joe was in the middle of a set," remembers Rupert. "He's told that there is a call for him in the bar. He just gets off the stage, no explanation and Peggy continues singing."

Joe drove his Mercedes from Bundoran a short distance to Ballyshannon, where Hucker was lying in the back of a car, moaning.

They drove down the street to a doctor, arriving at close to midnight.

"It's an emergency," O'Neill said, knocking on the doctor's door. "The man has no fingers."

The doctor opened up a blood-soaked bandage. Hucker took the fingers from his pocket.

Joe tried to explain that fireworks had gone off in Hucker's hand. The doctor knew Joe O'Neill and knew that fireworks would not blow three fingers off, sheared at the base.

He said that he would have to refer Hucker to Sligo General Hospital.

In Sligo, doctors could see almost immediately that the fingers could not be reattached. The bones were fractured, the veins ripped and the fingers shredded.

Meanwhile, in Belfast, the British army had arrived and sealed off College Avenue. A robot approached the taxi and leaned its video camera in the back door.

It revealed two and a half kilos of Semtex, still unexploded, and a timing device. Only the bomb's detonators had gone off. Had the Semtex exploded, it would have blown up the taxi and everyone standing nearby.

It was clear from the taxi driver's account that the man was badly injured, missing fingers and bleeding from his hand.

Sligo Hospital told the gardaí that they believed Hucker had explosives injuries.

Hours later, a group of gardaí arrived at the hospital.

Joe again tried to explain that fireworks had gone off.

He was immediately arrested under the Offences Against the State Act and taken to Sligo garda station.

Upstairs at the hospital, gardaí found Hucker lying on a bed, his arm heavily bandaged, just after a blood transfusion. He was pale and in shock but still conscious.

He was arrested and told he could remain where he was, under garda supervision.

Joe posted bail the next morning. He drove straight to the hotel in Bundoran where Rupert was staying.

Rupert was making last-minute preparations before going back to the US. He knew Hucker, and many other IRA members, from Joe's bar. Joe looked stressed.

"Dave, listen to me. A terrible scene in Belfast, Hucker's fingers were blown off. When are you going back to America?"

"Today."

"Good man. Army business. I need you to buy the biggest firecrackers you can find, blow them up and them send them to me immediately. Immediately, now."

"How is Hucker?"

"He'll make it. I need those firecrackers."

"Alright." Fireworks were strictly banned in Ireland. Joe needed the most powerful American firecrackers.

Back in the US, Rupert called the FBI field office in Chicago. Agent Buckley cleared it for him to buy firecrackers in a megastore, blow them up and send them to Joe for Hucker's alibi.

"You can't get fireworks in Illinois, but across the border in Indiana, they were on every street corner. So I just bought some big ones, let them off across from the trucking office and sent them to Joe. The FBI recorded the serial numbers of the package."

Joe visited Hucker in hospital to get their facts together and, with a solicitor sitting beside his bed, Hucker made a statement to the gardaí telling them that he was showing off Rupert's American firecrackers to his children on the beach when one went off in his hand.

On 17 May, when doctors said Hucker was well enough to move, he was escorted to Sligo garda station and immediately rearrested. Shrapnel embedded in his hand had matched that of the bomb fragments in Belfast.

Garda Detective Inspector Thomas Farragher said that when told he would be charged, Hucker replied, "I want to know why the emphasis is on an Irish citizen, and I am not guilty." Political offences had long been a difficult subject in the Republic. In the

1970s, it passed legislation allowing terror suspects to be tried in the south for crimes committed in the north. It was rarely used but Hucker's solicitor advised him to take it, as he already had IRA convictions in the north.

He had a one-year wait before his case came up in the anti-terrorist Special Criminal Court in Dublin.

"Hucker had just received a big compensation payment because he was hit by a car in Bundoran and he was determined to spend it, as he knew he was going to prison for a long time," says Rupert.

Maureen, who came and went to Ireland when her husband was there, remembers Hucker in the bar. "I didn't really remember him before this but afterwards, I sure did because he was missing three fingers and drinking really heavily."

Joe O'Neill and Declan Curneen, the two local Continuity IRA leaders, were close to Hucker.

They visited him frequently in Bundoran and told him of past martyrs – how the late aunt of Marian Price, the dissident IRA leader, had her arms blown off when her bomb exploded prematurely, but she never complained. As children, Marian and her sister, Dolours, would put their aunt's cigarette in her mouth and light it for her and she would sit back, puffing and tell them through the corner of her mouth when it was time to tip the ash and put the cigarette back in again.

The evidence against Hucker was overwhelming and the gardaí in Bundoran were adamant that Joe and the Big Yank had concocted the fireworks story.

Hucker pleaded guilty and was jailed for seven years.

Rupert had only been back in the US a few days when the FBI said they wanted to meet him.

Big things were happening in Ireland.

They agreed to meet at the truck stop.

Now devoted to the spying game, Rupert had been set up by the FBI with a new front office, where he was to capture recorded conversations with IRA financiers and gun-runners.

For the operation, Rupert had chosen a small trucking office close to downtown Chicago in an area called the Old Stockyards.

"The Stockyards was once the cattle and meat capital of Chicago. I used to haul meat from there where I was based in New York. Now it had really changed and it was rough. I would take the train there every day, carrying a pistol in my pocket," Rupert said.

Across the road from the stockyards truck depot was a small apartment building with an office at the front for a company called US 1 Industries, a legitimate trucking logistics company with whom Rupert had an agency contract. But the rent for it, security cameras and bugging devices were all paid for by the FBI.

In the parking lot across the road was Rupert's red Kenworth T600 truck, in which the FBI had fixed a listening device under the dashboard. He helped them install it and connect it up to the truck's electrical supply.

When the device was recording, a dashboard red light would switch on.

"At that time, the FBI really wanted results in Chicago. It was pretty obvious that a lot of money was going to the Continuity IRA from the city. They weren't interested in diesel-washing in Donegal or guys blowing their hands off in Belfast. They wanted to show their bosses they had this threat in Chicago under control."

Rupert's sole focus was now on the Continuity IRA's US support group, the Irish Freedom Committee, which was being run by the

Irish-born publican Frank O'Neill. Frank was close friends with Joe O'Neill in Ireland but they were not related.

The IFC was set up after Republican Sinn Féin and the Continuity IRA broke away from Sinn Féin and the Provisional IRA because they bitterly opposed recognising the southern parliament in Dublin. As far as they were concerned, they would bomb and shoot the British out of Northern Ireland, and only then could any parliament be allowed.

The FBI was urging Rupert to get closer to the IFC, which was gaining disillusioned Provisional IRA supporters in the US.

On 23 May, 1997, among the hefty truckers milling around outside the offices, one might have spotted Agent Buckley walking into Rupert's office. Intelligence from Ireland suggested the Provisional IRA would move towards a ceasefire. If President Clinton was to clinch peace in Ireland, the FBI would have to clamp down hard on Continuity IRA people like Frank O'Neill. "In short," says Rupert, "they wanted convictions."

*****

"Do you see that? What's that?"

Octogenarian Frank O'Neill is pointing at a photo of a dog on the wall of his Chicago pub.

"Patch, that's Patch." Patch was a regular at O'Neill's.

Frank would encourage her to climb up on a stool and push the pool ball with her paw. He would shout instructions in his booming Northern Ireland/Chicago accent until Patch knocked the ball into the pocket, and the bar crowd would cheer.

A TV assistant was in the crowd one night and Patch performed her trick in front of millions of people on the David Letterman Show.

"Ah, she's gone now," Frank liked to say. "Won't be long before I'm joining her."

Frank had closed his bar to the public but opened it at night for his fellow Continuity IRA supporters, people like David Rupert, and Irish American hardliners like Deirdre Fennessy, the glamorous daughter of a Chicago doctor, and her husband, Richard Wallace. There was also Catherina Wojtowicz, a conservative Irish/Polish American who would later become a major figure in the Tea Party movement.

"Frank would invite me up to his bar to have a chat but then some of his IFC friends would just happen to come along. What he was really doing was getting them to check me out, to see if they had seen me anywhere before."

A native of Carrickfergus in Northern Ireland, Frank O'Neill had a pencil moustache and tight haircut and was seldom without a suit and a smile.

Beneath his folksy republicanism, he raged against the Northern Ireland government, and wanted its destruction, as much for revenge as for ideological reasons. His writings of the time, contained in an Irish American magazine he partly owned, are tirades of anger and hatred, justifying the worst IRA atrocities with talk of job discrimination against Catholics in Northern Ireland.

O'Neill grew up in Northern Ireland in the bad days of Protestant British hegemony in the 1930s and 40s. Local elections, housing and jobs were rigged in almost every area to keep Irish Catholics from gaining any power. The Irish flag was illegal, the Irish language and sports viewed with official suspicion.

O'Neill moved south and joined the Irish army in 1943, hoping to convince military leaders in Dublin to invade the north and drive out the British, but nobody would listen.

"They just weren't interested, nobody wanted to know," he would later tell the Chicago Tribune.

He and several others were put on trial in the south of Ireland for IRA membership but he fled to Chicago, where he ran his bar until the mid-1990s. Like many of his generation, he was as pro-American as he was anti-British.

"I really, really liked Frank," says Rupert. "We just always got on. He was very relaxed with me. Deirdre Fennessy's husband, Richard, didn't like me one bit but as long as I said, 'Up the IRA' in the bar, I had Frank's protection."

A rift within the IFC was growing over whether Frank should give fundraising money directly to the Continuity IRA.

"The other groups in New York, Philadelphia and Boston wanted to give money to the families of Continuity IRA prisoners, so their children could have Christmas toys and clothes, but Frank wanted all the money to go directly to bombs and weapons," says Rupert.

"This old-timer in Philadelphia, she used to be in Cumann na mBan, the women's section of the IRA. She told me that if the money went to prisoner families, it still freed up the finances of Continuity IRA to do what they had to do. She was hoping I could convince Frank. But Frank never listened to that. He wanted money to go to the fight, nothing else."

Frank had been under FBI surveillance, and the close attention of Agent Buckley, for at least two decades.

Once, in 1993, while arresting one of Frank's supporters in a sting operation, Buckley accidentally left a $2,000 tape recorder in Frank's bar, which had been recording observations of people coming in and out. When he came back to get it moments later, it was gone. Frank denied all knowledge, despite threats of arrest. The incident made it into the Chicago newspapers and O'Neill often enjoyed taunting the FBI about the missing recorder.

The FBI even considered Frank a suspect in a Chicago murder because someone wrote the letters IRA in blood before dying. It emerged that the real murderer's name began with the letters I-R-A. "That made Frank mad as hell with the cops," says Rupert.

Rupert found infiltrating the Irish Freedom Committee easier than he expected, because he was coming from Ireland with the blessing of Joe O'Neill and the Continuity IRA.

"I had been living along the Irish border, helping supply bomb parts and knew a lot of IRA people by that point. The IFC were really impressed with my credentials."

While he was still operating from the Stockyards truck depot, the bureau supplied Rupert with a tape recorder for use at IFC fundraisers in Chicago.

"Many of the fundraisers were in Catholic diocese school halls and every penny we got was going towards explosives and weapons.

"Deirdre Fennessy's mother was always there helping out and she had no clue what was really going on. She said to me, 'This is for the IRA prisoners, right?' That was always the story they told people. I said, 'Yeah, that's what it is.' It was always meant to be 'prison relief'. It was only the upper people who knew that it was going to the army."

At the fundraisers, it was $10 in, with $100 for a raffle ticket, with a top prize of $10,000.

Joe O'Neill had been guest of honour at one of their annual dinners and told the crowd that Prince Charles would visit the site of Lord Mountbatten's death in Sligo. He told the crowd, to cheers, that the Continuity IRA had left a device for him that the prince would be lucky to avoid.

By 1997, because he was travelling to Ireland so often, always paid for by the FBI, Frank appointed Rupert as their under-the-counter bagman to take money they had raised to Joe O'Neill for direct use by the Continuity IRA.

"What they don't know is that the FBI is paying for all my trips to Ireland, but as far as they know, I'm going there because I'm making good money in trucking and I'm committed to the cause. So Frank makes me the bagman for an organisation that didn't want to leave any electronic records.

"That's it. That's the whole key to the story of how I infiltrated so deeply in Ireland. When you turn up with $10,000 five times a year, a lot of people want you around. So much has been written about how I infiltrated these groups and there it is – I was the man with the bag of money from Chicago and the doors opened up."

The FBI was delighted with this arrangement but was very clear – he could only bring to Ireland what was raised by the Irish Freedom Committee, the FBI would not be helping to fund the Continuity IRA.

Rupert's truck, now a mobile bugging device, was put to use around the US, recording IFC members. The first target was Joe Dillon, leader of the Irish Freedom Committee in Boston.

"They had tried to get him and Phil Kent, their guy in Canada, because the FBI had followed them to a depot on Long Island where they photographed them loading and unloading boxes. They got a search warrant and raided the place and found containers of IRA T-shirts that were being sold in Boston bars. That was a fuck-up so now they really wanted to get Dillon.

"So I drove down to Boston to see him and he's talking about buying up weapons to defeat Gerry Adams and the peace-makers but I just couldn't get him into the truck to record it. I said, 'Hey Joe, come into the rig, for a minute', but he kept talking. I asked again and he kept saying he couldn't stay but then kept talking. He did everything but get in the truck."

"The FBI realised that if you're not in the trucking world, you just don't jump in and out of each other's trucks for a chat or a sandwich, like me and my drivers would."

The FBI decided to try a different technology for Kent, once a major Provisional IRA gun-runner, who was now very active in the IFC. He lived in Woodstock, Ontario, and operated through the conservative Irish Catholic scene on both sides of the US/Canadian border.

"Their second attempt was with this bugged cell phone they gave me to record Kent. It transmitted directly to a recording device in an FBI car travelling behind me. Phil Kent came down from Canada and we're going out to a gun place in Valparaiso, Indiana.

"I pick him up in Chicago and I'm looking in the mirror all the time to see the FBI car, which has to stay close behind us to make sure it records. They couldn't make it more obvious that they are tailing us because they are driving a black SUV, like real typical FBI. I look in the mirror and they are about four feet from my bumper.

"Kent never noticed but I'm glaring at the FBI car in my mirror to say 'ease up'. I got Kent on tape talking about moving weapons but I never got to hear it. It went straight to the car behind us and to the FBI for analysis. That's the way it always went.

"The gun store was massive. They had every type of ungodly device. It didn't look like much from the outside, with canoes and outdoor equipment, and then you stepped inside to this superstore of weapons and military surplus.

"I took him out to see it because they had rocket-launchers there that were demilitarised, but like a lot of the bigger stuff in the store, it could be remilitarised pretty easily.

"We were looking at Barrett rifles. There was a rocket-launcher hanging on the wall. Phil's trying to get my attention and motioning up at it with his head like, 'This is what we want but I don't want to point at it.'

"At the time, you could buy 50 pounds of black powder, which is an explosive for guns. Just over the counter. There were also bullets for a Barrett rifle at $5 apiece.

"The FBI was waiting outside the store for us to take the ride home. Kent used to talk a lot about how he moved guns for the IRA in the Middle East and Cyprus but he had fallen out of favour with the Irish Freedom Committee because he would take their fundraising money to Ireland and make it look like he was donating his own cash to the cause, so that's why they favoured me.

"After I dropped him off in Chicago I had a meeting with Buckley and the FBI guys."

But Ed Buckley had been transferred from Chicago to Norfolk, Virginia.

"Nobody in the FBI had told me about Ed's transfer. Frank O'Neill was very old at the time and pretty much retired so he got a job working as a janitor for the Cook County sheriff's department in Chicago.

"He heard about Buckley's transfer because people in the sheriff's department, who he talked to all the time, were involved in the joint terrorism task force with the FBI.

"I asked my new FBI handler, Mark Lundgren, why they didn't tell me that Ed had been transferred. He looks at me real surprised and said, 'How did you figure that out?' I said, 'Frank O'Neill told me'.

"The FBI guys had a fit, they kept calling me and checking it. It was a nightmare for their internal security. A major terrorism funder like O'Neill had information directly from the joint terrorism task force about an FBI agent who had pursued him for years.

"That was the thing with the Irish American scene, it wasn't like Al Qaeda, with one side over there and our side over here. In every city in America, you had cops and all kinds of typists and administrators who were loyal to America but also loyal to the IRA. The FBI have got all this fancy equipment on trucks and in cars to record, and there is the number one target with a mop and bucket and he knows their movements even before they do.

"The FBI wanted to record IFC meetings. So I kept suggesting to Frank that they could use my office as much as they wanted but the problem was that they all lived on the north side of the city, and there is a big divide between north and south in Chicago. North-siders would never come south just for a meeting."

By the second half of 1997, the Stockyards office was starting to look like a bad idea for Rupert and the FBI. "Besides, I didn't like the office. It was hugely, hugely infected with cockroaches, which were coming from the apartment behind us, where one of Maureen's former employees at the convenience store lived. This woman didn't put out her trash and pretty soon cockroaches were taking over my office. I was talking on the phone and a cockroach climbed up the phone and onto my ear. It was disgusting. So I left everything behind in the office that day. I didn't want to remove any furniture that might be infected. The FBI thought we had some big sophisticated bugging operation going on in there, the only thing they recorded was me running from cockroaches."

It didn't matter, because Lundgren wanted to see him. There had been a development that would make the Chicago efforts seem almost irrelevant and elevate David Rupert to a space never before seen in spying. Lundgren asked to see him at a restaurant in downtown Chicago. David Rupert, trucker and spy, was about to go international.

CHAPTER 7

Rupert has his head thrown back in laughter. FBI agent Mark Lundgren is telling him a story about his single days.

By now, Rupert had a friendship with Lundgren that he never enjoyed with Buckley. Rupert, committed to Maureen, could live vicariously through Lundgren's tales of dating and chasing women.

"Mark was a funny guy, too, so I really enjoyed listening to his stories, and then going home to Maureen," said Rupert.

Maureen really liked Lundgren, who was always polite and impeccably dressed. "He and Dave just got on so well. Buckley was…" She searches for a word. "He was the kind of guy who would scratch himself all the time. I don't know if he actually did but he was just a bit unkempt."

Over lunch at a diner in downtown Chicago, Lundgren told Rupert that the British Secret Service wanted to meet him. It would more than double the pay he earned with the FBI.

News from Ireland suggested that the Provisional IRA was about to fracture between those who wanted peace and those who wanted war. The British urgently wanted him in Ireland.

Agents in London wanted an initial meeting to assess Rupert. They had been badly stung several times before. In October 1987, an MI5 agent, "Steve", had passed money to Stephen Lambert, a Derry republican, and requested a meeting. The agent told him that they were interested in spying on Martin McGuinness, a member of the IRA army council and the vice president of Sinn Féin. Unknown to MI5, Lambert was secretly recording the meeting and handed it over to a jubilant Sinn Féin, which played it at a press conference.

MI5 wanted to assess if Rupert really was an innocent who just stumbled into the IRA, or part of a much more sophisticated republican plot.

In July, unexpectedly, the Provisional IRA called a ceasefire. This time it would be permanent, it said, if Sinn Féin was allowed into peace talks. A deep and bitter split was emerging in the Provisional IRA, and MI5 wanted Rupert to tell them what was going on, and if the members who wanted to continue the violence would defect to the Continuity IRA.

Lundgren told him to expect a man called Norman at Heathrow Airport. He would be holding a coloured sign, as if picking someone up for a conference.

Maureen was finding the plot more and more intriguing and thought he should at least hear what the Brits had to say.

"I was a little concerned but also intrigued," she said. "David was always eccentric and larger than life, even from when I first met him. I felt if he could handle it, he might as well see where it goes."

Rupert flew into London in mid-August. Norman was waiting with the sign. He put out his hand. He had a warm smile and was sincere and earnest without being overbearing.

"And he was tall too," says Rupert, who carried a long and unreasonable resentment of small men. "They either knew I liked tall people or they guessed it," he said. "If he had been small, we would have started off real bad."

Norman was in his 50s. He had spied against the Soviets in the Cold War and was known for gaining information with his naturally easy manner. Now he was in charge of handling new recruits in the Ireland desk.

They walked to Norman's Daihatsu car, which was striking for Rupert because it was still not available in the US. It was only when they were on the motorway out of London that Rupert learned that they were going to Southampton, on the south coast of England. MI5 rarely took new recruits to London, where they might be spotted.

At a hotel near Southampton pier, Rupert dropped off his bags and rested. The room was spacious and open, with a view out on to the street near the sea.

Norman took him that evening to Joe Daflo's restaurant, across from the Mayflower Theatre in central Southampton. Over dinner, with enough noise around them to ensure they couldn't be heard, Norman asked Rupert how he became interested in Ireland and how someone with no Irish connections could end up being asked to move bomb parts for the Continuity IRA. Rupert ran through the whole story, as entertainingly as he could, about Linda Vaughan and his gradual move from womanising into violent republicanism.

"We got on real well. He was perfect for the job," said Rupert. "He was good company and he made you feel relaxed, like he was really interested. An acquisitional-type personality I called it from trucking – someone who is good at selling and getting you to trust them."

That night, Rupert couldn't sleep. It was a hot summer night and the heating in the room was running at maximum. He called reception several times but they didn't fix it. He stayed on top of the bedclothes, in his underwear, staring at the ceiling until morning.

"I think MI5 did that deliberately to keep me tired, because it's easier to tell if someone is lying when they are exhausted," he recalled. "I felt that they had used that particular room plenty of times before."

Rupert checked with other guests, who said that they had no problem with the heater in their room.

"I doubt we altered the heating in the room," says a former MI5 agent familiar with Rupert's case. "This is what I call 'goblin stuff'. Once I was told we caused it to rain in Islamabad to keep someone indoors. You hear all kinds of things we are supposed to have done. If only we had that ability."

The next morning over breakfast, Rupert was feeling groggy. Norman said he would look into the heater problem.

In the hotel garden, he asked Rupert what he would say if they wanted him to assassinate Ruairí Ó Brádaigh, the leader of Republican Sinn Féin and a member of the Continuity IRA's army council. "I could see he was just pushing me to test me," says Rupert. "I asked how much it would be worth to me."

Norman laughed and said they weren't in the assassination business.

He asked how Rupert assessed the Provisional IRA ceasefire and whether its members would move over to the Continuity IRA. Rupert said that there were already defections, but that the Provisional IRA breakaways might set up on their own.

That night, the heating in the room was just as bad and again Rupert stayed above the bedsheets, unable to sleep. He stared at the ceiling, and made a few more futile calls to reception, looking for help.

By the next morning, he was bleary and unable to think straight. He felt annoyed but tried not to show it. Norman had more questions for him about his background. Some of them were repeats from yesterday, others could be checked against information MI5 already had. Rupert felt he was being tested. "I just told the truth. Nobody can catch you out that way. Ninety-five per cent of what I told the IRA was also the truth."

Rupert was due to fly out the next day and would stay at a hotel near Heathrow that night. As they packed up to leave Southampton, Norman asked if he could show him a tourist site. He drove him to Winchester Cathedral. "I'd told Norman that I loved history and again, he might have been testing me, to see if I really did have the pastimes I said I had."

After a tour of the cathedral, Norman suggested they go for a stroll. They walked to a statue of Alfred the Great, whom Norman explained was Britain's first spy. He told Rupert a story about Alfred disguising himself as a travelling minstrel to enter the camp of Viking invaders called the Great Heathen Army. There, Alfred learned of their battle plans and left the camp waving and promising to come back. He slaughtered them in battle days later, saving England.

"I can still remember us standing by this statue and Norman trying to link what he was doing right back to Alfred the Great," said Rupert.

They drove to the airport hotel, where Norman asked for a double bed for Rupert. "Will you be sharing the bed?" asked the receptionist. "No, no, no, no," said Norman waving his hands. Rupert, behind him, starting sniggering. Norman turned around and started laughing too.

"I liked you, Dave, as a friend," he said.

They shook hands and Norman left. Rupert booked into the airport hotel and looked out over the bland office blocks and car parks around Heathrow. It was a kind of purgatory, neither the pubs of Ireland nor the trucking plazas of Chicago. He felt disjointed and wanted to come home to Maureen. On the flight back, there were empty seats all around him.

As usual, he was listening to an audiobook. This time it was *Schindler's Ark* by Thomas Keneally. A man with an English accent sat beside him and asked him what he was doing in the UK and if he had a good time. "The plane had plenty of seats all around and this guy is up beside me asking all these questions while I'm trying to listen to my book. I don't like talking to people on planes anyway, so I just shut down on him for the whole flight, but he was persistent.

"There were seats across the whole row, empty. To me, it was pretty obvious that this was a test of whether I had a big mouth."

"Yeah, that sounds plausible," said the MI5 agent. "We do try to check out if people are too talkative."

Back in the US, Rupert heard very quickly that the British secret service approved him for spying work. He was fast-tracked because he was coming in through the FBI and had been vetted by the Americans many times.

He agreed with Norman to work for the British for $50,000 a year, plus expenses, on top of the $30,000 he was making with the FBI. He also agreed that every time he was flying in to and out of Ireland, he would meet with his MI5 handler in London. He should also document everything on email and send it to MI5 and to the FBI – the beginning of a process that would stretch to more than 2,300 emails.

In a box store in Chicago, he bought encryption software, which he could share with MI5 and the FBI.

"People think you live in this big James Bond world but back then, email encryption was only beginning and we improvised a lot of ways of doing things," said Rupert. "The encryption package, it was 24-bit, now it would be in the thousands of bits."

With encrypted email, he learned from MI5 about a secret phone line for agents.

"They gave me this number to call in London in case of absolute emergency. The woman on the other end of the line sounded like a housewife answering the phone. They had a phrase and I would give a response so they knew it was me."

A week after his return to the US, the Continuity IRA exploded a car bomb in the small town of Markethill, in Armagh, which has a Protestant majority. It destroyed many businesses in a town that had been bombed several times before by the Provisional IRA. It was the Continuity IRA's way of signalling that if the Provisionals wanted peace, they would take over. Josephine Hayden, a Continuity IRA prisoner, was delighted. "We need more Markethills," she told the media. It was now clear. The car bombing of town centres would escalate in the coming year.

At his home in Chicago, Rupert got a call from Chris Fogarty, an Irish Freedom Committee member.

"Fogarty was completely hot-headed, always going on with conspiracy theories. He and Frank bickered and fell out a lot but always patched it up, because Chris needed Frank to listen to him."

Fogarty and Frank O'Neill had been questioned by Ed Buckley about a murder in Chicago, on the spurious grounds that the murdered man's sister was involved in civil rights issues in Northern Ireland. It became a notorious case and the murder had nothing to do with Ireland. The stress of the investigation drove the conspiracy-minded Fogarty into a mental vortex from which he never recovered. Although the FBI conceded that they should never have been investigated, Fogarty began to imagine bugging devices everywhere, and that someone in the Irish Freedom Committee was an FBI plant or working for the British.

"I had safety in numbers with Chris," said Rupert. "Nobody took his theories seriously, so if he said I was a spy, I would be just one of a dozen that day so I didn't worry."

Fogarty's suspicions had intensified back in January 1991, Fogarty and his wife, Mary, were at a meeting in a residence at the back of the Irish Wolfhound bar in Chicago. They had a new recruit, John Tuttle from Chicago, who was good at selling tickets for fundraising events. Everyone applauded him that day for the number of tickets he sold for an upcoming dinner. Then Mary walked over to her husband, sat beside him and pointed at her notebook. "Watch Tuttle!!" it said.

Chris Fogarty saw the note and stopped the meeting. "I immediately looked over, saw Tuttle and at that moment, he seemed to be aiming something, a revolver I thought, from underneath his coat, at our chairman, John Henegan. I immediately reached out my hand and pushed his hand toward the floor to deflect what could be a shot."

He pulled the device from Tuttle and found it was sophisticated bugging equipment. He shouted at Tuttle, "Who are you working for?", but Tuttle stayed silent. Fogarty called for a knife, then ripped out the lining of Tuttle's coat and found a transmitter insider. Within minutes, a team of FBI agents rushed into the room shouting, "Where's Tuttle?" They grabbed him and left in silence.

The next day, Chris and Mary Fogarty, Frank O'Neill and another Irish nationalist Anthony McCormack were charged with threatening the life of a federal informer and of supplying materials to the IRA. Mary: "The media had us charged with trying to supply surface-to-air missiles but that wasn't what we were charged with."

After an 18-month legal battle, the Chicago Four, as they became known, were exonerated by a judge. From then on, the Fogartys were highly suspicious of newcomers, especially ones trying to push them into weapon purchases.

Chris: "It was causing a split in the group. Rupert and Frank O'Neill wanted to buy weapons; we felt that buying weapons for the IRA was a one-way ticket to prison, so we wanted to go our own way. Frank was very contrite afterwards when he realised that he was being led by the FBI all along."

Chris and Mary Fogarty spent thousands of dollars buying a container load of Levi's 501 jeans. He wanted to send them to Ireland to help Continuity IRA prisoners. Rupert said he'd run it by Joe O'Neill when he got back to Ireland. Chris Fogarty: "501 jeans were the most sought-after clothing item at the time. We were thinking mostly of prisoners. We bought them commercially, a few hundred pairs and we did what we could for the prisoners."

Rupert also picked up $10,000 in cash from Frank O'Neill for the Continuity IRA and its prisoners. He was going to Ireland for several weeks, stretching through October and November and would report to M15 throughout his stay. First, he needed the fundraising money.

"I just had to stand there and listen to Frank go on about Gerry Adams selling out the cause and how the Continuity IRA would continue the fight. Then he handed over the envelope and said I was to give it to Joe O'Neill to do some damage."

When he reached Ireland in October, Rupert called in to Joe in the pub in Bundoran. Joe put the money in his jacket pocket. "Good man," he said.

Rupert raised the issue of Fogarty's offer of a container load of 501 jeans for the prisoners.

O'Neill turned to Rupert suddenly: "What the fuck are we going to do with a container load of dungarees? The army has pants, now we need money."

Joe was gaunt. He was suffering from diabetes and asked Rupert to take him to a faith healer in northern Donegal. Rupert drove him there in his rental car. People were queuing up to have the priest put his hands on them. Joe showed the priest his feet, which were swollen from diabetes. Joe prayed and blessed himself as the priest looked to the skies and asked God to remove the suffering, as he removed the suffering from Christ.

"It was strange to me that Joe was religious and yet he couldn't see anything wrong with the bombings and shootings. I asked him about it on the way back and he said, 'It would be a sin if it wasn't for the sake of Ireland.'"

Rupert then drove Joe from Bundoran to Dublin for the Republican Sinn Féin Ard Fheis (annual convention) in the second week of November. As vice president of the party, and as one of the party's few councillors, he had to be there.

It was one of the moments where my life intersects with Rupert's. I was also at the Ard Fheis. Security outside was very tight. Special Branch jumped out of unmarked cars to talk to anyone coming out of the hotel. I went out at lunch and two approached me. "We saw you coming out of the hotel. What business do you have there?" said one.

When Rupert left the hotel, he saw four men jump out of a car. "One of them ran at me and I thought I was being mugged so I pulled back my fist to punch him and he pulls out his badge and says, 'No, no, garda, garda.' I came so close to knocking him."

Republican Sinn Féin was suddenly relevant again and the bombing of Markethill showed that it had the violent intent.

The BBC was there, as was Sky News. "Do you have a paramilitary wing?" one TV reporter asked the Republican Sinn Féin leader, Ruairí Ó Brádaigh. "Well, we're not saying whether we have or we haven't," he said.

He and his party were deliberately old-fashioned and romantically republican. They were, and still are, against abortion and, to this day, are the only party in Ireland never to have endorsed same-sex marriage. At funeral services and commemorations, of which there were many, they often knelt down and said a decade of the rosary in Gaelic.

Theirs was a Catholic, nationalist politics of the 1920s. Old men got up on stage and denounced the partition of Ireland and peace talks at Stormont Castle in Belfast.

"The only way I'd walk into Stormont is with a barrel of dynamite under each arm," said one speaker, to thunderous applause.

Rupert was learning more and more about the party's conservative agenda.

"I remember there was this gay guy speaking and he was very obviously gay. He was a shorter, chubby guy and he was talking about human rights and, then, that everyone should have the right to love who they want. He was talking for about 10 or 15 minutes before Ruairí Ó Brádaigh and that crowd figured out what was going on.

"Ó Brádaigh says, 'That's enough now, I don't know if we want that human right.'"

The Chicago Irish Freedom Committee supporters flew in for the event, and Rupert had his photograph taken with them and with Ó Brádaigh.

After lunch, I met members of the boy scout group, Fianna Éireann, who were wearing their green uniforms and black berets. On the stage, to a standing ovation, they pledged their allegiance to the Continuity IRA.

Later in the lobby, the Fianna's leaders, the Ryan brothers, said with excitement that Ruairí Ó Brádaigh, the party leader, was coming in to say hello.

In the main function hall, David Rupert was being led around by Joe O'Neill, who was keen to show supporters that the US fundraising and support wing was working well. Rupert also stood at the top of the room and counted votes for the many resolutions calling for the withdrawal of British forces from Northern Ireland. His huge frame, as he stood there doing a head count of votes, was unmissable. "That was deliberate," he said. "Everyone in the Continuity IRA was in the room and I'm up there counting their votes. I wanted to show that I was at the centre of things, at the centre of the movement. I was central and they saw that."

*****

Cars pulled one by one into Ballyconnell House, a former Catholic boarding school in Falcarragh, County Donegal. The 80 delegates had rented a function room from Údarás na Gaeltachta, the Irish state agency that oversaw the Gaelic-speaking areas of the county and which now owned the school. Ostensibly, the delegates were there for a Sinn Féin Irish language seminar.

Unknown to Údarás, the Irish language meeting was a front. After killing 2,000 people over the past 30 years, the Provisional IRA was about to accept the principles on non-violence, ending its campaign on condition that Sinn Féin was allowed into talks with the British.

Under IRA rules, it had to hold a general convention to hear the views from units around the country. The last such convention was in 1986 and it was only done in the most extreme of circumstances.

The majority of the army council was behind Gerry Adams and those who supported the ceasefire. The majority of the executive, which appointed the army council, was behind Mickey McKevitt, a hardliner and the IRA's quartermaster.

Martin McGuinness, IRA army council member and the Sinn Féin deputy leader, was at this army convention, as was Brian Keenan, who oversaw the worst of the IRA's bombing campaign in England, which had cost 21 lives in the Birmingham pub bombings and five in the Guildford bombings among many other atrocities.

The dissident members arrived later. They included McKevitt and his wife, Bernadette Sands McKevitt, a sister of the IRA's most revered martyr, the hunger striker Bobby Sands.

Seamus McGrane, a member of the IRA's executive and a McKevitt loyalist, entered with them.

After several people spoke in favour of accepting talks, McGrane spoke, with the IRA constitution in hand, and gave a legalistic interpretation of why the IRA could never accept peace without a British withdrawal.

McKevitt, who controlled all the IRA's weapon depots, was next to speak. He loudly denounced those present and said that they were using jargon to disguise the obvious truth, that they were going to disband. He said that they were misleading the units present. He then got up and walked out, along with his wife, McGrane, and several others.

McKevitt was delighted, a senior garda told me later, because he was now the leader, and would wage the war he wanted.

A few weeks afterwards, he and his supporters reconvened at a sympathiser's farmhouse in County Meath to create a new army structure.

Liam Campbell, the South Armagh Provisional IRA leader, was appointed second in command. Campbell, now a millionaire from smuggling along the border, was softly spoken and always kept a neat appearance. He was clean-shaven, his hair always fixed, and well dressed. "He has a military bearing, you'd know he had some training," said a solicitor who had reason to fear him.

McKevitt appointed his wife, Bernadette, as third in command and she was to head their political wing, to be called the 32 County Sovereignty Movement.

McGrane, a stocky, moustached IRA veteran, was appointed director of training. He was instructed to set up arms camps around the country, as he had in the Provisional IRA.

In the IRA heartland of South Armagh, a showdown was coming. Sean Hughes, a local IRA commander, summoned Liam Campbell to a meeting. Campbell showed up with many of the local brigade to give support. Hughes backed down and Campbell left with his men. The split was now complete.

McKevitt held meetings in the following weeks with the leadership of the Continuity IRA, including Des Long, its chief of staff, and Colm Murphy, a wealthy builder, who agreed to act as liaison between the two groups. In reality, the Continuity IRA was becoming a feeder organisation for this new group. It would build the bombs and deliver them, but McKevitt would supply the equipment and take control.

The McKevitt group set up a checkpoint in Jonesborough in South Armagh, directed by Liam Campbell, to stop cars and show that they were in control. One of its masked Armalite-carrying members was asked by a motorist, "Who are you?" The masked man replied, "We're the IRA, The real IRA." The media immediately picked up on the phrase. The Real IRA was born.

On 6 November, Bernadette Sands McKevitt led a dozen Sinn Féin members in Dundalk to walk out of a meeting and join her new group. Both sides traded insults as she left.

State television did an interview with her, as did newspapers from all over Ireland, the UK and the US. Under Ireland's strict libel laws, reporters, including me, could only say that Bernadette Sands McKevitt was the leader of a new anti-peace group called the 32 County Sovereignty Movement and that it was linked to the Real IRA, which was led by "a former quartermaster general of the Provisional IRA". Libel lawyers in media organisations forbade us from revealing that the former quartermaster general was in fact Bernadette's husband, Mickey.

None of this had yet reached Rupert, who knew only that there was a split in the Provisional IRA.

"Joe O'Neill and all the Continuity IRA guys weren't exactly shouting about it to me," he said. "I was the money man from America and they wanted me only on their side."

After a long stay in Ireland, Rupert flew home to Chicago, after writing a long report on the Ard Fheis and the Continuity IRA's insistence, as always, that the fight must go on.

He and Maureen celebrated Christmas with Dorie, Maureen's daughter, and resolved that, when Rupert returned to Ireland in the new year, Maureen would come with him.

Throughout that winter, there were frantic talks between the Real IRA and Continuity IRA about waging an aggressive new bombing campaign.

In the new year, having taken some of the best of the Provisional IRA from its South Armagh heartland, and having won over the Continuity IRA to help deliver the bombs, McKevitt began.

CHAPTER 8

On 20 February 1998, a 500-pound car bomb exploded outside a police station in Moira, County Down. Seven police officers and four civilians were injured and it wrecked the centre of the town. It was a joint operation between the Continuity IRA and the newly formed and far more powerful Real IRA.

From their base in Dundalk, McKevitt and his group celebrated. They were now in charge. More Provisional IRA members started to come over to McKevitt, impressed by the calibre of leadership he was attracting.

Three days after the attack in Moira, a 300-pound bomb exploded outside a police station in Portadown, County Armagh, a town then famous for its contentious loyalist parades. The blast destroyed buildings across a wide area.

In March, they began the mortar attacks, first with what was called a "barrack-buster", a Provisional IRA-created giant mortar that fired like a cannon into police and army barracks. Two weeks later, there were two more mortar attacks in South Armagh, one at a police and army base, another at a British army watchtower.

Bernadette Sands McKevitt would appear before the media, saying that she didn't know who was in the Real IRA but adding that her position was to support those who were "engaged in armed struggle" and who were "protecting Irish sovereignty".

In Chicago, Rupert got a call from MI5. They needed him in Ireland urgently. After exhausted and often heated talks, all the parties in Northern Ireland were close to signing a historic peace agreement with the British and Irish governments. There was a mood of celebration, even jubilation, in Ireland that the Troubles might finally be ending.

By now, Bernadette Sands McKevitt had been expelled from Sinn Féin for calling the leadership traitors. She was interviewed by PBS in America, the BBC, and the *New York Times*. The international media often commented on how polite she was and how she had a striking resemblance to her brother, Bobby.

Rupert was told to fly to Ireland and to find out what was happening with the Continuity IRA. Police in Ireland and the UK were concerned that they would try to bomb Northern Ireland while the agreement was being signed.

He and Maureen flew into Shannon and drove north to Donegal. Since the closure of the Drowes, they had been renting a house in Tullaghan, paid for by the FBI, and so could slip quickly back into the local community. As soon as they were unpacked, Rupert drove north to meet Joe O'Neill, while Maureen met for coffee with her friend Pauline, the former bar manager.

At his bar, Joe took fundraising money from Rupert and said that the agreement would never work. He seemed excited, because this sell-out by Sinn Féin and the Provisional IRA would bring dozens of new recruits.

Talks in Belfast dragged on and on that day. After all-night talks on Easter Thursday involving the White House, Downing Street and a dozen Northern Ireland political parties, Tony Blair flew in to Belfast for the signing of a peace deal, soon to be called the Good Friday Agreement.

Congratulations flowed in from around the world. President Clinton said it was a historic moment in Irish history, while the Pope said the whole world was praying for Ireland.

It was the biggest news story in the world that day. The Agence France Presse reporter in Belfast, for the first time in his career, got to press a button on the AFP software that signalled to newspapers around the world that his article was the agency's top story.

The next day, as the country was celebrating, Joe O'Neill asked Rupert to call over. He sounded animated. He asked for a lift in Rupert's rental car because his own Mercedes was well known to gardaí.

"It was clear to me something big was up," said Rupert. "He told me to drive from Bundoran, all the way through Donegal to Letterkenny. When we saw a garda car, he covered his beard with his hand to disguise himself. When we got to Letterkenny, Joe told me to turn around and go back towards Bundoran. He was looking for roadblocks throughout the county.

A Donegal undertaker, who was also a Continuity IRA member, was storing a rocket-launcher in his funeral home. Under direction from the Real IRA, the Continuity IRA was to use it to blow up a police Land Rover on the other side of the border, either in Derry or Omagh. Time was of the essence. It had to happen that weekend, while the world's media were still gathered in Belfast and the peace agreement had the world's attention.

Rupert dropped O'Neill back at his pub, where he was organising Continuity IRA members to launch the attack, now that the roads were clear.

He drove quickly back to his apartment and emailed MI5, marked "Urgent" with the details of what was happening.

He also called them on a special hotline Norman had told him about, which was only for agents to pass on vitally important information.

The British called the Irish garda, who swamped the Letterkenny to Bundoran road with checkpoints. It would be an enormous international story if those who were becoming known as "dissident republicans" pulled off an attack within 24 hours of the peace agreement.

News of the garda clamp down in Donegal made the Irish newspapers but gardaí reassured the public that it was just routine security following the signing of the agreement. The rocket-launcher operation was called off and it was smuggled back to the funeral home.

For Joe O'Neill and his comrades, there was general suspicion that someone in the Real IRA had tipped off the gardaí about the rocket-launcher operation, or that they had a spy among them.

Mickey Donnelly, the Ulster chairman of Republican Sinn Féin, was adamant that there was a spy within the Continuity IRA.

Donnelly had a big beard and heavy-set eyes, with a warm lilting Derry accent. He was one of the first four members of the Provisional IRA in Derry in the late 1960s.

People in O'Neill's bar would say to Rupert, "Do you know Mickey Donnelly over there? He was one of the 'hooded men'."

In 1971, in the middle of a sustained IRA bombing campaign, the British had introduced internment without trial, allowing the army full martial power to arrest and lock up anyone they suspected of terrorism. In a single night, they snatched more than 340 men from their homes, including Mickey Donnelly. He was one of 14 who were taken to an RAF base in Ballykelly in Derry for a sensory deprivation experiment, in which they were hooded, blasted with white noise, told to stand in stress position against a wall until they collapsed, beaten and flung screaming out of helicopters only to land on hillocks a few feet down. The experiment lasted a week, before the men were sent to a regular internment camp.

The Irish government was outraged and took the British to the European Court of Human Rights, which ruled that Donnelly and the 13 others had been subjected to inhumane and degrading treatment.

Donnelly liked Rupert and soon asked him to be his driver. Rupert became a frequent visitor to his house.

"He told me about his torture experience but, to be honest, I wasn't listening all that hard. It was in the past and I was focused on what was going on right now," says Rupert.

Donnelly's experience of torture had left him furious with any republican who dared speak of peace. In his native Derry, just over the border in Northern Ireland, he angrily denounced the Good Friday Agreement as a sell-out and treachery, inflicted on the nationalists of Northern Ireland.

On the street, in newspapers and on the radio, he said the Provisional IRA were cowards who were now in league with MI5. Martin McGuiness, the Derry-based deputy leader of Sinn Féin, was nothing but a puppet, he said.

The Provisional IRA finally had enough.

Five masked men broke into his house in Derry, announcing "IRA – Provisional," and beat Donnelly with metal baseball bats while his family screamed in horror.

"They smashed my leg in a few places. I don't know how I did it but as one of the blows was coming down on my head, I caught the bat with my hand. The force ripped my thumb out of its socket," he said.

His son ran at them and was also beaten with the bats. His daughter was punched in the face.

Donnelly tried to stand up on his broken leg to fight them off. His leg bone was sticking out through the broken skin. He shouted at his son, Declan, "Run and get help."

Declan ran out the back door, banging into a hooded gunman standing watch. He knocked the man over with the force, then ran down the road. The group panicked and fled.

Donnelly appeared on the front page of nationalist newspapers, lying in a cast in his hospital bed. Then the BBC appeared, and Ulster Television, each documenting that he was attacked for opposing the Provisional IRA's move towards peace.

Rupert and Declan Curneen visited Donnelly at a cottage he was renting after the attack, which was located by a donkey sanctuary in Sligo, away from the threat in Derry.

"The injuries were a horrible, horrible sight but Mickey was a real hard guy. It made him more determined. He healed well and he was soon speaking out against Sinn Féin, in defiance of the Provisional IRA," said Rupert.

From his cottage in Sligo, Donnelly would get a lift from his sons to come to Joe O'Neill's bar in Bundoran and a lift around the area from Rupert.

Wherever they went, Continuity IRA members and republicans who were against the agreement shook Donnelly's hand and praised him for standing up to McGuinness and the Provisional

IRA, who they denounced as sell-outs to the British establishment. As his driver, it gave Rupert extra credibility.

As he sat there with his leg in a cast, many customers in O'Neill's offered him a drink.

"Mickey's stature went up and up after he was almost beaten to death," says Rupert. "He went right out there and called Sinn Féin traitors for signing the Good Friday Agreement and they almost killed him for it, so that really made him a martyr to the cause in Joe O'Neill's place."

In Joe O'Neill's bar too, that summer, was Seamus McKenna, son of Sean McKenna Snr, another of the hooded men.

Seamus McKenna, who served IRA prison sentences in the north and south, was surviving on the labouring work he got from Colm Murphy, a Continuity IRA leader, in the booming Dublin construction trade. He was an alcoholic and would disappear from work for weeks at a time to go drinking. Bundoran was his favourite place to go. Sometimes he took the bus, using a travel pass borrowed from a retiree in Dundalk.

He often drank alone, starting at 11am, consuming pint after pint of a Dutch lager that he said gave him less of a hangover than the Irish lager, Harp. I know this because I spent many hours drinking with him, trying to understand his mentality. He spoke longingly of Bundoran and Donegal, and how much he loved Joe's pub.

In 1998, McKenna had big sideburns and spoke with a thick border accent. He looked like a relic from 1970s Ireland. He was not a major figure within the Continuity IRA and Rupert might not even have met him at Joe's place.

The Continuity IRA used McKenna only for mixing fertiliser explosives and delivering car bombs to their targets. He was, in IRA parlance, "expendable". He knew that himself, and it was eating him up.

Picture him there, in the corner of O'Neill's bar, drinking by himself, trying to chat up the barmaids.

He is a small, insignificant man. He has no real relevance to this story, except that he is about to turn Ireland upside down.

CHAPTER 9

The morning of 15 August, 1998 opened with the promise of a late summer. Temperatures rose to the mid-20s, families drove in their thousands to the beaches of Ireland. Those who had gone abroad for August lamented their choice. The country was in celebratory mood. The republic's economy was booming, the ceasefire in the north was holding. A country whose economy had been crippled by outdated industry was flourishing in low-tax financial services and technology, and peace in the north was bringing a rush of investment.

That day, David and Maureen were climbing Benbulben mountain in Sligo, made famous by the poet W.B. Yeats. Down below them was the village of Drumcliffe, where Yeats grew up and where he is buried. In honour of his connection to the area, M15 had recently given Rupert the code name Drumcliffe Echo.

It was a warm, cloudless Saturday. That morning, I went hiking on the coastal path in Wicklow, between Bray and Greystones. On one side was a family of seals bobbing in the deep blue of the Irish Sea, on the other was the heather of the Wicklow Mountains. A narrow coastal path ran between them.

Along the way, I saw a piece of graffiti about David Trimble, the leader of the largest unionist party in the north, written with marker at a rest stop: "Trimble will Tremble When the Boys Reassemble. Up the IRA." It struck me as a little more advanced than most IRA graffiti. Whoever wrote it longed for militarism to replace the agonisingly slow and hostile talks in Belfast.

That summer morning, a friend of mine, Jerome, was walking into Dublin with his Spanish girlfriend, Anna, who ran her fingers through the air as she walked, to feel the warm summer breeze.

In England, my friend Ian was working as a hotel manager and had some overbooked guests to deal with.

As Maureen and David were beginning their climb up the Horseshoe, an outcrop at the back of Benbulben mountain, Seamus McKenna was getting into a stolen maroon Vauxhall Cavalier in a farmhouse in Carrickmacross, just south of the border. Beside him was a 19-year-old recruit, and in the back of the car was a 500-pound bomb.

Colm Murphy, the Continuity IRA's liaison to the Real IRA, had given one of his foremen's phones to McKenna the night before for use in the bombing mission.

Getting into a scout car ahead of them was Seamus Daly, a 28-year-old Real IRA member from Culloville on the Irish border, who communicated with the bomb car using Colm Murphy's own phone.

The same South Armagh bomb team had been adjusting their targets all summer. In June, they had left a car bomb in Lisburn outside Belfast but a phone warning from Liam Campbell, the second in command of the Real IRA, was given too far in advance and the police discovered the car bomb and defused it.

On 1 September, they parked a car bomb in Banbridge, County Down, with a much shorter phone warning. It exploded, devastating the town centre and injuring 33 people, including a police officer, who suffered a fractured skull. This was considered a big success in celebrations at Murphy's Dundalk pub, the Emerald.

An equally short bomb warning would be used for this mission. On the morning of the bombing they were told the target was Omagh, the largest town in County Tyrone. Unlike all the other targets that summer, Omagh had a Catholic nationalist majority and was chosen to spread the geographic distribution of the bombings.

The town was busier than usual. Peace had brought much more funding for community projects. There was to be a carnival in Omagh that day, which was attracting parents with young children. It was also close to the start of the new school year, and parents were coming into Omagh to have children fitted for uniforms.

As the car took off, eight-year-old Oran Doherty was joining a group of Spanish and Irish children on a trip to Omagh from Buncrana, just over the border in Donegal. They visited the Ulster Folk Museum, another museum that had sprung up with peace funds. At the last minute, the tour organisers changed plans to allow the children to do some shopping in Omagh, and to see the carnival.

Rocio Abad Ramos, a 23-year-old Spanish woman, was helping to lead the group.

21-year-old Aiden Gallagher finished up fixing a car at the family mechanic business and said he'd see his father later.

Avril Monaghan, 30, nine months pregnant with twins, was in town to celebrate the birthday of her mother, Mary Grimes, before Avril gave birth in a few days' time. As Avril and Mary talked, Avril pushed her 18-month-old, Maura, in a stroller.

Esther Gibson, a Sunday-school teacher, had walked into town to buy flowers for her church.

By 2pm, as the town was thronged with carnival lovers and shoppers, Seamus Daly parked the scout car in Dunnes Stores car park and waited. Seamus McKenna, eager to impress the young recruit in the car with him, drove up the main street to the courthouse, the intended target. But he had not considered that the carnival and good weather had brought a big crowd into town and the court car park was full.

He drove in a circle and parked the car on Market Street, outside S.D. Kells clothing shop, where parents were bringing their children for school uniforms. It was 2.19pm.

The 19-year-old opened the glove compartment and primed the bomb by switching up two toggle switches. A passer-by remembers him very carefully closing the passenger-side door. McKenna, always with an eye for the women, gave a passing woman a big smile. They walked a short distance around the corner to Seamus Daly's car and drove away.

A tourist, with his young daughter on his shoulders, posed for a photograph, right beside the bomb car, unaware of its contents.

As he drove away, Seamus Daly texted Campbell, in coded language, to say everything was in place.

Campbell drove to a phone box and, using latex gloves, made a warning call that there was a car bomb at the Omagh courthouse, using the Real IRA code word "Martha Pope", who was a member of the American delegation at the peace talks in Belfast. The name was also a play on Catholicism, as if the bombs themselves were blessed by the Pope.

The bomb call was serious enough for the police to start clearing the large numbers of people from the other end of town and direct them up Market Street towards the car bomb.

As they were chatting in the scout car, McKenna told Daly that there was no parking in the courthouse and that the bomb car was up the main street. He didn't know its name.

Daly called Campbell, who made a second phone warning, saying that the bomb was on "main street" in Omagh.

None of these men were familiar with Omagh, and didn't know the street names. Police were directing the public in tighter and tighter packs away from the courthouse and towards the bomb. There were two streets in Omagh that could be defined as the main street, adding to confusion. Shoppers were being pushed further up both streets when the third warning call came, in quick succession from the second, saying the bomb was 350 yards from the courthouse, on the main street.

There were now twice as many people at the top of Market Street than there would be on a busy Saturday.

Mary Grimes, her heavily pregnant daughter, Avril, and her granddaughter, Maura, went into Kells clothing store, walking right in front of the bomb car.

At 3.05pm, a senior policeman advised officers clearing the street to get people "well short of the courthouse" as there were three different locations for the bomb. As he was talking, the timer in the front of the glove compartment connected two wires, sending a full circuit that travelled through a wire to a booster tube at the back of the car, which was connected to a block of Semtex and 500 pounds of fertiliser explosive. A supersonic wave exploded, followed by thousands of pieces of metal and burning fuel erupting in every direction. It collapsed the drapery store, trapping the families inside under a falling roof. Mary Grimes, Avril Monaghan, and Avril's daughter, Maura Monaghan, 18 months, and Avril's nine-month-old unborn twins were killed instantly.

Bodies of children lay behind the bomb crater, their blood mixing with the water pouring from a severed water pipe. One volunteer who ran to the site found a decapitated woman and a dead mother clutching her dead baby.

Rocio Abad Ramos, who had rushed the children up Market Street during the bomb alert, was killed instantly. Four children died with her: James Barker, 12, Fernando Blasco Baselga, 12, Oran Doherty, eight, and Sean McLaughlin, 12.

Fernando's sister, Lucrecia Blasco, was hit in the face by burning fuel and metal and was scarred for life.

Breda Devine, 20 months old, was killed instantly. Her mother, who suffered 60 per cent burns to her body, was unconscious for six weeks before she discovered her baby was gone.

Some shoppers had been blown through shop windows by the blast.

Aiden Gallagher was lying on the street, barely breathing. Esther Gibson was dead.

One man jumped into the smoking bomb crater, pulling up rubble, crying and searching for a child.

Constable Geoffrey Eakin spotted the body of a man some way from the bomb with part of his face missing.

"I saw a young lady in shock, totally oblivious that her lower leg was on fire. A lot of people were on fire. I got a fire extinguisher out and basically went around putting the flames out," he said.

Police set up an emergency mortuary in an alley and each officer was allocated three bodies to attend.

The first body placed in PC Eakin's charge was that of a decapitated woman.

"There was no head on the corpse at all – just taken clean off. In contrast, the body of a small child appeared to be totally intact," he later recalled.

PC Allan Palmer remembered the scene at Tyrone County Hospital.

"People were running about with parts of bodies. Someone ran in and handed a limb to a constable," he said.

An amateur camera captured the immediate scene. It shows a middle-aged woman with blood on her blouse, lifting her shaking hands in the air. A crying Spanish student limps by, with blood pouring from her head.

Marion Radcliff, with glass still cut into her scalp, walked around the dust and rubble crying for her 16-year-old son, Mark. Volunteers broke sign boards from collapsed shops and used them as makeshift stretchers. Omagh Hospital was overwhelmed.

Helicopters arrived to lift the injured to Derry and Belfast.

Michael Gallagher, Aiden's father, remembers the helicopters lifting off, like something from the war in Vietnam in the 1970s, "but it was women and children they were lifting," he said.

The 5pm news reported that an explosion had killed at least eight people in Omagh. Phone logs showed a frantic round of calls between Campbell, Daly and the others as they asked each other what happened and then hurried home to dispose of evidence.

The death toll rose throughout the day – eight, then 12, then 16, then 18, then 21.

Elizabeth Gibson, searching for her sister in Omagh Hospital, remembered the blood-soaked hospital documents lying all along the corridor.

Michael Gallagher went to the hospital to visit his son Aiden, who was clinging to life. Doctors eventually came out and said that they were not detecting brain waves and that Aiden was fading. Michael went home to his family. They hugged, wordless, and cried.

Claire Gallagher, unrelated to Michael, was a talented young pianist who was planning to study music. She lay in a hospital bed, blinded for life. Over 200 people were injured, some with massive head fractures, others with missing limbs.

David Rupert was sleeping on the sofa of the apartment after the long walk up Benbulben. He switched on the 6pm news. An RTE newswoman reported that a bomb had devastated Omagh and that rescue workers feared that more than 20 were dead and the death toll was rising.

He called over Maureen. They sat and watched the footage in silence.

Eventually, Maureen uttered, "Oh my god, oh my god."

After the news, Rupert got up and drove over to Joe O'Neill's house, behind the pub. Joe, who had dreamt of a bomb to grab the world's attention, was looking scared. "He looked more worried than someone hearing about a bomb. It was a guilty look. He looked sick," said Rupert.

Joe told Rupert that the Provisional IRA, which had already nearly killed Michael Donnelly, would not stand for this disaster, and would start killing Continuity IRA members, and there would be mass round-ups by the police.

"I wanted Joe to tell me to go, and he did," said Rupert. "Go back to America, go quick and we'll talk," said Joe, and he closed the door. Where now was Joe O'Neill's romantic attachment to the Continuity IRA?

Rupert rushed back to the apartment and told Maureen. They packed up immediately. "We have never, ever got out of town that fast. It was a whirlwind. It was a sad and dangerous time," said Maureen.

David called the MI5 helpline. They said they would get him a flight as quickly as possible, anywhere out of Ireland. They called back. They were to drive to Belfast. They had a flight to Edinburgh, and then a flight to London.

I was coming back into Dublin after my hike. I was due to see a band in the city centre with my friend Jerome and his girlfriend Anna. Anna, who normally greeted me with a big smile, was waiting for me at the venue, her face stern. The show had been cancelled. "Why?" I said. "There has been a bombing in the north," she said. "Many English, Irish and Spanish people dead."

We walked into the bar. People were gathered around a TV screen watching in silence. More than 94 per cent of the Republic's voters had approved of the Good Friday Agreement in a referendum in May. The very people they were trying to stop had given their blood-soaked response.

I left the bar and walked home, passing my newspaper offices. A sub-editor came out for a cigarette, put his hands to his eyes and quietly sobbed.

In Omagh, the death toll climbed to 29, plus Avril Monaghan's two unborn babies. As she was due to deliver in a few days, most people now put the death toll at 31. The majority of them were children or teenagers. It was the worst atrocity in the 30-year history of the Northern Ireland Troubles, and it came after the people, north and south, had voted overwhelmingly for peace.

In England, my childhood friend Ian was in the staff apartments of the hotel, crying in front of the TV as the death toll rose.

That night, the bomb team gathered in Colm Murphy's bar, the Emerald, in Dundalk.

Kevin "Kiddo" Murray, a fat, squat Real IRA man who had helped relay the bomb messages to Liam Campbell, was pacing up and down the bar, looking concerned.

Seamus Daly and Seamus McKenna were drinking with Colm Murphy, with a practised lack of concern.

Terence Morgan, the building foreman whose phone Colm Murphy had borrowed the night before, noticed Seamus Daly laughing. He began to wonder if his phone had something to do with the outrage in Omagh. Daly came up to him and said, "It was you who brought the yoke to Omagh." Morgan said he looked at Daly in silence then walked away in disgust. He was appalled, but it was a vital clue.

In the days after Omagh, there was universal and unqualified revulsion. It rose above those of previous IRA atrocities to become something more – a tear in the national psyche. The country had never been so affluent, so self-assured, so willing to bury the certainties of nationalism and sectarianism. It was as if the bombers wanted to destroy not just a town centre, but the new national confidence.

In Dundalk, the McKevitts, who watched the scene unfold on television, fled their home immediately.

At the gift and T-shirt shop they owned in a Dundalk shopping mall, people began to line up to leave small toys and cards for the lost children of Omagh.

When Bernadette Sands McKevitt came back several days later, the management had changed the locks and ordered them out. Crowds cheered as she was escorted from the shopping centre.

In the White House, President Clinton, embroiled in the Monica Lewinsky scandal, vowed that he would visit Omagh during his upcoming trip to Ireland. Gerry Adams, the Sinn Féin leader, who for years had refused to condemn republican violence, said that he condemned the bombing unequivocally.

It is difficult to articulate the disgust and anger and helplessness people felt that week. It was a surge of energy that coursed through the country.

The sight of little white coffins being carried by sobbing grandparents convulsed the country.

The Irish newspapers, long frustrated with having to refer to the leader of the Real IRA as "a former quartermaster of the Provisional IRA" who had "close links" to a group run by Bernadette Sands McKevitt, broke all their libel rules in the aftermath of the bombing. McKevitt was named as "the alleged leader of the Real IRA" by the British newspapers, and the Irish papers quickly followed.

In Blackrock, the village just south of Dundalk where the McKevitts lived, local residents announced that they would lead a protest march to the couple's home.

Bernadette called a local priest, sobbing uncontrollably, saying she feared the protesters would harm her children. Mickey McKevitt took the phone and told the priest he had "no hand, act or part in the Omagh bomb". It was a lie, of course. He had carefully put together the Real and Continuity IRA teams to build and deliver the bombs. The priest told reporters what he had been told and that the family did not want their children harmed.

The next day, a more composed Bernadette was on national radio, saying in passive verbs that the bombing in Omagh "was condemned", without saying that she personally condemned it. When asked if she supported the Real IRA, she asked what the interviewer's agenda was in asking that question. The hardened IRA woman had rediscovered her composure and was back, as unapologetic as ever.

The Real IRA's spokesman called the Ireland International news agency anonymously, claiming responsibility for the Omagh bomb, saying that it was aimed at economic targets as part of "the war against the Brits".

The reporter read the statement back to him. "Do you want to say anything to the victims?"

"Yeah, and an apology to the victims," he responded.

That week, writers and artists struggled to find expression for the enormity of what had happened. Her whole adult life, Bernadette had carried huge respect among republicans because she was the sister of hunger striker Bobby Sands, the IRA's most revered martyr. Now, his death cult had pointed back at her.

Irish writer Dermot Bolger wrote a poem to mark the children's funerals, blaming the Sands cult for their deaths.

"Hovering like Christ above the mourners/The ghost of Bobby Sands smiled his boyish Bay City Roller smile/And held out withered hands/As they lowered each the coffin of someone's daughter or son/He called like the piper of Hamelin, Come, little children, come."

Paul Durcan, the republic's favourite poet, wrote a long, angry poem, in which he replaced the Catholic list of venerable names for the Virgin Mary with the birthplace of all the Omagh victims, followed by a second litany of their names, and a third litany of their ages. It had a powerful, repetitive, mournful effect.

He ended with a cry to the collective guilt of the Republic, long steeped in ambivalence towards republican violence. "Omagh have mercy on me," he wrote.

The Real IRA held an army council meeting in Dundalk to decide on whether to declare a temporary ceasefire, to give it enough time to reorganise. Bernadette Sands McKevitt and Mickey McKevitt voted in favour of the ceasefire. Liam Campbell, the man primarily responsible for the atrocity, voted against. He wanted to continue the bombing, regardless of public opinion, but lost the vote.

The group did call a ceasefire but refused to make it permanent. The rage of the public grew. People gathered in thousands in Dundalk, demanding the group disband.

Hillary Clinton wrote that the shock of the bomb reminded her of all the times she had met women from all over Ireland to talk about ending the Troubles. It was the middle of the Monica Lewinsky scandal, and in Omagh, she found common mourning.

"Now that's what I had to try to do in the midst of my own heartrending troubles," she wrote.

She, Bill and Tony and Cherie Blair walked the streets of Omagh in early September. Hillary was struck by how much Gerry Adams and other hardliners had softened their position since the bombing.

An Irish government representative met Mickey McKevitt, Bernadette Sands McKevitt and the leadership at Clonard Monastery in Belfast, warning them that if they didn't permanently shut down, they could expect the worst from the state. McKevitt immediately refused, saying that disarming would leave the Real IRA helpless to revenge attacks from the Provisional IRA. It was an excuse; he was already planning to restructure the Real IRA and begin a new bombing campaign.

In London, Rupert met Harold, his second MI5 handler. There was frantic activity in MI5 and the FBI.

Rupert was to gather as much information as possible about the Continuity IRA's involvement in the bombing.

The Irish garda was woefully ill-equipped to take down the leadership of a terrorist organisation. It had never convicted anyone of terrorist leadership or used wiretap equipment. It had never used an informer in court to accuse anyone of being a member of an IRA army council. It had spent years watching McKevitt's home without ever securing a conviction against him.

The Irish parliament, reacting to a public outcry, rushed through some of Europe's strictest anti-terrorism laws, which removed the right to silence in terrorism cases and allowed someone to be convicted of IRA membership on the word of a senior garda. It also introduced a new offence: directing terrorism, which carried a maximum life sentence, and allowed for the confiscation of farmland and houses if they were used for aiding terrorism.

The investigation into Omagh began on both sides of the border. It was to be the largest murder investigation in Irish history, involving interviews with thousands of witnesses, and tens of thousands of individual police actions.

A clerk who worked at a police station in Monaghan remembers the piles of paperwork. "It took up an entire wall, from floor to ceiling, just on Omagh."

Their single biggest problem was the decades of experience that McKevitt and the Real IRA had built up in defeating police investigations, and there was nothing directly linking Mickey McKevitt to the Omagh bomb.

What the southern police urgently needed was someone close to Mickey McKevitt, who could prove that he really was directing terrorism and bring Ireland's 30-year-long nightmare to an end. All of those close to him were completely loyal. They needed someone from the outside to come in and get close to him. MI5 believed they just might have the right person.

CHAPTER 10

Rupert drove to the ancestral home of US president Woodrow Wilson, just inside Northern Ireland, two miles south of Strabane in County Tyrone.

With peace funds, the house had been restored to its original condition. It was a pretty, red-doored, two-storey country house with whitewashed walls.

Inside were mementos from the Wilson family and a board showing the family tree and details of their journey from Northern Ireland to the White House.

Tourist figures had been hit badly by the Omagh bomb. There were few people around. A car pulled up. It was Andrew, an MI5 agent who was working on Rupert's case.

He walked to Rupert's car. Andrew lit up a cigarette. MI5 very much wanted to get the Real IRA leaders. He was intrigued by Mickey Donnelly, who was disillusioned with the Continuity IRA and defecting to the Real IRA. He listened and puffed as Rupert filled him in on Donnelly and his thinking. Rupert had told Donnelly that he was trying to buy a cottage in rural Derry or Donegal and wanted Donnelly's help in finding a place. He had the Drowes bar before, so he had credibility. It would give him a chance to talk to Donnelly and win his confidence.

Andrew nodded. He liked where this was going.

They drifted to talking about Linda Vaughan, Maureen and Rupert's glide through Irish women.

"Why do you like Irish women so much?" asked Andrew.

"Because they're easy to sleep with," said Rupert, laughing.

Andrew grimaced. "I should let you know that I'm Irish myself," he said.

"Oh, I meant no offence," said Rupert.

"I was scrambling, I remember that," said Rupert. "Turns out he was from just below the Inishowen Peninsula in rural Donegal. He didn't sound like it."

They both agreed it would be inadvisable for them to visit Wilson's home together, so Andrew switched to his own car and drove off.

The next day, Maureen, David and the still-injured Donnelly drove around the countryside, crossing over the border between Derry and Donegal, looking at cottages.

"How about this one?" said Donnelly as he pulled himself slowly out of Rupert's rental car and held up his crutch. David and Maureen also got out.

It was a quaint, isolated cottage in the foothills of the Donegal mountains.

Donnelly: "David had this little rental car that was way too small for him. He looked really funny in it. At the time, when we were driving around looking at houses, I thought it was ridiculous. It wasn't 'til later I started wondering, 'Why this particular car for such a big man? Is there something special about this car?'"

By then, Maureen and David had given up their house in Tullaghan and moved into an apartment a mile away in Bundoran.

It was among a group of holiday apartments near the sea. They both liked it and it was a good base from which to focus on Michael Donnelly, who was drifting further and further towards the Real IRA. Donnelly was impatient with the Continuity IRA and wanted revenge for what the Brits did to him, and to Ireland.

The day after he had driven around with Donnelly, Rupert looked in the passenger door of the rental car and found Andrew's cigarettes. He was furious.

"I couldn't fucking believe it. They were an English brand of cigarettes. I don't smoke, neither did Maureen. How would we explain that if Donnelly or Joe O'Neill or anyone had seen them in the car? It's one of those things that plants doubts. I called and wrote to MI5. I was pissed off."

It was to be a lasting change in the operation.

"I told them that from now I would not meet them anywhere in Ireland. I'd meet them in London or somewhere else or communicate by email but I didn't want to see their faces in Ireland, ever. I was really annoyed."

By now, David and Maureen had worked out an effective system for their spying business, reliant on nobody else.

Maureen would either join David at meetings or join him afterwards. In each case, he would say aloud his recollections of everything that had just occurred in the meeting and Maureen would write it down in the notebook as they drove back to the apartment in Bundoran.

Once inside, she would give him the notes and he would email encrypted details of the meetings to MI5 and the FBI.

When he was finished, they would take Maureen's notes and burn them in the sink.

"I was happy to play a back-up role," says Maureen. "It was a very sexist world they lived in anyway. It was nearly all men in Continuity and the Real IRA. Women stayed at home at looked after children."

Her husband gave her the nickname "99", the female assistant and love interest in the comedy spy show *Get Smart*.

More and more, Rupert was holding himself out as a self-made trucking millionaire, who could afford to take his wife to Ireland for weeks at a time. The money he was bringing from Chicago fascinated Michael Donnelly, who increasingly saw himself, in the post-Omagh turmoil, as the person who would lead violent republicanism on a new broad front of resistance to the British.

In February 1999, Donnelly, still recovering from his beating, invited David and Maureen for dinner at his house in Derry.

Donnelly was in a strange position: he hated McKevitt because of the Omagh bombing, yet he needed a ruthless, well-equipped leader like McKevitt to restart the campaign.

"Republicanism never recovered from Omagh," Donnelly told me. "Nobody was hostile to my face, but it knocked the heart out of it for me," he said.

"Were people like Mickey McKevitt reckless?" I ask.

"Yes, I have no doubt they were. You came across it all the time. They were isolated down south. Some of them had never crossed the border in 30 or 40 years. They thought that anything went, in terms of killing civilians, but living here [in Northern Ireland], we look at things in a very different way."

So McKevitt didn't see the human side of it? "That's putting it mildly, he didn't care," Donnelly says emphatically.

With the Chicago IFC's approval, Rupert would give Donnelly a few hundred pounds of fundraising money every time he visited, for Donnelly's family, and to fix his stalled Citroen car.

David and Maureen met Martina, Donnelly's wife, who had been one of the most committed female IRA members in Derry.

"She was such a kind, lovely woman," says Maureen. "I just couldn't imagine her getting involved in violence. They had a nice, clean house and adorable children. At dinner time, they blessed themselves and we said grace together. They were such good people and yet there was all this violence in the background."

Maureen was getting better and better at acting the American ingénue in Ireland. She behaved like she knew little of the IRA and was simply on holiday with her husband.

To this day, Michael Donnelly still does not know the extent of her role in writing out hundreds of pages of notes of her husband's recollection of meetings, including with Donnelly himself.

"Maureen was a lovely woman," says Donnelly. "A nice Irish-American woman who hadn't a clue about what her husband was doing in Ireland. She had a big personality and she was fun."

The four exchanged talk of family and the weather and the difference between Americans and Irish. Martina and Maureen stayed talking at the table, while David and Michael went out the back door to talk about "republicanism", as Michael Donnelly puts it.

"That's how it was from then on," says Maureen. "War was a man's business and I wasn't supposed to ask too many questions, that's how they saw it in Ireland."

The same week that David and Maureen visited the Donnelly home, Channel 4 broadcast a Continuity IRA propaganda video, in which it vowed that the fight against the British would continue.

Channel 4 said that the video had come from a Continuity IRA contact in Derry. It became the main source of footage of the Continuity IRA for the media and, today, a still from it features on the Continuity IRA Wikipedia page. It shows three men in balaclavas in front of an array of weapons, including a hand-held grenade launcher, an AK-47 assault rifle and a Magnum revolver.

When Rupert saw the video, he laughed. One of the men in balaclavas was wearing tear-away tracksuit bottoms with a white strip down the side and had snap buttons all the way down both legs.

"After the Provos broke his leg, Mickey always wore a pair of dark tracksuit bottoms with a white strip. They had buttons down the side so it could be opened and closed easily by the doctors and the dressing could be changed without having to take them off. So when I saw the video on the news, I immediately said, 'Hello, Mickey.'"

Donnelly smiles broadly when I ask him about the video. "I'm not in that video. My wife did buy me a pair of tracksuit bottoms when I was in hospital but it wasn't me."

Does he know who is in the video? He smiles again. "Well, you'd be surprised who is in it. It's a small world," he says.

Donnelly phoned Rupert shortly afterwards. He was setting something up. David was to come to a meeting in Derry. Maureen could come too. Some big people would be there.

They drove north to Derry in silence. It was raining heavily. They were led by car to a Victorian terraced house. It was dark and foreboding. The house was badly lit and the grey skies outside offered little light.

At the table sat Donnelly and Eddie McGarrigle, an Irish National Liberation Army leader who had been in a wheelchair since he was shot in 1984. McGarrigle, who would never walk again, was one of the most feared INLA men in the city. Beside him there was a female INLA member and another dissident.

Maureen and David sat down.

Donnelly introduced the Ruperts as the American fundraisers who could help with weapons. It was clear that he was trying to impress the group with his connections.

He and McGarrigle both spoke about the need to revitalise the armed struggle and how they would have to refocus and engage the community in a new wave of war.

Rupert could see that this was an important meeting. "I was told the guy in the wheelchair was high up in the INLA. I guessed he wasn't put in a wheelchair out of his own choosing. He looked pretty tough. I remember the room being really dark and the atmosphere was really dark."

Maureen: "We walked out of there and I thought, 'Oh my fricking God, is this the level we are at?' This was a turning point for me. This wasn't IRA songs with the good old boys in Joe O'Neill's bar. This was dark and sinister and absolutely terrifying. The woman terrified me as much as the guy in the wheelchair. I couldn't wait to get out of there and let David write his emails. I felt that there was a bridge being crossed here."

That year, Donnelly and Martina invited the Ruperts to their home several times. The house was under close surveillance by the British army, which kept a camera at the end of the street. "If I went to the shops, the camera would suddenly swing in my direction, so I knew they were watching," Donnelly said. Rupert felt the heavy surveillance on Donnelly might help him, if things went wrong.

Martina Donnelly was starting to observe David more closely. She had spent her adult life in the IRA and had some nebulous intuition about him, that he might not be who he claimed to be. Primarily, according to Michael Donnelly, she had noticed that Rupert collected receipts for everything he purchased, a claim Rupert denies. Donnelly said he began to notice that David would lead off conversations talking about importing weapons and would ask Donnelly what he needed from America.

One evening, after a meal and wine, Michael and David went out the back of the house to talk. Donnelly said that he was making good progress with Mickey McKevitt about starting a new campaign and wanted Rupert to meet McKevitt and his men.

They went back inside. Martina wished David and Maureen a safe journey on their hour-long drive back to their apartment in Bundoran.

Maureen got into the rental car with David and they drove off. As soon as they were on the road out of Derry, Maureen took out her notebook. "Today, Mickey Donnelly talked about…" began Rupert. Maureen wrote quickly.

Back at the Donnelly house in Derry, Mickey and Martina were cleaning up after the meal and putting the wine away. Donnelly was happy that Rupert seemed interested in moving away from the Continuity IRA and towards McKevitt's group.

As Martina was washing the dishes, she turned to her husband.

Michael Donnelly still remembers her words: "Isn't it funny," said Martina, "that a self-made millionaire like David collects receipts for the smallest things he buys. What would a multimillion-aire want to keep petty receipts for?"

"I said, 'Maybe that's the sign of a successful businessman,'" Donnelly recalls.

"She said, 'Well, maybe he has to give the receipts to somebody.'"

"I couldn't have been happier in my marriage and I knew my wife," says Donnelly. "She was well read and a good judge of character. I immediately listened to her. I tried to dismiss it from my mind but I started to think back. I remembered David reaching into his pocket for something and a big bunch of receipts coming out. It was a small doubt at first, but every time I spoke to my wife I thought about it and it began to fester."

CHAPTER 11

The Wolfe Tones, the IRA's favourite band, were playing before a heaving, sweaty mass in a community hall in Bundoran. Their most famous song, 'Celtic Symphony', was blasting. As usual, the lead singer turned to the crowd and cupped his ear. The crowd chanted back their support in unison, "Ooh, aah. Up the 'RA! Ooh aah. Up the 'RA!"

The Wolfe Tones attracted a large and rough crowd, a chance for IRA supporters of all factions to put aside differences and drunkenly hug each other to songs that celebrated the war against the Brits.

IRA sympathisers sold T-shirts and calendars from a table at the back of the room. The calendars had a different balaclava-wearing IRA member and a different weapon for each month of the year. July was the RPG [Rocket Propelled Grenade] shoulder-held missile, a weapon of such effectiveness that a west Belfast street has been renamed in its honour.

The bouncers on the door, as arranged by Joe O'Neill, were David Rupert, for height and strength, and a New Jersey bomb disposal squad officer, who will be named here only as Mr Gray (not his real name).

Mr Gray was a long-term Continuity IRA supporter. Every summer, he came back to Ireland to march in Republican Sinn Féin's hunger strike commemorations.

He was also an expert in bomb disposal and, by extension, in bomb creation.

After the last concert-goers were inside, Mr Gray chatted with Rupert. Through the design of the Continuity IRA, both doormen were Americans – Rupert the CIRA funder and Mr Gray the bomb expert.

Mr Gray talked about his contacts in the movement and how he was about to go to Belfast to meet Continuity IRA people, through Joe O'Neill's arranging, to share what he knew.

"So we just keep talking and I'm making a mental note of everything," says Rupert. "You have to be concerned about this guy because he's not some Irish American loud mouth. He has knowledge that could do a lot of damage."

Rupert has already been getting to know another police officer from New York, who also marches at Republican Sinn Féin events and is trying to encourage other police officers to do the same. He is also photographed in the Republican Sinn Féin newspaper, Saoirse.

"This second guy was of far more danger to me personally because he was from New York and he was in a position to run a background check on me and find out about the collapse of the trucking company and a lot about me locally. He had a girlfriend in Donegal and a wife in New York, so there was a lot going on with this guy."

That night, Rupert wrote a report on both men to the FBI Chicago office. They passed it on to New York and New Jersey FBI, which began an immediate investigation.

"The FBI were real interested in the bomb disposal guy. They asked me a lot of questions about him but didn't tell me what they were going to do. They never did," said Rupert.

While still in Bundoran, news came through from Michael Donnelly that Mickey McKevitt, the Real IRA leader, wanted to meet Rupert and Phil Kent, the Canadian IRA gun-runner, who had flown to Ireland. A date was fixed for Sunday, 29 July 1999.

At first, MI5 was incredulous that Rupert would be meeting McKevitt.

"They were cautious. They didn't want me to burn my contacts with CIRA if nothing was going to come of meeting McKevitt," says Rupert.

Rupert went back to the apartment in Bundoran and discussed it with Maureen.

"I thought, 'Oh wow, we are in a very different place now,'" says Maureen. "These people would kill us in a second if they knew the truth."

July 29 opened up with summer showers and warm spells between the heavy clouds blowing in from the Atlantic.

Donnelly arranged to meet Rupert at the bed and breakfast where Kent was staying. It was owned by an older Continuity IRA couple. Like Donnelly, they longed to move to the Real IRA and had told McKevitt that they wanted to make the switch.

Rupert knew the father very well, through Joe O'Neill, and learned that the man's teenage daughter, Mairead (not her real name), had a government job in Dublin. She also moved detonators and other bomb parts on the public bus from Dublin to Donegal, where they were assembled into bombs.

"I saw Dave leave to meet McKevitt," says Maureen. "I said, 'Great, you're going to meet bad people so they can bring you to really bad people.'"

At the bed and breakfast, Rupert met Kent, who was in a jubilant mood about meeting McKevitt.

Donnelly was concerned that Joe O'Neill might find out he was poaching Rupert and Kent from the Continuity IRA.

"I didn't want Joe O'Neill knowing about Phil Kent and our meeting," Donnelly said. "His people would have tried to put a stop to it."

That Sunday morning, Donnelly and Kent got into Rupert's rental car. Just as Rupert was about to leave the driveway, Mairead came rushing out of the house, got into the car and hugged Donnelly around the neck. She wanted to let him know, that if Donnelly was breaking away from the Continuity IRA to join McKevitt's more active group, he had her family's complete loyalty.

She got out of the car, almost in tears and Rupert drove out of the driveway and east out of Bundoran.

They were to meet McKevitt at the Slieve Russell Hotel in Ballyconnell, County Cavan, in the middle of the border region.

*****

As they crossed into Cavan, Kent said there were problems with Mr Gray. Rupert froze. Kent said that the FBI had dragged Mr Gray in for questioning about his Continuity IRA links and told him that he would be kicked out of the police and lose his pension if it was true.

Mr Gray was now back in Bundoran and angry because the FBI had said they saw him with Phil Kent. Mr Gray screamed at

Kent, accusing him of turning on him while in immigration custody in New York the previous spring.

Kent had managed to calm him down. He said they had been seen together at republican commemorations in Bundoran and that the garda must have passed on the information to the FBI.

Rupert nodded in sympathy. Inside, he was furious. He had only just told the FBI about Mr Gray and they had already busted him. He stayed calm – he would deal with it later.

They arrived at the Slieve Russell hotel and there was no sign of McKevitt. Donnelly needed to call him but his mobile phone was down. Rupert immediately offered his.

Donnelly called four numbers to reach McKevitt – one Northern Ireland mobile phone number to reach Maurice, a Real IRA man, and the southern mobile number and landline of Seamus McGrane, the Real IRA's director of training. Those numbers were now stored in Rupert's phone, to be passed on later to MI5.

In the final call, Donnelly spoke to McGrane, who said that he and McKevitt were watching the All-Ireland Gaelic football semi-final between Meath and Armagh.

McGrane said to meet them at 6pm at the Four Seasons Hotel in Monaghan. A little after six, McKevitt and McGrane arrived.

McKevitt had a disarmingly warm smile. A handsome man in his youth, his hair was beginning to recede and he kept a baseball cap pulled down over his face, as much for vanity as disguise. He had big eyes and spoke with the long drawl of the east coast border counties. He had been shot in both knees by republican rivals in the 1970s and occasionally had stiffness of the legs, but not on this day. He was in a very good mood.

McGrane had thick black hair and a moustache. He had swarthy features with dark eyes. His hair was short and straight but bristly and naturally stood up from his head. Rupert was struck by his intelligence and economy of speech. These men were different from the Continuity IRA. They were efficient business managers of the Provisional IRA for decades and had now broken off on their own.

Donnelly introduced Rupert and Kent as two very good republicans with a track record in the US.

It was clear to Rupert that McKevitt had already been briefed on both him and Kent. He kept his attention solely focused on Rupert, who introduced himself as the number two man for the Irish Freedom Committee in Chicago.

Like Rupert, McKevitt saw Kent as an ageing has-been, someone who had once set up arms deals all over the world for the Provisional IRA but who was now living on nostalgic stories and past reputation.

"Phil would start going on about the past and McKevitt would pull it right back to the present, and address it to me," said Rupert.

Donnelly had huge respect for Kent and was trying to edge him into the conversation. "I really liked Phil, I thought he was very wise. He just wasn't wise that day in bringing Rupert with him to the meeting," said Donnelly.

McKevitt and McGrane came straight to the point. They needed a US political and fundraising wing and wanted the Irish Freedom Committee to switch from the Continuity IRA.

McKevitt turned to the Omagh bomb. He told Rupert that it was a Continuity IRA operation and that he and his men had simply supplied the bomb parts. He was angry that Republican Sinn Féin had publicly denounced the bombing and distanced themselves from it. "They were supposed to share the blame but they turned tail and ran," he said.

Rupert saw that McKevitt was disciplined. He explained that the Real IRA was going well and was getting ready to strike but that it was weak in Belfast, where the Provisional IRA was at its strongest and was moving to peace.

McKevitt impressed Rupert. He seemed to be truthful and willing to admit where his organisation was weak. He wasn't like the loudmouths he had seen in the Drowes or in Joe's bar.

An hour into the meeting, McKevitt raised the issue of two members of a sleeper cell he was creating in Boston, who were there solely for weapon procurement and that more details would follow.

The final item on the agenda was procuring weapons on the global market. Kent, eager to get back into the conversation, mentioned that he had spent time in Cyprus and had obtained weapons in the 1970s, through the local leader of the Popular Front for the Liberation of Palestine. The man, said Kent, worked in architecture in the 1970s and his wife worked in an office.

Rupert cringed.

"And how do you know these people are even still alive?" demanded McKevitt.

"I don't know it for sure but they probably are," Kent said.

For Rupert, it was excruciating.

"Phil just came across as desperate to impress but he had nothing to bring to the table and they knew it. It was like he wanted McKevitt to say, 'You did big things for us in the 1970s, you're a hero,' but McKevitt didn't care."

There was a pause in the conversation.

Kent said he knew a Limerick businessman who owned him some favours and might be able to help.

There was silence at the table.

"Right," said McKevitt, staring back at Rupert.

McKevitt then mentioned that he had two men on the international market who were looking for some sophisticated new weapons.

Kent interjected that if the weapons were that sophisticated, maybe McKevitt and his men might not know how to use them.

"At this point, McKevitt and McGrane almost fell off their seats," said Rupert. "Don't worry, we'll know how to use them," said McKevitt. McGrane laughed with him.

McKevitt again directed his attention to Rupert, appealing for help in winning over the Irish Freedom Committee and its fundraising and support networks in the US. He said that the Real IRA was now referred to as Óglaigh na hÉireann (Volunteers of Ireland) or simply "the army" and that they were waiting for the anger surrounding the Omagh bomb to subside so they could begin a new bombing campaign.

Rupert said that he would do all he could to win over Continuity IRA supporters in the US and that he had already won over Chicago. "Good, good, good," said McKevitt. "We're going well."

It was coming up to 7.30pm. Rupert was keen to get out of there before Kent said any more.

McKevitt and McGrane left first. The hotel bar had no window in that section, so Rupert had to get up and walk a few feet to see if he could identify their car.

Kent, thinking Rupert was getting up to leave, told him to sit down and let McKevitt and McGrane leave first. Rupert had to think fast, so he said he had to go to the bathroom. From the toilets, he could see a red Volkswagen leave the hotel.

He walked back into the lounge and he, Kent and Donnelly walked back to Rupert's rental car. Kent was silent and sad.

Donnelly was excited. He had made that vital connection between the US fundraising wing and McKevitt.

Rupert was delighted because he was being brought in, quickly, to the Real IRA.

Rupert drove Donnelly back to Derry and then Kent back to the guesthouse in Donegal before making it back to his own apartment in Bundoran.

"I remember being really happy with the meeting but also pissed off that I had to drop Donnelly all the way to Derry city, which was way off the road home. I didn't have Maureen with me in the car to take notes, so I'm trying to keep all this information accurate in my head until I get home to her. I wanted Donnelly and Kent off my back and to start writing."

Back in the apartment before 10pm, Maureen made tea while he clicked on the computer and began to write thousands and thousands of words, more than he had ever written since agreeing to email MI5 and the FBI two years earlier.

"Big Day!" he began. "If I was worried about it being slow when I got here, it all changed today."

The message was addressed to both Paul, his new handler at MI5, and his friend Mark Lundgren in the Chicago FBI office. He detailed the entire day and every word he could remember but added a sharp admonishment to the FBI.

The arrest of Mr Gray, the bomb disposal officer, was "upsetting to me and I don't know what can be done about it". Mr Gray is "of course quite upset about seeing his pension disappearing," he wrote.

What scared him most about the arrest was that McKevitt and McGrane were lifelong terrorists, who were intelligent and very shrewd and had survived the worst of the Irish Troubles. They had improved their skills over decades and he pleaded with the FBI not to make any near-term arrests of anyone he mentioned in emails.

"There are new people that are going to come to the surface and you will want to pick up… if that is done, this new group of people are much smarter and it will wind up on my doorstep fairly quickly," he wrote.

The FBI assured him that they would be much more cautious in future.

Everything changed for David Rupert that day. He was now in what intelligence services saw as the most professional, well-armed and ruthless terrorist group in Europe. He was never as badly needed.

The geography of his life was also about to change. His entire experience in Ireland, from his first encounter with Joe O'Neill and Linda Vaughan, had been on the western Atlantic coast of Ireland, where the Continuity IRA was strongest.

The Real IRA was largely an east-coast phenomenon, mostly located north of Dublin in the border town of Dundalk and in the IRA heartland of South Armagh, just over the border.

He warned MI5 that night, "I see an entire new playing field now, probably much more dangerous, or at least I would have an entire new respect for my subjects," he wrote. "I think we need to rethink my cover, especially in the States."

The FBI gave a limited response but Paul at MI5 was ecstatic.

In a response email the next day, he peppered Rupert with questions.

Paul knew that within the internecine world of Irish republican politics, Donnelly, a republican hero, was unfiltered and ambitious and would soon find himself in conflict with McKevitt's overarching ego. The key challenge, Paul said, was to find a balance between the two men without alienating either.

Paul seemed to accurately know the psychology of Donnelly, the ambitious extravert, and McKevitt, more guarded but just as ambitious.

Overall, Rupert was delighted. There was now a real chance to infiltrate the Real IRA and get close to its leadership. "At this point," wrote Rupert to MI5, "I feel that the fire already has more than enough fuel so we will let it produce some heat."

CHAPTER 12

The InterContinental Grand Hotel rests in the centre of Paris, overlooking the Palais Garnier opera house. Paul, the MI5 agent, was waiting.

David and Maureen were staying at a hotel near Charles de Gaulle Airport. Maureen stayed in the room while Rupert took a cab to the InterContinental and met Paul in his hotel room.

He briefed Paul on the meeting with McKevitt and Paul handed him an envelope. Rupert was expecting $20,000 for his recent work in Ireland.

He lifted the envelope and weighed it in his hand.

"Seems alright," he said.

Rupert: "In the trucking business, you got used to weighing cash. You got an envelope, weighed it quickly in your hand and agreed to a shipment. If there was a problem later, you sorted it out, so I was used to dealing that way."

Paul wished him well and Rupert left the hotel room and went back to Maureen. Back at their hotel room, Rupert opened the envelope. Inside was a mix of dollars and sterling and it was ten thousand short.

Rupert flew into a rage. Nothing angered him like someone short-changing him or trying to take advantage of him. It brought back all the nightmare of the Drowes bar, and being stranded with no money, and of his bankruptcies.

It was happening again. The authorities were always trying to get him for tax, for insurance, for vehicle registration and were now short-changing him on the most dangerous time in his life.

"I was very, very hot about it. I called MI5 and the FBI, really really angry, saying this better get sorted out that very evening or I was walking away from the whole project. I called the M15 helpline. I was furious. God, I was so mad."

Rupert's rage immediately reached the FBI Chicago office, which was six hours behind in time. They promised to sort it out. "I told them they better sort it out, with dollars only. They can leave the sterling."

Lundgren said he would take care of it but it would take some time. David and Maureen flew back to the US and David went to the FBI the next day. From now on, he was on strike, even though his flight for his next trip to Ireland was already booked. Maureen and Lundgren urged him to go to Ireland but that he didn't have to work until Lundgren sorted out the money.

Rupert flew back to Ireland but was adamant he would not do any work.

Lundgren called Maureen and told her to meet him at a service station on a motorway outside Chicago.

"You have to imagine just how impossible David was with the FBI at that time. He would shout things to them all the time, he was very demanding," says Maureen.

Rupert does an about-turn and comes back into his living room when she says that. "Necessarily. I was demanding because I had to be," he said.

Maureen: "So I drove out there to the gas station to get the money from Lundgren and he hands over exactly what David wanted, in dollars, and I had to sign for it. I was going to sign my name but Lundgren said, 'No, just sign it Mrs Wristwatch.' That's how we discovered that David's FBI code name was Mr Wristwatch."

Maureen counted the money on the spot and called David to confirm. "I swear to God, it was like a hostage negotiation with Lundgren in the middle. I'm counting money, calling David in Ireland and saying, 'It's all here, he can go now.'"

Mr and Mrs Wristwatch. Rupert finally knew their code names. He already knew his M15 code name: Drumcliffe Echo. The FBI version was less poetic but easier.

He also got his money. "I was being a dick, I admit that, but if I wasn't, I could be completely ignored. Very few FBI agents go undercover, so they don't know what it's like to be facing castration, finger severing and execution if you're caught. That's what they are paying for."

Just when they had got that sorted out, there was another problem. The FBI Chicago office thought it would be a good idea if Rupert hired a yacht and asked Bernie and Mickey McKevitt out in it for a day's sailing. They wanted either the Brits or the Irish to bug the yacht. Whichever agreed, Rupert could steer the boat to that side of the narrow Carlingford Lough, which lies right between the two jurisdictions.

Rupert was militantly against the idea.

"I asked Lundgren, 'You want me to take them out on a yacht. Didn't I see that in a movie? Maybe McKevitt has seen the same movie. I don't know how to drive a fucking yacht, I'm not doing it.' The whole idea seemed like the backdrop to a cheesy Hollywood thriller.

"It was something out of the ordinary, and you can't do stuff that doesn't fit with other things around you. If I had been a big boat guy, maybe, but I wasn't. And suddenly I had this idea to go get a yacht? It was crazy."

*****

On 20 October 1999, after weeks of heavy surveillance, plain-clothes gardaí spotted known Real IRA men getting into a horsebox on a farm south of Dundalk with several young teens from the Fianna Éireann boy scout group.

They were followed to Stamullen, County Meath. A larger group gathered at the ruins of a crumbling, disused mansion. A local farmer, Seamus McGreevy, could be seen opening two galvanised sheets that covered the house's wine cellar. The group of ten, one by one, climbed underground.

At 9.30pm, after darkness fell, the garda Emergency Response Unit donned masks and black boiler suits and ran at the wine cellar armed with Uzi machine guns and pump action shotguns. They grabbed John McDonough, a Real IRA member from Dundalk, who was acting as lookout above the entrance and grabbed two others who tried to escape up the ladder from the wine cellar.

They threw down smoke bombs. One of the first to surrender was a crying, shaking 14-year-old boy who put his hands above his head, then a 16-year-old, both of whom were recruited by Alan and Anthony Ryan, the leaders of the Fianna Éireann.

The others inside agreed to surrender. Leading them out was Seamus McGrane, the Real IRA director of training, whom Rupert first met less than two months earlier. Five others also came out, including the director of firearms training, Martin "Golfball"

Conlon, one of the hardened South Armagh Provisional IRA members who had defected to McKevitt. Conlon was the only openly gay member of the South Armagh Real IRA. "He was gay and he didn't give two fucks who knew about it," one former comrade wrote about him online.

The Ryan brothers, under shouted instructions, also came out, along with Damien Lawless, one of the two nameless men who, McKevitt had told Rupert, were scouting the international market for weapons.

In the wine cellar, which was lit through a mobile generator, gardaí found a shoulder-held Russian rocket-launcher never seen in Ireland before, part of a large arms haul purchased by Lawless in the former Yugoslavia. They also found 40 detonators, bomb-making equipment, ammunition, an AK-47 assault rifle, a CZ 9mm submachine gun and CX pistol and ammunition. The 14-year-old told gardaí that he had been promised that he would learn some history and learn how to fire a gun.

In court, a garda described the rocket-launcher as "a very formidable weapon". It was clear that Lawless had already been successful on the international market and the group were training on the latest rocket-launchers and weapons, while teaching standards like the AK-47 and the submachine gun to the young recruits.

I was surprised the Ryan brothers were involved. I had known them for three years up to that time. They struck me as intelligent, if politically naive, and I thought that they would soon tire of Fianna Éireann's uniform fetishism and get jobs in Dublin's booming tech sector. It struck me how addictive the adrenaline rush of their clandestine world must be and how difficult it was to walk away.

David Rupert was back in Ireland, and agreed to continue the operation now that the FBI had handed over the money to Maureen.

The Real IRA had sent word through an intermediary that Rupert should go to the Fairview in Dundalk, a small hotel on the Belfast Road. From there, he would be picked up to meet McKevitt.

McKevitt's son, Stephen, pulled up in a new silver Alpha and took Rupert to the pretty seaside village of Blackrock, south of Dundalk, overlooking the Irish Sea.

Blackrock was where the newly expanding middle-class of Dundalk dreamed of living, close to the town but with long, pristine beaches, preserved sea marshes and open countryside to the south.

Stephen took him to a two-storey house with a low fence in the front. It was a pleasant setting, where a comfortable bank manager might live.

McKevitt greeted him with warmth and a big smile. Bernadette Sands McKevitt was down in Dublin, an hour and a half to the south, to lead a 32 County Sovereignty Movement meeting.

They went into the living room to talk. Rupert gave him $10,000 in fundraising money from the IFC.

Rupert thought that McKevitt would be upset about the raid on the wine cellar, and the loss of 10 people, but he was almost dismissive. "If it was a year ago, it would really have hurt us, but now, it's just a bruise," he said.

The loss of arms in the bunker was also not a big deal. He had taken far more from the Provisional IRA's bunkers and, after the Yugoslavia war and the Gulf war, Europe was flooded with cheap weapons.

The rocket-launcher found in the bunker, purchased in Yugoslavia, had cost less than £300 and there were many more.

He did, however, miss Seamus McGrane, his director of training, and Seamus McGreevy, the farmer who ran the bunker. Both were long-term friends. McGreevy, a former Provisional IRA member from Fermanagh, had moved down south to take over a farm. He was extremely loyal to McKevitt. He was a bachelor and devoted himself to farming and to the Real IRA. Any extra money he got went to help prisoners when they were released.

McKevitt was worried that the state might confiscate McGreevy's farm under post-Omagh anti-terrorist legislation because he was using it for Real IRA training.

It would not be good for publicity if the Real IRA released a statement saying that anyone who bought the McGreevy lands from the state would be shot, so he did it "the Irish way" and spread news locally that nobody was to have any part in the confiscation of the land, or its sale.

His biggest concern about the raid was that he believed the Provisional IRA, hoping to disrupt the Real IRA, must have tipped off the gardaí. (When he was released from prison, Martin Conlon, the gay South Armagh arms expert found in the bunker, was kidnapped, shot twice in the back of the head and his body dumped at the side of the road. Asked in an interview if it was responsible, a Real IRA representative said the organisation had no comment.)

McKevitt was confident and upbeat. The release of Provisional IRA prisoners had brought new recruits and he believed he now had the best of the bomb making "engineering division" on his side. His organisation was crippled and almost collapsed after Omagh but now it was back as strong as ever. It was on tactical ceasefire, he said, as a move to recover from mass arrests after Omagh, but was ready to strike hard against the British.

The big attacks would be in England and they would start soon in London, he said. The men were already in place and waiting.

McKevitt did nearly all the talking for three hours. Rupert nodded his head and laughed at the right moments.

"He was as relaxed as anyone in his position possibly could be. I liked him on a lot of levels, he was smart but there was this brutality behind it. It wasn't 'til you got away from him that you really thought about exactly what he was saying – bombs in England," said Rupert.

McKevitt mentioned two sleeper agents in Boston. The first was not a success because he drank too heavily and talked too much and was being thrown out of his apartment. The second was very different. He was a decorated member of the French Foreign Legion who had worked on a South African arms deal for McKevitt before being sent to Boston. In the IRA training camps, he had shown himself to be by far the best shot, and was an excellent assassin. He was too valuable to be brought to Ireland, where he might be caught, but would be recalled to assassinate "Tony Blair or somebody of that calibre" when the time was right.

What McKevitt really wanted, he said, was a spectacular attack against the British establishment, so notorious that it would generate headlines around the world and overshadow the damage caused by the Omagh bomb.

Frank O'Neill was flying in from Chicago that morning. McKevitt wanted him and Rupert to meet Bernadette the next day.

McKevitt shook his hand warmly. It was their first meeting alone. It could not have gone better, Rupert felt.

Another son dropped him back to the Fairview Hotel, where he booked for the night.

Up in his hotel room, he wrote a long email, warning Paul in MI5 that the Real IRA would start up their campaign again soon, that it would be aimed at military targets in the north and, more importantly, England, and specifically London, and that they were waiting for the right time to strike. It would give the UK authorities time to plan, and to find suspects in London. He also warned of a sleeper assassin in Massachusetts who would be brought back to kill a major British political figure.

His emails were developing their own dynamic. He was deeply immersed in dissident republicanism but didn't fully understand the politics. He repeatedly spelt Gerry Adams as the American "Jerry Adams" and used the abbreviation "JA". That suggested he was not reading much about the wider political context. He referred to leaks to the media as "press releases", leading to confusion in MI5, and he repeatedly called Michael Donnelly's ill-fated political movement the "Anti-Patrician League" instead of the "Anti-Partition League". In essence, if anyone intercepted any part of his emails, or fished them out of a bin, they would know an American wrote it.

Paul, in particular, showed great concern about security and about whether Maureen fully understood what her husband was getting into.

That night, life permanently changed for David Rupert. His email from the Fairview Hotel reached the top of the state security apparatus, as well as Tony Blair and the British cabinet. A cabinet briefing document was headlined "Real IRA ready to resume campaign, London likely target". Rupert was too wound up to sleep and continued answering M15's follow-up emails until after 4am.

The next morning, he woke up groggy.

They met at 11am in McKevitt's house in Blackrock. Bernadette Sands McKevitt was there, for her first meeting with Rupert. Tough-jawed, with a defining Sands flat nose she inherited from her mother, Bernadette had short dark hair and her clothes were either turtlenecks with a pendant or just plain and inoffensive. Bernadette bore a close resemblance to her brother Bobby. And, as Bobby Sands' sister, Bernadette was republican royalty. She herself had been mentioned in Bobby's smuggled prison communications. She had joined the IRA after her brother was jailed for possession of weapons in the 1970s and visited him frequently when he was first in prison.

In the 1970s, the Provisional IRA gave Bernadette an incendiary bomb to smuggle into Belfast city centre, past the city's new security gates. When she got to the centre, one of them went off, setting her coat on fire. She threw it off and fled, with IRA protection, south of the border to Dundalk, which had become the IRA's southern headquarters. When Bobby went on hunger strike to gain political status in 1981, she campaigned for him in the south. When he was elected an MP, the world's media gathered to watch the unfolding drama. He died, aged 27, on 5 May 1981, after 65 days on hunger strike. Around 100,000 people turned out at his funeral and Northern Ireland was convulsed by riots and shootings. Bernadette, wanted in the north, had to watch it all on television from Dundalk. The night after his death, the Grateful Dead dedicated the song "He's Gone" to Sands at a concert in Long Island. In India, the opposition party stood in silence for him, and the Longshoreman Union in New York implemented a 24-hour boycott of British goods. Some 5,000 students marched for Sands in Milan, while protesters occupied the British consulate in Ghent, Belgium. Over time, five French cities named streets after him. The British embassy in Tehran, to this day, sits on Bobby Sands Street, a deliberate insult. In Havana, there is a memorial to him. The mural of him on the side of the Sinn Féin building in Belfast is one of the most photographed images in Northern Ireland. He is as iconic an image for the IRA as Che Guevara is for the Cuban regime.

When Bernadette denounced the Good Friday Agreement, many joined her, simply because she was a Sands. "My brother didn't die for cross-border bodies," she said. "He died for a united Ireland."

Rupert found her very friendly and polite, not a hothead or visibly angry. Many people, including Republican newspapers, noted the close resemblance between Bernadette and her brother, which made her all the more iconic.

"She kept a clean house, she had well-behaved children," Rupert recalled. "She looked like this neatly-dressed suburban mom except that she would turn on you in a heartbeat if she thought you'd crossed her."

They were joined at the meeting by McKevitt's second-in-command, Liam Campbell, who had been the officer commanding the Provisional IRA in South Armagh, one of the most respected positions because South Armagh was as close as the IRA had to an independent republic within Northern Ireland. Hundreds of soldiers, police officers and civilians had been killed there and the IRA operated largely with impunity.

Campbell was known as a fearless and ruthless fighter, who had kept the British pinned down in South Armagh for decades. He also ran its cigarette and alcohol smuggling business, which brought in millions in profit, for him and for the cause.

He grew into the IRA in South Armagh. His older brother, Sean, blew himself up while planting a landmine in the 1970s. The family had heard the explosion and just assumed it was another IRA bomb until a priest and neighbours came to the house. Liam Campbell was banned from Northern Ireland from his early 20s because of his heavy campaign of bombings. Northern Ireland was right behind his house. He was not shy of publicity – he was photographed in the Irish Press newspaper, jumping over his back wall, one inch inside the Republic of Ireland as the photograph was taken.

He had a visceral energy and would arrive at McKevitt's house at 8am and say, "Let's go to Cork to meet the volunteers", then drive 200 miles to Cork, hold a meeting, drop McKevitt home and drive to Derry, 150 miles away, for another meeting.

Like Bernadette, the death of his brother gave him the stamp of official republican martyrdom. His family held an annual commemoration for Sean Campbell. Liam made it clear that Sinn Féin and the Provisional IRA were no longer welcome.

With McKevitt's approval, he directed all Real IRA operations and made the botched and imprecise warning calls before the Omagh bombing. Shaking hands with Rupert was, essentially, the person primarily responsible for the worst atrocity in modern Irish history.

Frank O'Neill had flown in from Chicago and was the last to join the meeting.

McKevitt had a big announcement – that he was going to appoint a US representative to the Real IRA army council. The representative wouldn't have voting rights, but they would be there for full transparency, so that they could see how the fundraising money was being spent and report it back to America.

This, he said, would avoid the "old Provo shenanigans" in which millions in US fundraising money went unaccounted.

O'Neill immediately looked at Rupert. "This is our man," he said, as Rupert travelled back to Ireland four or five times a year.

"This was a huge opportunity," says Rupert. "But I wasn't sure how the FBI and MI5 would feel about me on the ruling council. I said, as vaguely as I could, that we would have to report back to the members of the Irish Freedom Committee and see what they say."

O'Neill and McKevitt liked the answer. He was not rushing in. They could wait a few months until the bombing campaign began. Both McKevitt and Campbell assured him that the campaign in England would start soon and that a US representative could verify to American supporters that the money was being well spent.

Over tea, the four of them discussed their most immediate problem: Rupert was in serious trouble with the Continuity IRA for defecting to McKevitt's side.

Rupert was expected to go to the Republican Sinn Féin Ard Fheis in a few days. He already received word through Joe O'Neill that Des Long and the Continuity IRA army council were unhappy and wanted to speak to him.

Bernadette suggested Rupert should go, otherwise the Continuity IRA army council would feel betrayed and might take action against him. She felt he should be diplomatic and explain the decision he had taken, with Frank, to move to the Real IRA.

McKevitt immediately overruled her, saying that there was no way he should go down to Dublin, as the CIRA would try to get him back and "badmouth" the Real IRA.

McKevitt looked at Rupert. His underlying anger began to show. "If they threaten you," he said, "we will have people call at their doors and threaten to shoot them."

David Rupert, trucker, was now stuck in a tense stand-off between Ireland's two most prominent terrorist groups. Both wanted him, and the money and support he offered, and the threat of violence grew.

They all agreed. Rupert should not go to Dublin.

McKevitt told Rupert to go to Joe O'Neill before the Ard Fheis and explain to him that he was moving his fundraising to the Real IRA.

Rupert drove westward across the country the next day and met Joe in his bar. O'Neill's tone was harder than it had ever been before. He was depressed anyway about losing his seat on Bundoran council; Rupert's sudden defection to the Real IRA was adding to his sadness.

"Joe told me that they had taken me in on trust and that I was now taking everything from them," said Rupert.

He mentioned that McKevitt was reshaping the Real IRA and wanted Republican Sinn Féin to be its political wing.

"Over my dead fucking body," said O'Neill. "We have our own thing going."

It was the last conversation Rupert would ever have with his old friend. They had known each other for seven years and it was time to say goodbye. Time for Rupert to move on to bigger things. They shook hands and Joe escorted him to the door.

Rupert drove away, listening to an audiobook, and booked into the Carrickdale Hotel on the Old Newry Road in Dundalk, where Frank O'Neill was staying.

That night he couldn't sleep. He tossed and turned, wondering if the Continuity IRA leadership would accuse him of robbing army funds. This was a very serious situation – he was essentially stealing all of their US fundraising and support operation and moving to McKevitt, all because MI5 wanted him to get closer to the Real IRA.

The next day, he took Frank from Dundalk down to Dublin Airport and told him to take a taxi from there into the city centre for the Ard Fheis. "Alright," said Frank. "You do what you gotta do."

Rupert: "I left there immediately, drove all the way up to Bundoran to get my stuff from the apartment and left immediately for Dundalk. Bundoran was Continuity IRA people and Dundalk, on the other side of the country, was Real IRA people, where I'd be safer. I was driving along thinking, 'I'm safer with the Real IRA, as long as they don't know I'm FBI and MI5' and that all made sense to me."

*****

The car pulled up at a house in Dundalk. Stephen McKevitt told Rupert to walk inside.

He was being led into his first bomb team meeting. They were at the very top of the engineering department preparing bombs for Northern Ireland and London. McKevitt was already there. He wanted to show Rupert, and the American support base, how it all worked and to obtain their support in getting bomb parts.

It was just two days after his meeting with Bernadette and Liam Campbell in Blackrock.

"It was a lot more serious than I wanted my mind to believe. If you thought about how serious it was, it would eventually show up somewhere in your reaction," said Rupert.

He was focused on remembering as much detail as possible.

As he walked in the short driveway, he noted the number on the door, the second last house on the row.

"We were in a council row house on the outside of Dundalk. It was projects, you call them in the US."

Inside were McKevitt and two of the Real IRA's main bomb-makers. As always in the IRA, they tried to match an electronics expert with the man who makes the fertiliser or Semtex bomb. Both are needed to build a sophisticated car bomb or mortar.

The electronics engineer, called "Dent" by the others, was well dressed, handsome and had a goatee beard. The bomb maker, Frank, (not his real name) was scruffy and badly dressed. He looked like a farmer and was from South Armagh.

McKevitt began the meeting and invited Dent to lead the discussion.

Dent explained that the wine cellar had been raided after the gardaí had blocked the signal of the walkie-talkies used by the Real IRA lookouts, who couldn't notify the team in the wine cellar that the gardaí were there. After decades of walkie-talkies, the team would now switch to digital radio and would need Rupert to source them in the US.

They were probing Rupert's knowledge of components and electronics and McKevitt gave him a list of bomb-making equipment to get in America.

As the number of items grew, Rupert asked McKevitt if he could take notes. McKevitt said yes.

Rupert wrote it down on a notebook as the team called it out:

Two clean laptops to be used with public phone hook-ups for remote detonation. The laptops should also have voice distortion for coded warnings, as the police had recorded the panicked bomb warning before a car bomb detonated in Banbridge, injuring 33 people.

They also wanted digital radios with US frequencies, so that the Irish police could not interfere; parking meter timers for bomb detonation; black powder for "barrack-buster" mortars; marine magnets strong enough to hold eight pounds, to attack ships in a harbour; voice synthesisers; encryption software; giant-sized flash bulbs for bomb detonation; catalogues from spy supply stores, and model rockets and remote-control helicopter catalogues.

They wanted to be able to drop bombs on police and army barracks using $5,000 model helicopters.

They also wanted GPS devices and four personal organisers.

Frank had a copy of a specialist news brief called Interception Capabilities 2000, a trade publication for the bugging and interception business. Rupert asked to have a look and kept it in his hand as he talked.

Afterwards, they discussed a machine shop in Cork where the group was trying to make Barrett .50 calibre sniper rifles, which were extremely long and difficult to import. It was easier to make the barrels themselves and smuggle in the rest of the gun from America.

Rupert: "I could buy a Barrett over the counter in my local town in the US but they were too hard to bring over to Ireland."

The meeting broke up after an hour and a half.

The two bombers left first. Nobody ever drove their own car to the meetings, they all left with supporters who pulled up at the house, picked them up, and left quickly.

After they left, Rupert sat with McKevitt for half an hour.

Mickey explained that Dent and Frank were known as Lilywhites – they had clean criminal records and weren't known to the police, similar to the bomb team in London.

He wished Rupert well in the States and told him to report back. Stephen picked up Rupert and drove him back to the Carrickdale. Rupert still had the bugging magazine in his hand. He flicked through it.

It was coming up to Christmas. Time to go home and celebrate with Maureen and the family. It was clear from the meeting that there would soon be bombs in England. MI5 prepared for a bombing in the new year, based on Rupert's assessment. The assessment was passed on to the home secretary and the cabinet.

In the US, the FBI's response was far more subdued and it was clear that they would let the Brits run the operation. Mark Lundgren sent back a short email to Rupert.

Of the coming bombing campaign, he wrote:

"You have struck the lightening once again. I'll say a prayer for all of Ireland and Britain tonight… sounds like the shit is about to hit the oscillator once again."

CHAPTER 13

The church manager's windows smashed into the kitchen and the blast blew the doors off their hinges. It was 3am and the bomb could be heard over a wide area of rural Derry. The manager's children came crying down the stairs. Patients in a hospital 50 yards away woke up and got out of bed to see the wreckage outside.

The Real IRA announced its return with a bomb at Shackleton army camp, which was breached by entering the Church of Ireland grounds next door and cutting a hole in the barracks' fence.

The bomb, made up of three gas cylinders packed with explosives and a sophisticated Mark-19 timing unit, was placed against the wall of the accommodation block of the Royal Welsh Fusiliers. The accommodation block was damaged but nobody was killed. It was a near miss for the British army.

The attack was symbolic – in 1982 the INLA had planted a bomb in a pub outside Shackleton barracks, killing 11 British soldiers and six civilians.

It was February 2000. The same month, the Continuity IRA phoned in a bomb warning before blowing up the back of a hotel in Fermanagh. The bomb, placed under an oil tank, blew out the gable wall of the hotel and collapsed the ceiling in the kitchen and the toilets. Hot oil rained down on guests' cars, setting them on fire. It was the Continuity IRA's third time bombing a hotel in Fermanagh.

Two days later, Rupert flew in to Ireland to be initiated into the Real IRA army council. He had the approval of Frank O'Neill in Chicago but it was causing a serious split with representatives in New York, who wanted to fund Continuity IRA prisoners and to keep the organisation legitimate.

McKevitt's son, Stephen, picked him up at the Fairways Hotel in Dundalk. Stephen was late and Rupert was getting worried. As he waited, he could see what looked like a white Daihatsu Rocky with number plates from nearby Kildare. Two middle-aged men were inside and they were peering at the hotel.

Stephen pulled up at the entrance quickly and jumped into the foyer, telling Rupert they had to move. They got into his car and sped off. Stephen said he was so late because the Irish anti-terrorist Special Branch were following him and he had to drive into Dundalk centre to lose them and then drive out to the hotel. Rupert told him the bad news – that there was a car outside the hotel. "That's them," said Stephen. He pulled up at a junction just outside the hotel and watched until a line of cars came down the road to them, then spun out in front. The Special Branch were hemmed in by the five or six cars following in close procession behind Stephen and he sped off quickly to the McKevitt house in Blackrock.

His father greeted Rupert warmly and greeted news of the chase with a shrug.

Rupert dropped $10,000 in an envelope on the table, along with the video conferencing equipment and the digital personal organisers requested by the Real IRA's engineering department.

"Why isn't your wife with you?" asked McKevitt. Maureen was afraid to come. Rupert had to think fast. "Oh, she's on her spring healthy eating and exercise kick so she's at home working on that."

McKevitt thought the Continuity IRA bombing of a Fermanagh hotel, yet again, showed their incompetence. He was laughing about it to Rupert, who laughed back. "Couldn't they even find an army barracks to plant it in?" McKevitt said.

As they sat down to tea, McKevitt said he was thinking of shooting Michael Donnelly because of his leaks to the media.

McKevitt had asked commanders from each area to collect information on the home addresses and movements of senior Provisional IRA figures, as there was likely to be a bloody feud between the Real IRA and the Provisional IRA and they needed to prepare for assassinations. Donnelly had collected information on Gerry Adams' country house in Donegal but had then leaked the information to the *Sunday World* newspaper, which did a big spread on Adams' champagne socialist lifestyle. McKevitt wanted to know how Rupert would feel if the Real IRA killed Donnelly. Rupert said he didn't have a problem with it, as long as it was justified.

Approving assassinations. Who was Rupert by now? He was more confident than he had ever been in his life, finally finding the excitement he had always craved. Like Walter White in *Breaking Bad*, he had escaped suburban drudgery for a new, dangerous life that had affirmed his masculinity and reaffirmed his marriage. But was he, as Maureen feared, getting too familiar with the world he was inhabiting?

That morning, Rupert drove back to the McKevitt family home in Blackrock. There, as arranged with McKevitt, he spent the entire day setting up a new 32 County Sovereignty Movement webpage and online video conferencing system for Bernadette, who was alone in the house.

She used an external hard drive for sensitive material she didn't want the police to see, and wanted Rupert to protect her computer, while giving the 32 County Sovereignty Movement's webpage a new look.

While working on the computer, Rupert looked over the table and tried to memorise the books he saw in the McKevitts' home office. He noticed a pocket guide for hotels in Yugoslavia and a detailed roadmap for Belle-Isle-en-Terre on Brittany's Côte-d'Armor. Like many republicans, McKevitt found an affinity with the Celtic nations, and visited Brittany by smuggling himself out of the country in the well of a trucker's lorry.

Rupert: "I was trying to take in all I could while working on the computer. His office was 8ft wide and 14ft long maybe. I made a note of books that might be of interest to M15.

"Bernie left and I was all alone. I knew that Mickey had a lot of security video cameras in the house, some of them maybe hidden, so I only dared to go as far as the toilet and back to the computer. I felt he would review it later."

Bernadette came back later and talked about her children and made tea as he worked. At 6.10pm, Stephen said he was ready to bring Rupert. Bernadette wished him good luck.

He got into Stephen's car and they drove north to Gyles Quay, a long, curved beach on the Cooley peninsula, just south of the border. Stephen said little on the way. Rupert grew tense.

"I honestly thought maybe this is the time I get killed," he said. "It was absolutely ink-dark out at the beach, no lights. You couldn't even see your hand."

"There he is," said Stephen. A white pickup in the car park flashed its lights. "He'll take you from here."

Rupert walked across the car park and got into the pickup. "A white pickup truck. There weren't many of those in Ireland at the time. They were kind of a desert jihadi thing."

The man took him up through a country road and into the remote mountainous townlet of Lordship on the foothills of the Cooley Mountains.

He was talking to Rupert about the area. Rupert was nodding his head, trying to memorise the route. They turned right up a steep driveway to a whitewashed farmer's cottage. Inside was a woman and a young child of 10 – Rupert couldn't make out if it was a boy or a girl.

The woman made tea and tidied up in time for the army council meeting. She smiled and said little. It was her husband's business.

It was the home of a Real IRA member from Louth who farmed cattle and who was trusted enough to host army council meetings and store, under fields where the cattle roamed, some of the Real IRA's most sophisticated weaponry.

Within a few minutes, Liam Campbell came in the door with a big smile for the woman of the house. Behind him came Kieran McLaughlin from Derry, the Real IRA's finance chief and a gunman trained in some of its best weaponry. With them came Maurice, a Real IRA man from the north. Rupert focused, trying to remember their appearance. McLaughlin was in his 40s, about 5ft 6, 190 pounds, receding hair. Maurice looked like he was in his 30s, "very modern, looked like a college boy," according to Rupert.

There were just three of them. They wanted to assess Rupert before he met the full army council.

Campbell led the meeting. They were especially grateful to Rupert, he said, who had done more for them in just three months, through winning over US supporters and providing technical support, than Michael Donnelly had in nine months. They all expressed their disappointment that Donnelly, a republican hero, talked so loosely to the media. It was clear that Donnelly was in big danger.

Campbell raised his arm over his head. "Mickey was up here," he said. "Now Mickey is down here." He lowered his arm down to his hip.

They sat at the kitchen table and poured themselves tea. "What would improve support in the US? A bigger campaign?" asked Campbell.

"Of course," said Rupert. He told them that as the Real IRA was back attacking the Brits again, they should strike in their own time, and not when Sinn Féin's peace talks in Belfast presented an opportunity.

The three of them seemed happy with that answer. Campbell said they were waiting for Sinn Féin and the Provisional IRA's final disgrace by agreeing to destroy their weapons and then win over more of their members.

The joke was, said Campbell, that the Real IRA had taken so many weapons from bunkers that the Brits would have to give Gerry Adams some weapons to hand in.

They all laughed in unison.

Campbell outlined that they were hit hard by the Omagh bomb and had been on tactical ceasefire, but were ready to restart a major campaign. Rupert, referencing his truck business, said it was good to lie down for a while when you are beat.

Campbell and McLaughlin looked at him in horror. They both protested that they didn't just lie down after Omagh, they worked like hell, travelling around the country to reassure volunteers that the fight would go on and that it was only a setback. They had taken the army back to where it was now.

They seemed almost angry with Rupert. He backtracked, defining his statement three or four times, saying that it was only a pretend lying down until you could come back up again, like he did in the trucking business.

Campbell told Rupert, defensively, that 30 per cent of the army council had voted against the ceasefire after the Omagh bombing, including him.

Let's pause there for a moment. The man who made the botched warning calls, who caused police to lead families toward the bomb, not away from it, who committed the worst crime in Northern Ireland's history, had voted against even a sham ceasefire in the aftermath of its outrage. Rupert was puzzled by him. Where did this callousness come from, when even the most hardened like Mickey and Bernie McKevitt wanted a temporary halt?

He had to move on with the meeting. They were very interested in getting the latest spying equipment from the US – especially bugging detectors and computers that had electronic timers suitable for detonation. Rupert asked if US computer parts would be compatible with detonation from Irish phones. Campbell told him they weren't, but some phones on mainland Europe were and could be adapted. A European phone, calling an American laptop, leading to detonation of an attached bomb.

The meeting broke up after an hour. Kieran and Maurice, the two northerners, had to drive back to Derry and Belfast.

The woman peered around from a backroom where she and the child had stayed for the meeting. "Are ye alright?"

"Fine, thanks," said Campbell with a smile.

The farmer came from the back of the house to take Rupert home. As Rupert was walking on the driveway, he noticed a red car with a Dublin number plate. He only had seconds to commit it to memory. All his years in high school of memorising school books to compensate for his astigmatism had its use. He kept the number in his head and played it over and over as the farmer talked.

He told Rupert that the view over the mountains was beautiful but he had gotten used to it and needed to see it with fresh eyes again. They drove through the darkness back to the hotel.

David Rupert had gone from Continuity IRA hanger-on to trusted confidant to bomb-part supplier and financier, had crossed over, through Michael Donnelly, to the Real IRA, and was now in its army council – the most successful spy in Britain's long and bloody history in the Irish Troubles. Many had died trying to get to even the first layer of Irish republicanism. He had penetrated them all and was now at the centre. MI5 was ecstatic.

The next day, Mickey Donnelly, who knew he was being ostracised by the Real IRA army council, was composing a letter to the Irish Freedom Committee in America, concerned about a possible spy.

"Re: David Rupert," he wrote.

CHAPTER 14

Jimmy Taff had David Rupert pressed up against a wall. "You're a spy. You're fucking FBI.

"I fucking knew there was something up with you. You're a fucking tout."

"Calm…"

"Don't fucking tell me to calm down. It's right here."

Taff held up a newspaper. Rupert held out his hand slowly. Who had exposed him?

He took the newspaper.

"You were Hillary Clinton's boyfriend and you're living in Washington."

"What the fuck are you talking about?"

"Hillary Clinton got you into all of this. You're working for the US government. The Clintons wanted peace so they got you into this."

"Hillary Clinton's boyfriend? What the fuck are you talking about?"

"I've told Maguire about you. Read that," said Taff.

Rupert began to read from the newspaper. It was an extract from Gail Sheehy's new Hillary Clinton biography, *Hillary's Choice*. It said that Hillary's first serious boyfriend, the "ruthlessly handsome" David Rupert, met her in Washington the summer of her junior year, and confirms that they had protected sex and suggests she tried marijuana.

It also mentioned that David Rupert was from upstate New York and was now living in Washington.

Rupert smiled widely.

"This is fucking ridiculous. I don't know who this other David Rupert is, but he's not me."

Rupert read more of the article.

"So you're saying you're not David Rupert from upstate New York?" said Taff. "This fella has your address, ye are the same age."

Rupert: "The David Rupert in the book was from Syracuse, which is 160 miles from where I grew up, and we were pretty close in age. I said to him, 'Listen to me, I've done a lot of things in my life but Hillary Clinton wasn't one of them.'"

"I was laughing about it because I wanted him to see how ridiculous it was, that there must be photos of this other David Rupert out there somewhere and that I'd never lived in Washington in my life."

Taff began to calm down. "So you're not Hillary's David Rupert."

"Absolutely not, we don't mix in the same circles."

Jimmy Taff (not his real name) sang folk songs in the pubs of Bundoran. He needed Rupert for his latest venture – making leprechaun hats.

Novelty stovepipe leprechaun hats were becoming popular for Irish soccer fans at matches and Taff saw an opening.

He had applied for an Irish government grant to begin manufacturing. Rupert had agreed to write a letter, using the real name of his trucking company, claiming that he was an American interested in distributing the hats across America and that there was a guaranteed market.

Taff knew that if Rupert reported him to the Irish authorities, any chance of a grant was gone.

There was an awkwardness between them that Rupert tried to cover over with laughter. "That's a fucking good one."

Taff asked if the letter still stood. "Yeah, of course. I'm still buying fish from you, right?"

Taff said he would check Rupert's story and said goodbye.

Rupert had only gone back to the apartment in Bundoran to get some more possessions.

He belonged in the east coast now. He drove back to Dundalk and booked himself into the Carrickdale Hotel.

McKevitt met him in the lobby. It was just a few days after the army council meeting.

McKevitt told Rupert he needed two tiny .25 ladies' pistols, the type that could fit into a book or a small purse. It looked as if he was going to send someone to spring McGrane and dozens of other Real IRA members from prison. Rupert said he would try to get them in the US. It illustrated McKevitt's taste in guns. He hated AK-47s, Armalite and large rifles – too cumbersome and ineffective. He wanted ones that were smaller and easier to manoeuvre, suitable for urban warfare.

The next day, he waited in the lobby of the hotel. It was time to meet the bomb team again.

Stephen McKevitt pulled up and took off to the south, in the direction of Dundalk town. Along the way, Stephen told of his romance problems. He was dating a woman whose father was a Special Branch officer and her father was furious about it. He forbade his daughter to ever contact Stephen again. Stephen asked around town and discovered that the married police officer was seeing another woman. He took photographs of the man leaving a pub with the woman one night and sent them to him. The father's objections ended and Stephen was seeing his girlfriend again.

They drove through a maze of small council estates and back to the house where the first engineering department meeting had taken place in November. By now, Rupert knew it was called Oakland Park because he had retraced his steps. The owner, unknown to him, was a Real IRA member named Eoin Quigley, who put his home at the disposal of the bomb team.

It was as grim-looking as ever. Rupert got a better look. A street of terraced houses in a cul-de-sac with a lane at its end leading to the back of some of the homes.

Unknown to anyone arriving at the meeting, the gardaí had launched a major security operation and were across the road at the start of the lane, watching those going in and out of the meeting. MI5 had not shared details of Rupert's movements with them but they had been following McKevitt around Dundalk for decades. Surveillance had increased sharply in recent months because of the resumed Real IRA campaign. They parked an unmarked van on the street and several officers in unmarked cars. Photographing people going to meetings was still beyond their capabilities so they took notes of those entering.

Det Garda Fergal O'Brien had been hiding in the back of the van since 6pm and was looking out of the back window at the house, which was just 30 yards away.

At 7pm he saw Stephen McKevitt drop off David Rupert at the house. He knew Rupert to see and identified him in his notes as "tall and broad".

Half an hour later, Mickey McKevitt arrived in a car driven by Alan Browne, a Real IRA member from Dundalk. Campbell had led the last bomb-makers' meeting, and now it was up to McKevitt.

Inside the house, McKevitt greeted Rupert. The main topic of the meeting today would be an update on remote detonating techniques.

The men in the engineering team loved getting the latest technology. They read up on manuals and websites, always looking for the latest, the most sophisticated. They had come from the best of the Provisional IRA and they were competitive, almost to the point where they had forgotten about human victims – it was about creating the best, most modern bomb that would make all other engineers notice.

The chief electronics engineer, Dent, wasn't there; he was sick, Mickey said. Rupert wondered if they were telling him the truth or if he was off planting a bomb somewhere. He was replaced by a second man, Simon, who was well dressed, softly spoken and politely mannered. "He was the Liam Campbell-type. I liked the guy," Rupert said.

The other bomb-maker, Justin, he hadn't seen before. The man was extremely sharp and very good at computers and electronics. Each of the pair had a team who worked for them but only the top people were invited to engineering department meetings.

Rupert handed over the PGP encryption software that the bomb team had asked for in November. It had been with M15 for a month before it was handed back to Rupert. Justin lifted it up, looked at it and walked over to Rupert.

"How do we know that this isn't hacked?" he said.

Adrenaline coursed through Rupert's body. "How do we know it isn't doctored?" Justin said again.

He was confrontational, angry and suspicious.

He was right up to Rupert. One question after another. "Someone could have hacked into this, I don't even know this company." He looked down at the software package.

It was the most terrifying moment of Rupert's time in Ireland. What did they know? These men were electronics experts. If they examined it, they might find something from MI5 buried in the software's programming.

"Still to this day, it was the scariest moment of my life. Every time I think about it, I freeze," said Rupert.

Rupert's only way out was to do what he had done so many times before when he was in trouble. He got angry.

"Look, Dent asked for it. I brought this thing through Irish customs, I sure as fuck am not bringing it back through US customs. If you don't like it, if you think it's compromised, then throw it away. It's not my fucking responsibility."

McKevitt came between them. He explained to Justin that the engineer Dent had asked Rupert for this specific encryption program. If Justin wasn't happy with it, they would put it aside until Rupert came back to Ireland, which would give them time to check out its security.

He was calm and measured, trying to defuse the situation.

Rupert said that, when he went back to America, he didn't expect to get an email from the army council informing him that a bomb would go off in London at a certain time and date, but he needed secure emails so he could let them know when he was coming to Ireland, and expect that they could make arrangements for him, without the Brits knowing it.

Justin backed down. He could see McKevitt was on Rupert's side. It wasn't Rupert he was questioning, he said, it was the security of the software and potential for hacking.

They all sat down to discuss updates.

It was then, as everyone calmed down, that Rupert learned that he had inadvertently supplied very useful bomb parts to the team by giving the four digital personal timers to McKevitt.

Until now, he had been stalling on their numerous requests for bombing equipment from America, telling them that he was working on getting supplies without detection. On this visit, he had already come with $10,000, set up the political wing's website and supplied four personal organisers. It was enough stalling.

"I'd supplied them with the timers only because I thought that they needed them for organisation purposes. Turns out they had taken them apart and were using their internal timers for long-term bombs, the ones that could be planted months in advance."

He knew that the FBI's lawyer would be furious. He was under strict instructions: do not supply bomb parts from America. He would have to explain it.

He tried to tell the engineering department that the personal organisers were really good because they could store more lines of data than others, but nobody was listening. "They couldn't give a fuck what they could do, as long as they could be reset for bombs," he said.

McKevitt also mentioned that the bombs they were designing could be triggered by calling a mobile phone. They had tried one out already in a joint landmine operation with the Continuity IRA. The Continuity IRA called the number to test it and the bomb went off. McKevitt said he was angry about it because he felt they did it deliberately to undermine him.

McKevitt had an updated list of supplies for Rupert. As in November, Rupert asked if he could take notes. McKevitt said yes, but that Rupert would have to be careful where he put the notes. Rupert said that he would transfer a written list to his computer and encrypt it.

McKevitt, with help from Simon and Justin, began:

Remote control model helicopters, parking timers, marine magnets, infrared detection devices, bug sweeping gear, two clean laptops, detonators and cords, broad spectrum radios, mercury switches, laser/fiber-optic cable, black powder and handguns.

Rupert said he would try his best.

The meeting was adjourned.

Outside, the men left in other people's cars. McKevitt stood outside the house talking to Rupert.

McKevitt was delighted that Rupert had stood up to Justin. "If he talked to me like that I'd tell him to go fuck himself," he said.

It was the first time that the gardaí had seen the pair of them together in public.

Gardaí later tried to suggest that Rupert deliberately brought McKevitt out to be seen by them, and even said that later in court, but he is adamant that is not true.

"I didn't even know the gardaí were there," said Rupert. "I would have been upset if I'd known they were there because I didn't trust them. It had to be a very tightly held operation with the Brits because the gardaí were a sieve for information."

Gareth Mulley, a bomb team member, arrived in a blue Ford Fiesta at 9pm and David Rupert left in it.

On the way home, Rupert was shaken. His confrontation with Justin left him unbalanced and paranoid. Mulley would later be jailed for 10 years for building a keg bomb similar to the ones for which Joe O'Neill sought Guinness kegs. At the time he met Rupert, he was learning new techniques from Simon and Justin and was happy to chauffeur the American, who he had heard a lot about.

Rupert made it back to the Carrickdale Hotel. He went to his room to write, but couldn't. He felt exposed, wondering what M15 had put on the encryption disk and if Justin would find it. Why had Justin been so aggressive? Did he suspect something? Was he talking about Rupert to McKevitt and would someone on the engineering team send the disk for special analysis? He imagined the interrogation in South Armagh, and the torture and that final bullet and being dumped out on a border road late at night.

He left the hotel and did what he did his whole life when he was stressed: he put an audiobook into the cassette player and he drove for hours.

He passed the house where the army council meeting took place, just to confirm where it was. Eventually, he drove back to the hotel to deliver his report, later than usual.

"Sorry for the delay," he wrote. "I think my nerves are about gone for this trip. A good drive and a book on tape always calms me down, I have had both and I am ready to report."

The next day, he had to shake out his fears.

He noticed that the Real IRA leaders were starting to relax a bit: they were not as intensely security conscious as they had been. Liam Campbell picked him up in his own car. He had his 10-year-old daughter in the back, bringing her to a Real IRA meeting.

They drove back to Dundalk, to a row of houses. Rupert noted the door number on the way in.

Campbell came in behind him with his daughter. Inside, they met a 65-year-old man named Bernard, who had white hair. The presence of Campbell's daughter led the conversation. Bernard mentioned that he went to New Zealand every winter to be with his own daughter. Rupert saw that as a potential way of identifying him.

The two men led Rupert to a back room, while Campbell's daughter stayed in the front room to wait alone, while Daddy was having a meeting.

Campbell explained to Rupert that he invited his daughter and his other kids on meetings because it threw gardaí off the scent and he would buy the kids ice cream or sweets in exchange for them coming along in the car. As with Joe O'Neill's smuggling operation to a school, that Campbell would take his daughter from their nice farm along the border and bring her to a Real IRA meeting had a lasting impression on Rupert.

"I always liked Liam, he was polite and well dressed and smart, he was a farmer but he had this college professor look – but I thought a lot less of him after that. Bringing his daughter and leaving her there was a marker for me."

In the back room, Rupert met two other men, neither of whom got up to greet him. They both had brush cuts and moustaches but weren't similar enough to be related.

The taller of the two, Noel, was a senior member whom they were sending over to the US, to arrive in Chicago in April. Noel would explain to their US supporters that Rupert was now in charge and that he was the liaison to the Real IRA, or, in their language, "the army".

Campbell was in an upbeat mood; he needed the US trip to be a success so that the Real IRA could have a true US support wing.

The meeting broke up soon. It was simply so that Rupert and Noel could recognise each other.

Campbell called his daughter from the front room. He was a family man, who seemed to love his children.

They drove back to the Carrickdale in good spirits. Campbell had a big broad smile and laughed easily. Rupert was struck by how Ireland's most wanted man was so at ease.

He arrived back at the hotel, turned around and waved goodbye to Campbell and his daughter, who both waved back. He watched her leave, a little girl on a day out with her daddy.

A source close to Campbell insists that he did not bring his daughter to meetings and that he tried to keep his children separate from the Real IRA.

A member of the Real IRA army council insists that by now they began to see Rupert as a braggart...

"McKevitt thought Rupert was the greatest thing ever and was trying to get everyone to meet him. But I could see that he wasn't delivering. He talked and talked about it but he didn't bring the goods. That week was a turning point."

The next morning, Rupert checked out of the hotel. He had a meeting in the foyer with McKevitt who told him to be imaginative in America and to think big in suggesting ideas to the engineering department. He himself, in the Provisional IRA, had come up with the idea of leaving a bomb in a flashlight beside an army checkpoint. When a curious soldier picked it up, it blew his arm off.

The flashlight has a special relevance later on – it should have been a warning for Rupert's MI5 handlers.

McKevitt told Rupert never to be afraid to suggest something, that nothing was ridiculous. Then McKevitt left, wishing him well.

Rupert still had one last mission before he left Dundalk.

He went to visit Colm Murphy, who was suffering from severe depression after he was charged with the Omagh bombing. Murphy, a multimillionaire builder, had always been lively and charismatic, and his bar, the Emerald, was a shrine to fallen IRA heroes. Now he was shunned in Dundalk, and his business was falling apart.

McKevitt told Rupert that Murphy was suicidal. Seamus McKenna, the man suspected of driving the car bomb into Omagh, told me that he also noticed a profound shift in Murphy, who seemed distant and "quite odd".

"I thought I was going to prison for the rest of my life. I wasn't in a fit state," Murphy would later recall.

Rupert had met him briefly in November. He was a small man with brown hair, short legs and tough, builders' arms. He was suspected of killing over 20 people, on top of the 29 killed in Omagh. He was part of the Provisional IRA's South Armagh brigade and was a major suspect in the Kingsmill massacre in 1976, in which 10 Protestant workers were taken off a bus and shot dead. Murphy moved to the US and was jailed for five years there in an FBI sting for setting up an IRA arms deal. While he was in prison, he was protected by the Italian mafia, who identified with him as a Catholic.

He was deported back to Ireland, where he set up a successful construction business that did all the brickwork for Dublin's financial services centre. He was at the heart of the Celtic Tiger boom and picked up many other government contracts, including the science building at Dublin City University. All the money he made, he put into buying up property, including the Emerald.

But after Omagh, his natural vigour and excitement was gone. He lay in bed in the mornings, afraid to make business calls. A close relative suggested anti-depressants, but he resisted. He was charged with conspiracy to cause an explosion in Omagh but other charges were likely. He expected to be charged with 31 counts of murder and to be jailed for over 600 years. He wasn't to know it at the time, but he was to be convicted of conspiracy to cause an explosion in Omagh, but it was later overturned on appeal.

When Rupert met him in the Emerald on 20 February 2000, Murphy barely spoke, staring into the distance. He seemed "shy and hard to talk to," Rupert told MI5.

When he spoke, it was one complaint after another. He wanted McKevitt to restart a major bombing campaign as soon as possible or Murphy would "lose face" with his own men. The Continuity IRA was ready and wanted McKevitt's bombs and equipment, and Murphy "couldn't hold them back" for much longer.

He wanted a bombing campaign like an old spinster might seek a dance hall – to reclaim something that no longer made sense. He seemed listless and indifferent. What once seemed glorious to him now seemed pointless, and yet his bar was still full from one wall to the next with IRA memorabilia. He was becoming what he hated most about the Continuity IRA – a nostalgia buff.

Murphy railed against Republican Sinn Féin leader, Ruairí Ó Brádaigh, who could have made a powerful army out of the Continuity IRA but had "blown it".

The Continuity IRA was a disgrace, he said, and all Republican Sinn Féin were self-serving.

Rupert tried to keep it sympathetic and said that Murphy had many supporters in the US who knew that he could beat the case.

Murphy was embarrassed that the subject was even raised. In police interviews, he had confidently claimed he had never been to Omagh and had nothing to do with the bombing. Days later, police revealed that they had analysed phone mast records, which proved that Murphy's phone travelled up to Omagh and back down to Dundalk at the exact time the bomb was planted. He was compromised and was facing life in prison.

Rupert talked and talked, pleading with him to think of his sister, Angela, and his family, saying that the Brits had set him up and that it was time for him to fight the case. It was Rupert's trucking sales pitch brought to a new and tragic landscape.

Murphy, distractedly, listened and said that he would do what Angela wanted him to do. "That's great news," said Rupert. "You can't let them get you down."

Rupert clasped his arm.

Murphy agreed that he would defend himself in the largest criminal investigation in UK history.

"Thank you," he said simply.

CHAPTER 15

Back in the US, Rupert was busy repairing the house and doing the garden. He drove a tractor mower up and down the garden all weekend, listening to an audiobook about American forces in World War II.

As Maureen and Dorie chatted at home, he drove to an Irish pub in Forest Park, Chicago for an IFC meeting and to appeal for weapons. It was Sunday, 19 March 2000.

He wanted to see Frank O'Neill before the others arrived and to brief him on the trip to Ireland.

Carl O'Connor [not his real name], an increasingly regular attendee was also there, talking to Frank.

O'Connor was a business journalist and by the far the most middle-class and educated of the Chicago group. He acquired his Irish republicanism from his good friend, the unfortunately named George Harrison, the Provisional IRA's most prolific gun-runner.

The FBI estimated that Harrison moved 100,000 rounds of ammunition and 3,000 weapons, including rocket-launchers and heavy machine guns, to Ireland in the 1970s. The IRA had given him his own unit of men for transporting weapons by sea.

At his trial on weapons charges in 1982, the prosecutor told the jury that Harrison had been gun-running for six months. Harrison objected.

"Mr. Harrison is insulted," Frank Durkan, his lawyer said. "He wants the court to know that there has not been a weapon sent to Northern Ireland in the last 25 years without Mr Harrison."

He was acquitted after convincing the jury that his mission was approved by the CIA, which refused to come to court to deny what was obviously an invented story.

Harrison strongly opposed peace in Northern Ireland without a British withdrawal and sided with Republican Sinn Féin when the split came.

When I worked for an Irish American newspaper in New York, we would occasionally get letters from him, signed "George Harrison, Continuity IRA".

O'Connor was far more discreet and even-tempered.

Rupert, with army council observer status and having been appointed US coordinator for the Real IRA, was keen to assert that he was now in charge.

To show his new status, he told Frank and Joe that he had been given a list of weapons that the Real IRA wanted. McKevitt immediately needed two .25 ladies' pistols, he said.

Rupert had discussed weaponry with the IFC many times before, but nobody had ever volunteered to go out and buy them. It was always seen as something that Ireland sorted out directly.

Frank O'Neill was too old for gun-running anyway, so Rupert could discuss the subject knowing nothing would come of it.

O'Connor, the business journalist, said he would go to Fetlaws, a gun dealership in Indiana, and buy the guns.

Rupert was in real trouble if he did. The FBI had repeatedly warned him: do not buy any weapons for the Real IRA. The case against its US fundraisers could be thrown out if he did. It was bad enough that he had given the Real IRA personal organisers with long delay timers.

Rupert tried to dissuade O'Connor by telling him that it was a bad idea, that any guns would have to be off the street and untraceable.

He thought that was the end of the problem.

Three days later, O'Connor emailed him, saying he wanted to see him for breakfast that morning. It was usually Rupert who prompted the meetings with IFC members. He was concerned.

Rupert contacted Mark Lundgren in the FBI. Mark told him that if it was about the guns, Rupert should try to dissuade O'Connor as best he could.

Rupert drove to a diner for breakfast with O'Connor, who had already made a deal to buy two .25s and needed $400 from IFC funds to get them. This was bad news.

Rupert had the money, because he was on the way to the lumberyard to buy wood for home repair. He was stuck – if he didn't give O'Connor the money, it would arouse immediate suspicion and show Rupert up as a bragger rather than a real army man. He had requested the guns, so why wouldn't he want them?

Across the table, he gave the $400 to O'Connor who put it in his wallet.

O'Connor said he would email Rupert with a place to pick up the guns.

Rupert had prompted a very respected business journalist to buy specialist handguns to be used by the Real IRA, probably to help a mass breakout of prisoners.

He tried one last attempt to scare O'Connor out of the purchase. "How do you know they are clean?" he said. "They're clean," said O'Connor. "Or at least they will be because the serial numbers are being removed."

Rupert contacted Mark in the FBI again and told him what happened.

Lundgren was furious.

He couldn't believe that Rupert had just handed over the money like that – this was clearly enticing someone to procure weapons, someone who wouldn't have bought any weapons if Rupert hadn't opened his big mouth about being the big fucking man in Ireland.

It was the angriest Lundgren had ever been with him. Lundgren contacted his superiors, and the FBI lawyer, Jim Krupowski. More and more superiors got involved, including the head of the Chicago office. They were all mad. Rupert's instructions were clear – leave the gun-running to the gun-runners.

Rupert: "We had an awful row about it. They wanted me to go back and get the money from O'Connor and make sure he didn't go through with it. I said I just can't do that. I have to have some opening to do weapon deals otherwise I'm going to be uncovered.

"When I said that, they got into a big tizzy. They were all back and forth about it to each other – if O'Connor got the guns, how were the FBI going to deal with it?

"I knew this was a mess. This was exactly what the FBI had told me not to do, that a prosecution would not hold up, that the whole bureau could be in trouble for entrapment. O'Connor should be left out of the picture. He wasn't one of the big players."

Rupert apologised by email to both the FBI and MI5, saying he didn't see the problem arise as O'Connor did not fit the profile of a gun-runner. "He is college-educated, not someone that I could have dreamt of getting me this type of thing," he emailed the FBI. Rupert was uncharacteristically apologetic, while warning that it was inevitable in the world in which he was operating. "So, though I am sorry it happened, it is bound to happen again. All I can do is try to be more careful," he wrote.

There was an even bigger problem. Noel, the mysterious senior Real IRA figure, was coming to the US from Ireland on 22 April, just a month away. O'Connor would likely boast to Noel about his role in getting the specialist pistols for the operation. That would immediately show that Rupert hadn't delivered the weapons.

Rupert told the FBI by email that he would warn O'Connor to keep his mouth shut to Noel about this top-secret operation that only a few people should know about. The FBI were unimpressed.

Lundgren worked through the day to sort out a solution as soon as possible.

They told Rupert to go to lunch with O'Connor and tell him that Rupert already had the pistols from another source and to get the money back.

"Make sure to get the money back," said Lundgren.

Rupert invited O'Connor to lunch the next day and told him he already had two pistols. "Really?" said O'Connor, always well mannered. He agreed to cancel his own deal, after Rupert told him he had found the exact match for McKevitt's request.

O'Connor seemed undisturbed and was happy to help out. He handed Rupert the money back and called someone to cancel the deal.

Rupert was extremely relieved and put the money in his pocket straightaway and kept talking over lunch.

What would prompt a business journalist like O'Connor to go out on the streets of Chicago to buy untraceable pistols for foreign terrorists? Boredom? Suburban ennui? Breaking out of the clichés and euphemism of bland business journalism and living the gritty language of the streets? All of the above?

When I asked O'Connor for an interview, he googled me and read about my various escapades reporting in the Middle East.

"That sounds rather staid compared to what you usually work on," he wrote. He never did do an interview, but his emails to Rupert and Rupert's recording of the meetings are still intact.

Rupert saved the FBI from the mess he had created. Still, in email after email he raised the same point – how was he to be the Real IRA's representative in the US without buying weapons? It was a question the FBI could not answer. It was one that prompted them to reconsider this project. At some point there would have to be a discussion with MI5 about pulling Rupert out of the field. He already had enough evidence to convict McKevitt and some of the major Real IRA players for directing terrorism, and was soon to meet the Real IRA senior representative flying into Chicago. How long could he keep up this ruse without supplying a single weapon or bomb component from the long list the engineering department had given him?

He also had another concern. Michael Donnelly had written to the Irish Freedom Committee in New York and Chicago, expressing his concerns that Rupert was a spy. Some of the anti-Rupert faction had sent the letter to McKevitt, demanding his opinion. He sent word back that it was nonsense, that Rupert was solid and that Donnelly was bitter that he was being kicked out of the army for insubordination. It was very lucky for Rupert that Donnelly was viewed so negatively by the Real IRA leadership. Donnelly was right, of course, but he was also a loose talker. His very habit of denouncing spies was saving Rupert's life.

*****

On 23 April 2000, FBI agents positioned themselves in an unmarked van at O'Hare Airport in Chicago.

Rupert drove in, parked in the airport car park and walked to arrivals, without looking at the van. Bernadette Sands McKevitt had supplied him with the flight number.

As he waited in arrivals, he realised he had left his FBI-supplied recorder at home and didn't have time to go back and get it. It was a serious error. He would just have to take notes.

Noel came into arrivals and Rupert nodded at him before walking out of the airport alone. Noel followed a few hundred metres behind as Rupert walked to the car park.

The FBI spotted them. An agent lifted up his camera and snapped furiously. Now past the airport security cameras, the men were talking. Rupert, much taller, in knee-length shorts and T-shirt, Noel in jeans and long shirt, walking to the car.

Rupert realised immediately that there was a serious problem. He couldn't understand a word Noel was saying. He had a very thick Tyrone accent, spoke very lightly and his moustache appeared to hide a cleft palate because his voice was so indistinct.

Rupert: "Half of Tyrone was in Bundoran during the summer so I was used to the accent. It's a thick accent, but he was way beyond that. I didn't understand one word."

He consoled himself about forgetting the recorder – the man's accent was so thick that there was no way the FBI would understand the tape even if he had it.

As they drove into the city centre, he began to acclimatise to the man's voice. The man's full name was Noel Abernethy, he was 30 and from Dungannon in Tyrone. He joined the IRA when he was 15 and was jailed in the early 1990s for possession of explosives.

He was also tied into Liam Campbell's cigarette smuggling operation, which moved tens of millions of cigarettes every year, to both Britain and Ireland.

The father of Abernethy's girlfriend, Orla, had been shot dead by loyalists just a few years before as indiscriminate revenge for the murder of one of their leaders.

Abernethy had proposed to Orla the night before coming to the US and she had said yes. He was in a good mood.

He was looking forward to married life, though his commitment to the Real IRA was unflinching, even after the killing of 29 civilians in Omagh, just a few miles from his home in Dungannon.

He complained to Rupert that the Provisional IRA were now getting weak, that in a recent punishment shooting they had shot the victim six times with what they called a "six pack" – shooting him in the ankles, wrists and kneecaps. Abernethy felt this was unduly lenient. The man was a suspected informer, he said, and should have been "put to sleep".

Rupert nodded his head.

"Yeah," he said. Informers should be executed.

The FBI followed them to Frank O'Neill's house. Rupert dropped Abernethy off and, to the puzzlement of the FBI, rushed back to his own home to get his recorder and sped back again.

IFC members gathered at the house, where Abernethy informed them about the Real IRA bombing campaign in Ireland.

Abernethy spoke for two and a half hours, answering everyone's queries.

He was conscious of the fact that, until Rupert and O'Neill's recent intervention, all of these people had been Continuity IRA supporters and that he should downplay its role in the struggle.

Every mortar and bomb attack in Northern Ireland this year had been Real IRA, he said, apart from the bombing of the hotel in Fermanagh, which was Continuity IRA.

"The Continuity IRA is a figment of the imagination of about a dozen men," he said firmly.

The Provisional IRA was bigger than the Real IRA but was being dismantled as part of the peace deal. Abernethy told the guests that South Armagh Provisional IRA volunteers had told the leadership that if they surrendered even a single bullet, there would be a mass defection to the Real IRA.

There is some truth to this boast. There were large parts of South Armagh's two battalions that were on the brink of breaking away, but were wary of McKevitt, Campbell and their history of mistakes.

"What can we do from America?" one person asked.

"Money," Abernethy said. The army needed all the money it could get. The Real IRA had to buy untraceable cars for operations and if security was compromised, they had to send the cars to be crushed and start all over again. It all cost money. And propaganda: they needed vocal support in the US.

Rupert asked his own question – why had Abernethy travelled under his own name and why had he come through Dublin and not continental Europe? Abernethy said that McKevitt told him Rupert himself had suggested using his own name to avoid hassle at the airport.

Rupert was happy with the response: it showed that McKevitt trusted him.

After the meeting, when the others had left, Abernethy, Rupert and O'Neill had a chat about guns. The sharp admonishment from the FBI not to buy weapons was fresh on Rupert's mind. The gun situation in America, he told Abernethy, was very bad following the Columbine school shooting and other massacres. You could still buy a truck-load of weapons if you wanted, but it was now easier to trace back to the purchaser.

Abernethy said he understood but they would find a way.

Abernethy also said that Donnelly was already on his way out of the army and that his "stirring the pot" about Rupert had not been credible.

Rupert was relieved. He, Abernethy and Frank O'Neill were able to laugh about it together. Donnelly the crank. Donnelly the paranoid. Donnelly the absolutely correct.

Donnelly: "Did I send a letter to people in American warning them about Rupert? Absolutely I did. They went to McKevitt and he was saying, 'Oh don't mind Donnelly, he's feeling left out because I took Rupert from him.' So they have themselves to blame."

Rupert passed on Abernethy's travel plans to the FBI – he would fly to Boston the next morning and call at IFC supporter Joe Dillon's house. He would have meetings with a senior member of the Catholic fraternity, the Ancient Order of Hibernians, and other Republican-leaning groups and then Rupert would drive him to New York on Tuesday to meet supporters there. Abernethy would fly back to Dublin on Thursday.

Then the Chicago field office called Rupert and hit him with something he wasn't expecting – he was to wear his recorder and tape Abernethy for the rest of his time in Chicago and Boston, but he was to switch it off at the New York state border because they didn't want the FBI in New York to know what they were doing.

For all their talk about working by the correct protocol, Rupert was amazed.

At this point, it was one year and four months before 9/11 and 18 months since President Clinton promised to help defeat the Real IRA in the wake of Omagh. The FBI was so caught in its own territorial disputes that it wouldn't share anti-terror information, even internally.

Before Rupert drove down to Boston to pick up Abernethy, the FBI had another request – stop singing. It was a habit Rupert had picked up to keep himself awake during long-distance trucking. Pop, country music and Irish rebel songs had filled his previous car recordings with Phil Kent, Joe Dillon and Frank O'Neill.

He had to learn to be quiet, except for conversation.

For the next two days, the Boston field office followed Abernethy to his meetings, using the itinerary supplied by Rupert.

Abernethy had flown to Boston and needed a lift around Massachusetts and then New York. In a motorway layby, Rupert switched on his recorder and collected Abernethy. They drove through Massachusetts and Connecticut. Along the way, Abernethy explained the cigarette business and its distribution, and the structure of the Provisional IRA and the Real IRA.

As they were coming close to New York, he switched to talking about fertiliser bombs, similar to the one used in Omagh, and how to construct them.

Rupert: "He gave me a full description of how to build a bomb. The mix of the fertiliser, you should use 18-6-12 and not 0-30-30, because of its explosive effect, how to use a timer, the whole thing.

"What could I do? I was under strict instructions to switch off the recorder before crossing the New York border. If I didn't, the Chicago office would have to tell the people in New York what they were up to, and they didn't want that."

When he saw signs that they would soon be crossing over to New York, Rupert told Abernethy he was thirsty and pulled into a filling station.

"So I stopped to get a soft drink and went into the bathroom and shut the recorder off, by pressing a paperclip into the side."

He got back into the car and Abernethy continued talking about building bombs.

He dropped him off in New York to meet the lawyer, Martin Galvin, and some of the New York supporters who had defected from the Continuity IRA.

He then waited around the city for Abernethy to finish.

Rupert dropped him off at the airport in New York, and said a final farewell. Abernethy reminded Rupert that he should meet soon with the sleeper agent they had in Boston, the one that they would bring back to assassinate Tony Blair or some major target.

Rupert wished him good luck on his flight back to Dublin and drove back to Chicago.

That night, under Abernethy's insistence, he called a phone number listed for a house in Worcester, Massachusetts. As instructed by Campbell and Abernethy, he identified himself as "Dale" and asked for "James Smyth".

An American woman immediately recognised the code name "Dale". "I've been waiting for you to call," she said.

CHAPTER 16

There was a loud knock on Michael Donnelly's door.

He checked the spy hole and swung it open. It was Liam Clarke from the *Sunday Times*.

Most of Clarke's off-the-record information about the Continuity IRA and Derry republicanism had come from the veteran republican.

Donnelly: "Liam was desperate for a story. He got like that sometimes. He said he had nothing for Sunday and did I have anything interesting?"

Donnelly, who had written to the IFC to warn them that Rupert was a spy, was still hurt that McKevitt had ostracised him for leaking information to the media and for taking Rupert from him.

"You should check out a guy called David Rupert," Donnelly told Clarke.

Clarke got out his notebook and began to write while looking at Donnelly. David Rupert.

"Who is he?"

Donnelly: "I said he's a money man from America, bringing a lot of cash over here. He's part of the Irish Freedom Committee. Liam jumped at it, it saved him that week. I knew him a long time and I knew the system. There was an ex-admiral in the *Sunday Times* and if a story was stopped, Liam would say, 'The admiral stopped it.'

"He looked into Rupert and said it was a great story and it would be in on Sunday. Then he phoned me and said that the admiral pulled it. For some reason it was sensitive but then he said it would take a few weeks and it would be published."

Clarke began calling around, convinced that Rupert must be a multi-millionaire who was supplying his own fortune to the Real IRA.

Donnelly suggested Clarke call John McDonagh, an IFC leader who hosted the pro-Continuity IRA radio show called Radio Free Éireann on WBAI, New York's popular liberal station. McDonagh was also beginning to wonder about Rupert, but also carried a burning resentment that Rupert had successfully convinced much of the IFC to move from supporting the Continuity IRA to the Real IRA.

McDonagh: "Rupert would come to New York and say we should be supporting this and we should be supporting that. I thought, 'Who the fuck is this guy? He's not even Irish American. How did he get into this and who put him in charge?'"

McDonagh was a Continuity IRA loyalist and was also suspicious that Rupert seemed to hand out laptops to a lot of people.

Meanwhile, Dorothy Robinson, one of the leaders of the Irish American republican group Clan na Gael, was also developing her own suspicions about Rupert. Robinson, who lived in Philadelphia, was one of the most bloody-minded US-based Irish Republicans. A *Daily Mail* reporter bought a ticket to a Clan na Gael fundraiser in New York that year to see what they talked about. Robinson got up and proposed a toast to the IRA members who had bombed Lord Mountbatten, Prince Charles's great-uncle. The 250 people at the fundraiser clapped in approval and raised their glasses with Robinson; some were prominent lawyers in the Irish community.

She had been friends with Rupert but disagreed with the split in the IFC and was still loyal to the Continuity IRA. She also found Rupert's sudden rise in the movement very strange.

That year, she flew to Ireland to talk to Mickey McKevitt directly. Her main focus was Rupert and her concerns about him. McKevitt dismissed it and said Rupert was "solid". Robinson was known to be opinionated and headstrong. She told McKevitt that he should back the Continuity IRA and their ideology and that he was running his campaign the wrong way. McKevitt was furious. He got up and walked out of his own living room. Robinson stayed in the room, having a polite cup of tea with Bernadette. Rupert was saved, but how much longer before McKevitt began to listen to the growing chorus of suspicion?

Rupert drove from Chicago to Worcester, Massachusetts, on 24 April 2000, listening to Dan Brown's *The Da Vinci Code* along the way. The FBI had already booked him a room at the Holiday Inn and spent the morning bugging the room. Armed FBI officers were poised in case anything went wrong.

James Smyth met Rupert in the hotel room at 5pm. This was the man that the Real IRA had set up in the US, in preparation for the assassination of Tony Blair or another major British establishment figure.

He was as Rupert expected – lean, military build, Northern Irish accent, very serious and knowledgeable about military hardware. He was about 35 and came from a very hardline republican family.

In Rupert's hotel room, and with the FBI listening, Smyth told Rupert he had already sent handguns to Ireland but needed an untraceable mailing address to post Glock handguns and bomb timers. He needed Rupert to get a safe address from McKevitt. Rupert said he would sort it out.

He handed Smyth a military catalogue and asked him to choose what he wanted from it, saying that IFC funds could pay for it. Smyth flicked through it and said he would come back to him, and took the bomb component list the engineering department had given Rupert. He left shortly afterwards, saying he'd be in touch within a month.

The FBI were happy with the meeting. The conviction of someone plotting to kill Blair would be good for the agency.

The agents came into the room to congratulate Rupert.

He is reluctant to talk about how the room was bugged.

I press him several times, but he resists.

"It's trade craft and obviously there will be certain people reading this book who would like to know that information, so I can't."

In May 2000, as suspicion about Rupert mounted, Maureen had one of the proudest moments of her life. She and David flew down to Bloomington, Indiana. Dorie had graduated from law school. Maureen had dropped out of high school and was pregnant with her as a teenager. She had raised her without a husband, put every penny from the truck plaza towards her education, had never travelled so that Dorie would one day have a profession, and here she was with a law degree.

"I cried. It was an immense day," said Maureen. "David came down with me and I was just glowing with pride. David and I are in the spy business and it all felt so strange being surrounded by all these people in Bloomington who had normal jobs. Dorie's graduation was like our rock of sanity with all the madness going on in Ireland."

A week later, a bomb exploded under Hammersmith Bridge in London.

The blast woke people a mile away and left a major split on the city centre side of the bridge.

The Real IRA didn't manage to collapse it but it was the best effort yet in the IRA's long history of attacking the bridge. Long lines of traffic queued up at other bridges in the following days. News reports showed tailbacks and angry truck drivers.

It took two years of intermittent repairs before the bridge was deemed safe and it still has weight restrictions in place 18 years later.

The target was symbolic – the IRA had set two suitcase bombs on either side of the bridge in 1939. One of the bombs exploded, a support column collapsed, but the other needed to explode to bring the whole bridge down. A hairdresser coming home from work spotted a suitcase with smoke billowing out of it and flung it over the bridge into the water. It exploded, sending a 60ft jet of water into the air. The hairdresser was later appointed MBE for his bravery. The Provisional IRA returned to the same bridge in 1996 with the largest bomb ever planted in mainland Britain. It was nearly all Semtex, designed to destroy the supports of the bridge. The detonator went off but for reasons still disputed within the IRA, it failed to explode. By coming back for a third attempt, the Real IRA was signalling the longevity of the cause.

MI5 contacted Rupert – finding the London cell was now an absolute priority. Could he find out anything from McKevitt about who was responsible and when the next attack would be?

They had known since Rupert's meetings in November that the London cell was using young "lilywhites" with no criminal convictions and with no known republican connections. In America, Smyth was in a great mood because of the scale of the attack. He asked to speak to Rupert in Worcester. Again, Rupert drove down there and the FBI bugged his hotel room.

Smyth came into the room with a big smile.

"Smyth was very, very excited about the Hammersmith bomb, it got publicity in the US and it showed that the Real IRA were back in London," said Rupert. "It was even more exciting to him that the Real IRA now had untraceable lilywhites in London and would soon be striking again."

Now Smyth said he needed $5,000 to $10,000, to buy weapons and bomb components from the military weaponry catalogue Rupert had left with him.

Rupert was in a difficult situation – he was taking legitimate IFC funds and diverting them to buy weapons and bombs.

But the FBI believed that it was a different scenario from that with O'Connor – Smyth was a Real IRA member and was not being induced to commit crimes.

Rupert told him he would get the money and would be in contact. Smyth, who lived just minutes from the hotel, said they would meet again when he had the weapons, and left.

It was time for Rupert to return to Ireland.

MI5 wanted a meeting first. They were deeply concerned. The Provisional IRA had previously caused billions of pounds worth of damage in the financial district of London, had bombed the Conservative Party conference in Brighton, had bombed many restaurants, pubs, shops and parks in London, and the Real IRA were determined to continue with the England campaign.

On 18 June, Rupert flew from Chicago to Paris for a meeting with Paul at a hotel room near Charles de Gaulle Airport.

They agreed that the London bomb cell and McKevitt's direction of it was a major priority for the trip. They planned out how Rupert should raise the issue without forcing the conversation.

Because of the meeting with Paul, Rupert missed a connecting flight to Dublin and had to travel the next day. Mickey and Bernie McKevitt were getting very worried when he failed to arrive in Dublin. Bernie said she sensed something was wrong – that he had been arrested, or worse.

When he got to Dublin, Rupert sent word to them that he was all right and would see them soon in the Carrickdale Hotel, where Real IRA supporters were gathering for the annual 32 County Sovereignty Movement AGM. That same day, police found a primed Real IRA bomb on the grounds of the residence for the Northern Ireland secretary of state, Peter Mandelson, at Hillsborough Castle. It was designed to kill him and as many members of the Northern Ireland parliament as possible. It came just weeks after a Real IRA cell were caught trying to deliver a car bomb to Hillsborough to destroy the parliament building.

Wiping out the parliament was almost as important a goal for the Real IRA as bombing London.

On the night of 22 June, Rupert was in a frustrated mood. Real IRA members were coming in from all over Ireland for the 32CSM Ard Fheis in the same hotel as him and McKevitt spent the evening talking to senior leaders in the bar downstairs.

Rupert paced up and down his hotel room waiting for a call from McKevitt. Eventually, he got a knock on the door. It was Martin Galvin, the attorney and Real IRA supporter from New York. He tried to hide his disappointment.

"Dave!"

Galvin annoyed McKevitt. He was always talking, always discussing. He called their home every single day from New York to talk to Bernadette. He was also political and McKevitt hated politics – he wanted bombers, not talkers.

Rupert was also getting impatient with Galvin, who "talked and talked and talked" for an hour and a half about republicanism and the internecine politics of the Irish-American scene.

Finally, they were called downstairs. This was Rupert's big chance to talk about the London bombing campaign with McKevitt, if Galvin would just go away.

McKevitt was still in the hotel bar with some of the Real IRA leaders. He had never greeted Rupert so warmly. He loved him as a brother: they were both blue-collar, smart men who wanted action. Galvin was a soft-handed personal injury lawyer and never a member of the army. Judging by his body language, McKevitt wanted Galvin to leave.

"We thought you were lost," McKevitt said, of Rupert's late arrival into the country.

Rupert said that he had gone through Paris to avoid British security forces.

"Good move," said McKevitt.

He said he had reassured Bernadette that Rupert was fine. "I told her that he's just doing things the way they are supposed to be done," McKevitt said.

Galvin was careful to keep his law licence by avoiding any direct talk of bombings. He sensed Rupert and McKevitt were going to talk about London. He asked if he should leave the table.

Rupert didn't want to look too eager to discuss army business and said it was OK if he got another drink with them. Galvin stayed chatting until 10pm. Rupert was getting more and more tense. He knew he had to find out about the London cell before it was too late.

Eventually, Galvin got up and said he would see them at the AGM the next day.

"All right, good luck," said Rupert.

As soon as Galvin was gone, Rupert rolled his eyes. The two men got down to talking about the London cell.

McKevitt was elated about Hammersmith. He was really impressed with the London cell.

Hammersmith was difficult, he said, because there were many security cameras around the bridge, so they used Irish republican truckers with legitimate reason to be passing over the bridge to do the reconnaissance over several days, and the truckers helped transport the bomb into place. The truckers had also deliberately stalled on the junctions near the bridge in the aftermath, to maximise the traffic chaos.

McKevitt called over two more drinks.

They had sent over known Real IRA members to wander around London, attracting the attention of the security forces while the real cell, the lilywhites, planned and planted the bomb.

"But the Brits have now caught on to this," McKevitt said. "We're going to have to mix up the pattern a bit with something new." Rupert tried to remember the exact words for filing later.

Most of all, McKevitt was happy with the leaders of the engineering department, whom Rupert had met twice.

They had designed a new type of switch to detonate the bomb and it would be used for bigger targets in London. The engineers had no criminal records, like the London cell, and would keep the gardaí totally confused.

He told Rupert that the AGM would be all day the next day but said that Rupert wouldn't see much of him for the rest of his trip because McKevitt would be "away on business".

Rupert felt it was likely that McKevitt would be smuggled by container truck to London to speak to cell members and oversee new attacks.

As always, he was making a big effort to downplay the Continuity IRA, which had recently fired mortars into an army barracks in Fermanagh.

The mortar was "only a little fellow" but the media had overblown it and made it look like it was the size of a truck, he said.

McKevitt also talked about his recent arrest after the London attack and how he was treated very well by the gardaí, who knew that if he was ill-treated, their homes would be burned down. Other arrestees had been very badly treated. A senior garda punched one of their Dublin members very hard in the face, he said.

Rupert briefed him on the situation with James Smyth and the weapon procurement, using IFC money.

When the London situation had escalated, Smyth would be brought in for an assassination, McKevitt said. From hints dropped, it was clear that whatever Smyth's real name was, he was hiding under at least two layers of false identities.

Then McKevitt let slip an important clue – there were several cells in place in the UK. The first would plant a bomb, then, with London on edge, the cell would make several hoax bomb calls, using the recognised code word, until the second team was ready to set off its bomb and the second team began the hoax calls, causing chaos, and a third team prepared their bomb, in an ever-rotating cycle.

Rupert said he thought it was a really good idea.

The two friends ended their two-hour chat at midnight.

Rupert was happy with the meeting but furious with Galvin for delaying the talk. He still didn't get enough time to get more details about the London bombing campaign. He never liked to rush conversations – it would take another hours-long conversation with McKevitt to get more details.

In a hotel room just two floors above where the Real IRA leadership were drinking well into the night, Rupert wrote a long email to MI5 and the FBI.

"Kind of a fucked-up meeting," he wrote, before complaining about Galvin's unending chattiness.

Rupert was taking his job more and more personally. If the Real IRA managed an atrocity in London, it would be blamed on him.

Paul in MI5 sought to calm him and assure him that the information was very important, especially that truckers did the reconnaissance on Hammersmith Bridge before the bombing and how they had deliberately clogged the traffic afterwards.

It was "very interesting" that McKevitt was going away "on business" after the AGM and M15 would try to figure out where he was going.

That same night, Rupert drove up to Donegal, leaving Dundalk after midnight. The Continuity IRA couple, who farmed and kept a bed and breakfast, had now defected to McKevitt, along with their young daughter, who had a good government job in Dublin.

They had hosted Mickey and Bernie McKevitt for dinner and pledged their support and the use of their house and land for attacks and weapon storage. "They are 100 per cent," McKevitt had told Rupert.

Rupert had left some of his medicine in their home and wanted to collect it first thing in the morning. As he drove, the pressure of breaking the London cell was having its effect. He was seeing potential paramilitaries and IRA members everywhere.

At 1.30am "exactly", he saw four or five men with a ladder up against a telegraph pole on the A4 motorway, between Fivemiletown and Enniskillen in Fermanagh. There were no lights or markers on their van and they didn't appear to be servicemen. One was "about 45 to 50, thick dark hair, about 160 pounds, about 5ft 8 and wearing farmer-type clothing. Looked suspicious," he wrote to MI5.

Was he becoming Mr Security Guard, mall cop of Ireland? His emails at the AGM the next day were littered with talk of his importance within the Real IRA. Regarding Noel Abernethy, now back from the US, he wrote that he didn't see him because he was lower in the rankings than Rupert. "I am considered way above Noel Abernethy and would have no reason to deal with him," he wrote, and later referred to "us big guys" having talks.

He picked up his medicine, had a chat with the family and left early for the drive back to Dundalk. That morning was spent at the McKevitts' house, working on the 32CSM website.

Before they left the house for the AGM, Bernadette very firmly told Rupert that he must address the hall and tell their supporters that they had American backing.

Bernadette wouldn't listen to any of his arguments that he didn't like public speaking.

"Go out there and speak up for us and tell people we have support in America," she said. For the first time, he saw a flash of anger in her. It was a side she rarely showed, unless she felt her place in the struggle was undermined.

Rupert said he would. When they got to the hotel, there were Special Branch officers in four cars at the entrance. Rupert was stopped, while the McKevitts were waved on. After they took his name and address he was allowed to continue inside.

The AGM itself was a one-day talk shop of republican hot air and rhetoric. The chairman of the committee, Francie Mackie, never offered anything but waffle. "We as Irish republicans have challenged the legitimacy of British interference in Irish affairs…" he said. An undercover BBC *Panorama* film crew was in the hall to record for a documentary on the Omagh bomb suspects.

They filmed Liam Campbell as he left the hall.

A Real IRA army council member was nearby. "They had a small camera looking up. Nobody noticed it," he said.

"And now, all the way from the USA, would you please welcome, on behalf of the Irish Freedom Committee…"

Just like counting the votes at the Republican Sinn Féin AGM, Rupert felt this gave him good exposure as a republican. He took the microphone.

"Thanks Bernadette. I'm very honoured to be here, among so many great Irish republicans…"

He spoke for a few minutes, promising that the war against the Brits had the full support of Irish Americans and the movement in America was very proud of the armed struggle.

His speech got a big applause. He waved and sat down.

Delegates came up to him afterwards to shake his hand. Amid the dour northern accents of the Real IRA, he was a colourful novelty.

The 32CSM sent out informal word among members that the post-AGM social drinks were moved to a bar in Dundalk but to make sure the gardaí didn't find out. Then they deliberately let it slip to the gardaí that the social was in Colm Murphy's bar, the Emerald, leaving the gardaí waiting outside there all night. McKevitt thought the duplicity was hilarious.

Rupert was still focused on breaking the London cell. He was tired but decided to go to the social and see who was around. The bar, in the centre of Dundalk, was crowded with Real IRA members and their supporters. As soon as he arrived, he heard an English accent. He was immediately drawn to it. Could this be a cell member?

The man's name was Simon Poot. He was a government social worker from Manchester who helped maintain the 32CSM website and ran their operations in much of England. As a government worker, he had access to very sensitive information, including addresses of police and leading government officials.

It took Rupert several hours to get the man's full name. He memorised it to pass on to MI5.

Simon, who wasn't Real IRA but was mixing with its members, was with a man called David, who travelled with a press card.

Rupert was training in on any reference to London.

Someone bemoaned that the Hammersmith bombing got more coverage in America than in Ireland. This other David said that those near the bomb sure heard about it because it was so loud. Rupert began to wonder if he knew more than he was saying about the attack.

He bought a few drinks, then left the event and took a taxi back to the hotel to write up his notes about London.

He was exhausted and fell asleep.

The next morning, Sunday, he came down to have breakfast at the hotel. He was greeted by the ever-chatting Galvin.

As he had breakfast, he got a text from Bernadette. "Did you see the *Sunday Times*?"

He got a copy at reception. There was a front-page article by Liam Clarke about how Real IRA supporters were stepping up their presence in England after the Hammersmith attack and were planning to picket the home of home secretary Jack Straw.

Then it mentioned that the Real IRA had a prominent American multimillionaire supporter named David Rupert, who owned a trucking company and who had donated a fortune to the cause and was given special access to the Real IRA. It was straight from Mickey Donnelly's mouth.

Rupert panicked.

Campbell was already calling McKevitt, warning him that Rupert was now "hot" and would draw attention to them.

McKevitt was furious that his US liaison was now exposed in the media.

Meanwhile, Nancy, a neighbour of Rupert's family in Madrid, was on a coach tour of Ireland with a group of retirees. At her hotel room in the south of Ireland, she picked up a copy of the Sunday Times.

She was stunned to see Joebe was the chief American funder for the IRA. She scanned the article and sent it back to her family.

Within a day, everyone in Madrid knew that Joebe was a terrorist mastermind.

Rupert was frustrated. Just when he had to get close to Campbell and McKevitt to find out more about London, his cover was blown.

"I didn't know it would go like this," Rupert wrote to MI5. "I've got an army council meeting tomorrow, and things just might be fucked."

CHAPTER 17

Mickey McKevitt and David Rupert stood at the southern side of the inlet looking across at the hated state of Northern Ireland.

Between it and them sat a heavily gunned British navy ship.

It was anchored in the mouth of Carlingford Lough, on the most easterly dividing point between Northern Ireland and the Republic. It was meant as a deterrent to republican dissidents, and as a show of strength. Its presence, just a few miles north of the republican heartland of Dundalk, was a constant irritant for McKevitt.

"What we need is a suicide bomber," he said.

"I wish we had volunteers like that."

He turned to Rupert. "We're working on something to blow that ship to pieces and the Brits won't come near here again."

They were going to have an army council meeting the next day. He wanted Rupert to discuss it.

Rupert made a mental note. McKevitt seemed serious about blowing up the ship.

The next day, 26 June 2000, Rupert was told to come out of the side entrance of the Carrickdale Hotel, across from the leisure centre, in front of a line of trees that blocked the view from a British observation tower.

Although the Carrickdale was a few hundred metres inside the Republic, the number plates of cars going in and out could be read from the tower. Locals believed the tower was built there to watch people going into the Carrickdale and the line of republican-controlled bureau de changes and petrol stations that dotted the road.

Today was to be Rupert's second army council meeting. As before, McKevitt was only letting him meet a few members at a time.

Stephen and Mickey McKevitt pulled up in a brown Toyota Corolla later that day. A Real IRA sympathiser who had a garage gave the McKevitts free use of his vehicles, so they confused the British and Irish security forces almost every day.

They drove into the countryside, up into the mountains to the whitewashed country cottage where Rupert had been for the previous army council meeting. Stephen McKevitt dropped them off at the bottom of the long driveway, which gave Rupert time to study the house.

There was a van from a forestry chainsaw company outside. There was also a Dublin-registered 1994 Toyota Corolla in the driveway. He memorised the number plate as he and McKevitt walked towards the cottage. He said the number over and over to himself as they approached the door.

There was also the same white four-wheel drive that brought him to the army council meeting the last time.

An attractive woman opened the door. Rupert had no trouble memorising her appearance immediately.

Inside the living room was Kieran McLaughlin and Dominic, a dissident republican living in the Letterkenny area of Donegal.

Liam Campbell came in after them. He was smiling about the *Sunday Times* article. "You're famous now, Dave," he said, but made it clear that he would have to keep his distance from Rupert for a while until any extra surveillance had died down.

"Well," Campbell said to McKevitt, jokingly. "What have you done with this big financial contribution that multimillionaire David Rupert gave to us?"

Everyone laughed except for McKevitt.

He was in a rage about the article. He was furious that John McDonagh in New York had contributed to it and he also blamed Donnelly, who should be shot, he said.

He turned to Rupert. His tone was tense. "Listen, you deny any knowledge of this, ever. If anyone asks, you don't know anything about it."

Rupert noticed the stark difference in personality – nothing ever seemed to bother Campbell, whereas McKevitt was far more tightly wound and took problems far more seriously.

But he felt that most of the men there were like Campbell: they could see the lighter side of it, and it gave Rupert some battle scars that helped him bond with the army council.

He did worry, he told them, that the IFC in Chicago would see the newspaper article and think that Rupert was claiming their contributions as his own, much as Phil Kent had in the past.

McKevitt said not to worry about it because he would make sure the people in America understood.

He turned to Rupert, angrily. Rupert was to buy no weapons, and James Smyth was to buy NO weapons, without McKevitt or someone from the army council going over there to approve. If they had ideas for good calibre weapons, James Smyth could test them in advance, he said. He was walking up and down the room.

Again, he said that they wanted large Barrett rifles from the US to continue the Provisional IRA's sniper campaign in South Armagh.

He would go over to America himself, he said. Which did Rupert think was a better way to get into America without being detected – Newfoundland and then the US-Canadian border or El Paso and the US-Mexican border?

Rupert said that, as a trucker, he had crossed the border at El Paso with little difficulty and it would be a lot easier.

"Good, good," said McKevitt, still distracted. "I want James Smyth based down there, you go test the border for us and then set up with a place for him to live down there."

McKevitt was concerned – the gardaí had figured out the Provisional IRA were still importing weapons by mail from a cell of sympathisers in Florida.

It was all over the media.

The gardaí also knew that one address in Meath was being used that wasn't on the Provisional IRA's list, so they knew it must be going to McKevitt. He was concerned that Smyth would be exposed in a big arms clampdown in the US and wanted him moved to El Paso, where McKevitt could meet him.

He was still annoyed about the newspaper article and vowed that Mickey Donnelly would pay for it.

The fact that Mickey Donnelly openly admitted to me for this book that he was the source of the article says something about his personality. As with the Provisional IRA, his attitude was "Come and get me."

They talked more about newspaper stories. Campbell noted that the papers said the Real IRA used satellite photos, now commercially available on computer disk sets, to check out a barracks in Derry before a recent bombing. McKevitt, starting to thaw out, turned to Dominic and said perplexed, "Did you?"

Everyone laughed.

The entire media commotion left little time to talk about the London cell.

The group agreed that things were going well in London and would gear up for bigger targets, but revealed little else. They had another problem – two senior members of the bomb-making team were supposed to be at the army council meeting but there was no sign of them.

They waited and waited. They were growing increasingly worried that the two had been arrested and that the gardaí might raid the meeting. Campbell looked visibly upset. They waited a few more minutes.

Campbell and Dominic decided that using their mobile phones would be too risky, so they drove off to a phone box.

They came back 10 minutes later. Nobody was answering. Something was wrong.

They decided to get Rupert out of there and carry on with the meeting, which they could say was 32CSM if they were raided.

The woman of the house, the one whose attractiveness Rupert had noted, was called to the front room. She and her family carefully avoided being in the room when the meeting took place. Campbell asked her to drive Rupert to the Carrickdale. She got her car keys and took Rupert back to the hotel. Rupert was trying to talk to her but she didn't say much.

Back at the hotel, he wrote a report on the army council meeting. Paul was very pleased and said he would locate photographs of Dominic to show to Rupert when he returned to London in a few days.

As soon as the meeting was over, South Armagh Real IRA members called around to people close to the Dublin-to-Belfast railway in Meigh, County Armagh.

They told the locals that there would be a bomb on the railway line but not to worry because it would be small and would not hurt any civilians. They knew the community distrusted them after Omagh and wanted to assure republican areas that there would be no mistake.

On the night of 29 June, a bomb destroyed the rail line, causing havoc and mass cancellations of Dublin to Belfast trains.

The following day, McKevitt agreed to show Rupert around the area, so that he could choose a rental house.

Rupert felt it was important to have a house in the area and to be trusted. It was also a good way to understand McKevitt's movements in the area.

They got into Rupert's rental car to drive around looking at houses. "So you heard about the railway?" said McKevitt.

Campbell and his men had detonated it to test the security force reaction, he said. The Real IRA had spotters there all day, studying the pattern by which the Northern Ireland police and army dealt with the situation and seeing if they had air support.

"We'll do a few of these," said McKevitt. "They may use a different pattern next time but then we'll find the rotation of how they move," he said.

They drove out to Clogherhead in north Louth, overlooking the Irish Sea, to view property for sale and rent.

McKevitt loved the area. It was a beautiful coastal village and the people around here were good, solid republicans, whereas the republicans of Carlingford Peninsula were fanatics, either for or against the Real IRA. He didn't want fanatics, he just wanted solid people, he said.

After they finished looking at houses on Carlingford, he told Rupert to drive a bit further along the border road, to the road overlooking Narrow Water Bridge and Warrenpoint on the other side of the inlet.

It was a spot that always made McKevitt happy when he was stressed: it was the site of one of his greatest accomplishments.

They sat on a car on a hill, looking down on Narrow Water, which lies just inside Northern Ireland. It was here that, in 1978, McKevitt had dreamed up the following year's double-bombing that killed 18 British soldiers on the same day that Mountbatten was blown up in Sligo.

They got out of the car and McKevitt pointed out all the points, like a battle historian recounting a great victory.

They had watched troop movements for months, and saw the soldiers had to use the border road to get back to base. He pointed out where the first bomb was planted at the side of the road and how they could watch it all unfold from the hill on the southern side, without ever having to go into Northern Ireland. Brendan Burns, one of their best bomb-makers, pressed the button as the bus was passing a haystack mounted on a truck. The bus was blown up and fell on its side. The nearest rescue point would be an old lodge house, where the soldiers carried the injured and called for help. Burns picked up a different device and pressed the button. The lodge house blew up, killing the injured and their rescuers.

McKevitt clasped his hands. "A great operation," he said. It was a major career booster for him in the Provisional IRA and had greatly impressed IRA leaders in Belfast. Best of all, on a busy road, there were no civilian deaths. He seemed nostalgic. It was a glorious time for him.

They got back in the car and drove back to the hotel.

McKevitt was trying so hard to impress Rupert.

They had tea for an hour back at the Ballymascanlon House Hotel.

He knew by now that the BBC were coming around to Campbell's house and that a major documentary naming Omagh suspects would soon be released.

McKevitt said that they had a shadow army council and engineering team in place, in case he and Liam were arrested at the same time. "I hope it doesn't happen, but it might," he said.

Back at the Carrickdale, Rupert didn't have time to write down all the real estate addresses he visited with McKevitt, so he wrote a quick note to MI5 saying that he would deal with it later as he had to reduce what he was now calling "exposure time" – the time when he was writing his spy reports and could be exposed if someone came into the room.

Late that night, he discovered that the bomb team couldn't make it to the army council meeting because they were being tailed by the Special Branch and had to duck back into Dundalk. Campbell told him they would reconvene the meeting at the cottage the next day.

After breakfast, the cottage owner picked up Rupert and drove up into the mountains once more.

In the cottage driveway, Rupert walked slowly so he could pick out the Dublin number plate of a black Nissan Sunny car.

Dent and Frank, the bomb team leaders, were there.

Both were wearing white gloves as they examined and explained new bomb components to Campbell.

Both were happy with Hammersmith but thought they needed to develop new detonating techniques. It was as if they didn't realise they were in the Real IRA, or had come from the Provisional IRA, but were in a hobbyist club for people who liked to construct explosives from every imaginable type of electronics, each competing with the other for the best adaptation and best bomb technique.

They were having an argument when Rupert came in. Frank wanted to adapt a mortar bomb detonation system similar to that used by Hamas in Gaza. Dent thought it was a stupid idea, too cumbersome and not modern enough. Dent was always well dressed and well mannered. He spoke about giving lectures and Rupert believed that he was a college professor. He listened closely as they talked about getting components. Dent told him about an electronics shop that was run by a man from the border area who would let them buy what they wanted, no questions asked, and that it was a back-door system of purchasing electronics without being traced.

Campbell listened attentively, then divided out expenses for them, in wads of cash that were in dollars for one and British pounds for the other. Rupert, watching carefully, realised that they were from different sides of the border.

If only he had their real names.

Campbell supplied Rupert with a handwritten address of a car valet service in county Kildare where he could ship guns and bomb parts when he got them from James Smyth. The valet, run by a Real IRA member, had been used several times before. The guns from America came in with other business envelopes. Guns were wrapped in lead to avoid metal detectors. They were hidden in the company's offices until the time was right and moved quickly up to one of the weapon teams in Meath and Louth.

It was a major find for Rupert.

Through this meeting, he also discovered the details of McKevitt's plan for the navy ship in Carlingford Lough.

On his last visit to Ireland, he was asked to co-ordinate with Smyth in getting marine magnets that would work underwater. He now learned that they were for attaching bombs to the underside of ships in Carlingford harbour. They needed them soon, so they could attack the ship.

He wrote down a list of all they needed from America for the bomb parts: Untraceable computers, sports radar guns, encryption software, a specific type of flashbulb, Intertec mechanical switches, software for military rockets already in their possession, stun guns, a white noise generator, a digital voice changer, a scanner for detecting humans nearby, so that they would not get caught at training camps again, and a GPS receiver so that they could locate their own arms bunkers.

Frank, digging at the regular members, said they shouldn't be using X-marks-the-spot to find their own bunkers in the 21st century.

Campbell laughed at this and said he didn't use Xs for weapon bunkers.

The men broke up the meeting after an hour. Rupert said he would do what he could to get the components.

But things were beginning to get uncomfortable. "It was just more Dave," said an army council member. "Always with the waffle, not delivering. I had lost faith in him by that point. I couldn't understand why McKevitt was so insistent on him."

A few days later, Rupert moved down to Dublin for a small break before going back to the US.

M15 had booked his hotel in advance. It was the five-star Shelbourne Hotel on Stephen's Green in the centre of the city.

He woke up the next morning and looked out over Stephen's Green.

"I must have been doing something right, this was really one of the best hotels I was in."

He lay there on the bed, in a hotel bathrobe, eating room service and flicking through Irish TV.

Then he got a call from Mickey McKevitt on his untraceable phone.

"Well?" said McKevitt. "When are you on your way to Mexico?"

CHAPTER 18

The morning sun rose over the Mexican hills and the heat bleached the roads. A gauze of dry, muggy air pushed against Rupert's skin. He was alone in Ciudad Juárez.

He stopped off at a café and with a little broken Spanish, ordered a coffee and checked his phone. No word from James Smyth. Nothing. He was getting concerned. Had the FBI jumped too soon? Was Smyth in custody?

On the other side of the Rio Grande river lay El Paso, Texas.

Rupert was to check a safe route for McKevitt to enter the United States from Mexico, as the Real IRA army council had agreed. He was struck by how easy it was to drive over to Mexico and back to the United States without a search. Smuggling McKevitt across wouldn't be a problem.

Ever since the huge shipments from Gaddafi in the 1980s, McKevitt had been quartermaster of the Provisional IRA. He was insistent, to the point of obsession, on seeing any major arms shipment himself before purchasing. He loved that world. He loved the feel and excitement of weapon purchases. For the Real IRA, he had smuggled himself out of Ireland to South Africa,

Bulgaria and Croatia to look at weapons. Now he would go one step further, and finally see the huge US gun market for the first time. "I'm very hands-on with weaponry," he told Rupert. McGrane and Campbell had also noted McKevitt's schoolboy excitement for major arms deals.

McKevitt told Rupert to take the funds for his trip to El Paso from the IFC prisoner relief fund. Rupert used it to stay at a five-star hotel in El Paso.

"I wasn't paying for it, so I didn't care," he said.

All those fundraisers and lotteries in Chicago were keeping him in luxury on the Mexican border. Every day, he would drive across to Ciudad Juárez, have a coffee, check the route for smuggling McKevitt back to the US and then drive back to El Paso. Ciudad Juárez was so close to El Paso that, along with Las Cruces in the neighboring US state of New Mexico, they formed the largest bilingual and binational work force in the Western Hemisphere. For smuggling, it was perfect.

Rupert drove back over the bridge to El Paso, imagining if he had McKevitt hidden under a seat at the back. No checks, no searches, it would be easy.

He went back to the hotel in El Paso, lay on the bed and flicked through the TV stations. After an hour, he went out to the corridor. He saw men in suits with guns coming towards him. He must be busted. This could ruin everything. He was instantly mad with the FBI for not giving him cover.

An agent approached. "What's going on?" said Rupert. "Visit to the hotel by Governor Bush," said the man with the gun. He was secret service. Nothing to worry about. Bush was running for president. As governor, he had won over the Democratic town of

El Paso and now he was coming to appeal for votes in his election fight against Al Gore.

Rupert went back up to his room and left a message on Smyth's mobile phone.

His second function in El Paso was to find accommodation for James Smyth in Texas so he could escape the scrutiny of Boston and set up an explosives and gun testing range in the desert. It would also be easier for him to meet McKevitt there. "I drove out myself into the desert, looking for a good place to test weapons. Obviously, it had to be far enough into the desert that nobody could hear it," Rupert said. "Our research and development facility, as I called it."

Smyth called back an hour later. "Why aren't you down here?" said Rupert, leaning against his car out in the desert. He knew Smyth carried huge respect. He couldn't be mad at him.

Smyth paused at first, and stumbled, but then told the truth. He didn't want to go through with the move to El Paso. He was in love. McKevitt had sent Smyth to South Africa to intercept a Provisional IRA arms shipment. When the Provisionals found out about it, they were furious and were going to shoot Smyth, so McKevitt sent him to Boston. Now Smyth had met a beautiful American woman and didn't want to move to El Paso.

"I just don't want to go," Smyth said.

"Where are you now?" said Rupert.

"In Canada."

Rupert knew McKevitt would be furious. So did Smyth.

"You're supposed to be down in El Paso. What's in Canada?"

From his days in the French Foreign Legion, Smyth loved speaking French with Québécois, the closest North America had to a French ex-pat scene. Quebec had many former legionnaires like him, and he was with this girlfriend, showing her around a French-speaking island in Quebec.

"You know someone's not going to be happy about this."

Pause.

"Yeah, I know."

Smyth had tried to reach a compromise, by volunteering to bring his girlfriend, who had military experience, into IRA operations.

McKevitt had rejected it completely. He didn't know anything about this woman and Smyth was never, ever to discuss operations with her.

Meanwhile, she was putting pressure on Smyth to show real commitment. He knew everything she said made sense. He was sick of being moved around the world at a click of McKevitt's fingers. First Ireland, then he lived in South Africa, then Boston, now El Paso. He was still on for assassinating Blair, but moving to Texas was a step too far.

"Alright," said Rupert.

He called McKevitt to say that the parcel wasn't going to be delivered to where it was supposed to be, because of a woman.

McKevitt was furious. He couldn't believe that Smyth, the most militaristic, the most loyal, would disobey an order, and for a woman.

The good news from Rupert was that the place they talked about was perfect and easy to get to from the other side.

McKevitt said he didn't give a fuck.

He couldn't shoot Smyth – he was far too valuable. So that made McKevitt look weak, which angered him even more.

Rupert told him that Smyth would be up in French-speaking Canada for a while. McKevitt said, "What the fuck is he doing up there? You tell him he has to go where he is supposed to be."

When Smyth came back from Canada, Rupert drove to Boston to explain the seriousness of the situation and also to give him some rocket-launcher software that the army council were seeking.

He met Smyth at the Holiday Inn in Worcester. The FBI had wired the room and were listening. It wasn't a long meeting. Rupert did not want to get caught in the middle of the difficulty between McKevitt and Smyth. He knew Smyth was well respected and that it would eventually blow over. So he just reiterated what McKevitt had said and that he was angry. Smyth said that he understood, but that he had to have some kind of life and he couldn't keep his secret from his girlfriend forever.

Smyth picked up the software disk from the table and left.

The FBI agents came into the room. They were close to a prosecution but needed to see Smyth deliver weapons to Rupert. It had all got sidetracked by woman problems.

Rupert assured them that it would happen and drove back up to Chicago.

Back in his study at home, he sat down at his computer to write a report for MI5.

Sitting on the table beside the computer was the disk he was supposed to give Smyth.

In his haste to get out the door, he had packed the wrong disk. Smyth now had a disk that contained Rupert's notes that he used before sending emails to M15 and the FBI. He believed they were the ones about his last trip to Ireland.

"I can only describe it as several days of hell about what was on the disk. I was petrified of what I had sent him and had no idea what to do! So I called Smyth and told him I'd made a mistake and would get the right disk to him. But I did it in the middle of a lot of chat about McKevitt."

Maureen desperately tried to reassure him that there was nothing damaging on the disk. Even if there was, Smyth would never find it in the folders and sub folders. If he did find it, Rupert could always say that it was his note-taking of meetings so he would know what to get for the Real IRA.

Rupert had a long, tense drive back down to Boston to exchange disks with Smyth, telling him he was on his way to a meeting with Joe Dillon and the other Boston IFC supporters.

"I got it back into my car and I was sweating. I hadn't been able to sleep, I was so worried," said Rupert. "I didn't know if Smyth was going to whack me when I got down there."

In Ireland and Britain, the Real IRA's attacks were getting more and more daring. They fired a giant barrack-buster mortar at a British army barracks, dropping 80 pounds of high explosives and causing extensive damage.

Then on 9 July, a team drove a car bomb to a British army base. But they thought they were being tailed and security was extra tight, so instead they drove the car bomb into Stewartstown, a predominantly Protestant, unionist town.

The bomb ripped through the town centre, destroying shops and damaging the police station.

McKevitt was furious. The Real IRA had assured members after the Omagh bomb that there would be no more car bombs in town centres. Immediately after Stewartstown, some very skilled members who had defected from the Provisional IRA announced they were quitting. McKevitt and Campbell tried to persuade them to stay. McKevitt wanted everyone involved in the Stewartstown bomb to be court martialed for disobeying his commands. He worked hard to win back members who walked away. They eventually relented. The focus must now be on London.

On 19 July, security forces carried out a controlled explosion of a bomb left at Ealing Broadway train station, sending flames spiralling into the air. Police had to shut down Victoria and Paddington railway stations and stop the London Underground, causing disruption to hundreds of thousands of people.

Then on 21 September, the London cell pulled off a major coup: one of its members fired a shoulder-held rocket-propelled grenade at the Vauxhall headquarters of MI6, the international spying organisation of the British state. The attacker jumped on the back of a motorbike and the two men escaped. The bombing caused extensive damage and generated news around the world. It was a warning to Britain's vast spying system – we will get you.

McKevitt, watching the scenes on TV from his home in Blackrock, was elated. Those members who had walked away after Stewartstown came back, congratulating McKevitt on his brilliance.

It was embarrassing for MI5 and the gardaí. It was clear that, as director of operations, Liam Campbell was behind those who led the attack. He was kept under almost constant electronic and physical surveillance.

In early October, the Ruperts were getting ready for another big trip to Ireland. On the morning of 3 October, they checked on Irish news sites and found some big news.

That morning, at 5am, the Republic's Emergency Response Unit broke open the door of Campbell's house, which was just feet inside the border. Armed gardaí ran to the back of the house to make sure he didn't dive over the back wall into Northern Ireland.

Inside the house, they found a secret trap-door leading to a storage room. They also found forensic suits for bomb-making and latex gloves and walkie-talkies.

Campbell barely had time to put on his trousers. He was dragged out of the house still in his bare feet and with a shirt barely on over a bare chest.

At Kells garda station, he was reminded that after Omagh, new legislation meant he no longer had the right to silence. Now, a negative inference could be drawn from silence to questions about IRA membership. He still said nothing. He was told that gardaí believed he was a leading member of the Real IRA. He still said nothing. The gardaí wrote it down. For the first time in Irish history, silence was evidence.

The arrest was a blow to McKevitt.

Nobody could replace Campbell's enthusiasm for the fight: he had the same energy in his 40s that he had when he was 17. But while McKevitt liked him, he also quietly blamed him for Omagh and began to wonder about him and the reasons for his enthusiasm.

Far worse was to come that month. The Provisional IRA had long tolerated the Real IRA along the border. It was too strong to oppose there. But in Belfast, it kept the Real IRA tightly suppressed, even picketing the homes of its sympathisers. Now, tension was building. A new, restructured Real IRA was bombing many barracks, and even M16 headquarters, and was getting an upsurge of support among disaffected youth in republican West Belfast.

The young mostly looked up to Joseph O'Connor, 26, a Real IRA member who was working on rights issues for the growing number of Real IRA prisoners.

O'Connor was close to McKevitt, who saw him as the man to win over West Belfast.

O'Connor's grandfather, Francisco Notarantonio, was a leading Provisional who had been shot dead at his home by loyalists 13 years previously. The Notarantonios, one of several Italian Catholic families in West Belfast with several IRA members, were one of the most influential families in the community. The Provisionals hated that O'Connor had gone over to McKevitt.

On the night of 12 October, O'Connor spotted a group of Provisionals out the back of his house, watching him. He and a friend went inside, bolted the door and didn't come out.

The next day, O'Connor and his friend were in a car outside his mother's house in West Belfast. Two men ran toward them. O'Connor struggled to free himself from his seat belt as his friend jumped out of the car. The two gunmen ran up to the car window and shot O'Connor several times in the head. His body slumped in his seat.

At the same time that it was happening, Maureen and David were flying into Paris. MI5 had booked them a good hotel, and they decided to take a few days' holiday.

Maureen: "The Paris hotel was just fantastic. They even had a bottle of champagne waiting for us in the room. Because our value to MI5 was getting better and better, the hotel rooms were getting better and better."

Maureen, who had lived her entire life within a five-mile radius of the truck stop, was now holding hands with David as they inspected the paintings of the Louvre. The Impressionists were her favourite. She sent a postcard from the museum to her family back home. Then they walked around the Eiffel Tower and Sacré-Coeur.

While Maureen read at a café, David met Paul at the InterContinental Hotel. David was upbeat, even ribbing Paul about the Real IRA attack on M16. Rupert said, "You sure took one up the ass from McKevitt." Paul laughed back. "Yeah," he said nodding. "We sure did."

David and Maureen flew from Paris to Dublin and drove up to Dundalk, to stay at the Carrickdale Hotel.

There were frantic and intense negotiations between M15 and the FBI that day. The FBI wanted arrests as soon as possible. It had a big reason for expediting the case – the Clinton administration was coming to a close, and with it would come an end to the most Ireland-focused administration in the history of the United States. In January, there would be a new president, with a new focus on the justice department.

MI5 explained that its agents had never given evidence in Irish courts, that they wanted Rupert to continue feeding them information so they could disrupt bombings.

To go to court would involve a reworking of everything they did and a new, open and accountable MI5. The argument matched a new thinking in MI5, that in the post-cold war environment, they had to make themselves relevant to law enforcement, rather than operating on a level above it.

All of this continued as Rupert met McKevitt on 18 October at the Fairmont Hotel in Dundalk. Maureen stayed in the hotel room, reading and watching TV.

"I used to watch *Judge Judy* and other shows you could get on Irish TV – it passed the time," she said.

Rupert and McKevitt drove from the hotel to McKevitt's house in Blackrock. Rupert dropped off $6,000 in fundraising money, plus a new computer for McKevitt, which he began configuring with software. But this time, McKevitt questioned the money. Why was there only $6,000 this time?

He looked at Rupert fixedly. "He got a little pissy with me, frankly," says Rupert. "I said, listen, we need money for the El Paso thing and James Smyth's been buying up weapons."

Still, McKevitt was happy with the new computer Rupert gave him. His own one was slow and dying.

They drove to a restaurant on the north side of Dundalk, which was McKevitt's new safe hang-out. It was owned by a supporter.

At the restaurant, McKevitt went through recent operations. Stewartstown car bomb: a catastrophe that had cost them good volunteers, disgusted that the tactics of Omagh had returned. Those responsible for driving the car bomb into the town centre would be punished. Attack on M16 headquarters: absolutely magnificent and had won back those who had walked away after Stewartstown.

The barrack-buster attack on the military base had caused major damage and showed they were stronger than ever. He seemed very happy with progress.

Rupert felt, in this great moment of bonding, that it would be a good time to raise Dorothy Robinson's claims that Rupert was a spy.

McKevitt instantly dismissed it. She had met him about Rupert's alleged spying and he told her it was nonsense. He knew she was a Real IRA supporter but Rupert was on a level way above her and the IFC members in New York and Philadelphia, who were still loyal to the Continuity IRA, anyway. In his emails Rupert recorded McKevitt as saying that Rupert was "solid". "Don't worry about the likes of her," he said.

The arrest of Liam Campbell was a loss, McKevitt said, but Campbell was too trusting of people and may have been betrayed. However, as a result of the arrest, McKevitt had to take over the investigation into the murder of Joseph O'Connor. When he drove up to Belfast, all the Real IRA members in the city wanted to meet him and were demanding revenge, he said. McKevitt insisted on meeting only Maurice and other army council members in the city. Their attacks on the British had big momentum and they couldn't afford to get into a feud with the Provisionals, who felt weak because they had to give up most of their weapons under the peace agreement.

McKevitt said he had ordered the Real IRA to take the man who had been in the car with O'Connor to a safe house for questioning, where the man swore he had nothing to do with the killing. "If you are lying to us, we will shoot you," McKevitt said, and let him go.

On James Smyth, he was very, very disappointed. He didn't give a flying fuck if Smyth's girlfriend had military experience – she shouldn't be involved, and he should go to El Paso.

Rupert brought the news that Smyth had moved address.

"Where did he move?" said McKevitt.

"Across town, Worcester," said Rupert.

It just made McKevitt madder. He put down his drink. "Across town? Is he stupid? I told him to go to El Paso."

Rupert, trying to lighten the mood, said that in trucking, when a man messes up like that because of a woman, they say he is "drowning in pussy". McKevitt laughed. He liked that description. No harm would come to Smyth – he was a good soldier.

He leaned in, as he did when he had something big to say. They had real momentum now, and were winning over members every day. What they needed now, though, was a state sponsor, a new Gaddafi to take it to another level.

Rupert suggested Slobodan Milošević in Serbia, who hated the western governments and had huge supplies of weapons. McKevitt dismissed it – it wouldn't work with Milošević. Someone bigger, like Saddam Hussein, he said. Someone who could deliver.

How would the Iraqis possibly get involved, Rupert asked. "I don't know," said McKevitt. "But we'll just have to keep plugging along until they do."

In London, Paul and the MI5 team were delighted with Rupert's news that McKevitt was looking for Saddam Hussein to step in as the new terrorism sugar daddy to replace Gaddafi.

Paul's emails were never as exuberant as they were on the night of 19 October. He was already talking about the end of Rupert's deployment – but first, Rupert would have to leave McKevitt with the idea that Rupert was working with him on finding a foreign sponsor.

He shouldn't over-discuss it, but should drop it into the conversation that he was trying to find the right contacts.

Paul also warned him not to discuss it with James Smyth when he got back to America – this was way above the head of a mere assassin.

"Again, we go back to the issue of not asking too much and not offering too much," Paul wrote.

At the time of Paul's response, Rupert was in McKevitt's home, putting additional software onto the new computer. Mickey and Bernie looked very happy with it. The computer had first gone through FBI and M15 hands, but nothing traceably.

Rupert wanted Bernie to let him install software so that she could lock files on her computer against any police raid, but she resisted.

She had an external drive and could pull it out at short notice whenever there was a garda raid.

There was one other computer matter – Smyth had inspected the rocket-launcher software and given it back to Rupert to give to the engineering department for Hamas-style rocket attacks on British barracks.

The software was still in his hotel room and he wanted to hand it over to the army council as soon as possible, Rupert said.

McKevitt replied that he'd send someone around the next day to pick it up.

He was delighted with this new technology. He left the house in a good mood while Rupert stayed there, working on the computer.

Things were very different when he came back an hour and a half later. He was in a foul mood. There was tension throughout the house. He just stood around Rupert, waiting for him to leave. He was flushed and clearly stressed.

The meeting, with other Real IRA chiefs, was likely about Campbell's arrest.

Bernie looked concerned. Rupert packed up quickly but couldn't find his hat. He had never seen such tension in the house. Perhaps somebody at the meeting had said something about him?

He found his hat in the home office and left quickly.

"It was kind of a cluster-fuck night," he wrote to Paul from his hotel room.

On 21 October 2000, he went as usual to the Fairmont Hotel, to pick up McKevitt, who was back to his jovial self. Whatever had happened at the meeting was forgotten, or at least put aside.

The mood change was noticeable, but also puzzling.

McKevitt asked Rupert to drive to Carlingford Lough, between the Republic and Northern Ireland.

"Look," he said, pointing over at the clear view. "The navy ship is gone."

Rupert looked across at the unrestricted view to Northern Ireland. The navy ship had been moved miles out to sea.

He froze.

On his last trip to Ireland, the army council said it wanted marine magnets to blow up the ship, and McKevitt lamented the lack of suicide bombers to do the job. Now, the ship was suddenly gone. It was clear MI5 had told the navy to move it. He felt betrayed.

McKevitt told Rupert to drive south, through Drogheda and then out to Newgrange, the megalithic tomb where, only on the winter solstice, light comes in through a chamber window. It was built before the giant pyramids of Egypt, when the Irish were a high civilization, before the Brits came and ruined everything, McKevitt said.

Next, there was a short drive to the site of the Battle of the Boyne in 1690, where the Irish were defeated by William of Orange, signaling the end of Irish control of their own country, and the plantation of the country into English, Protestant estates.

Rupert nodded. McKevitt liked explaining things to him. They were genuinely good friends. They trusted each other.

"I just put everything else aside when I was with him. With Mickey, I was army 100 per cent and I didn't think about my other life, except to gather information as it came," said Rupert.

McKevitt was adamant – they had to find a foreign sponsor now that things were going well. Some members had gone to two left-wing "human rights" conferences, one in Tbilisi, Georgia, the other in Geneva, Switzerland, hoping that state agents would make contact, but they hadn't.

McKevitt said he needed Rupert to help him find foreign agents, to think big and come back to him, that they could work on it together.

They drove back to the hotel. Along the way, Rupert said that a journalist loyal to the Real IRA, and an IFC member, wanted to interview McKevitt. He thought it was a good idea that Rupert guide her in what questions to ask.

Rupert said he'd see him for dinner in a few days' time with their wives.

Back at his hotel room, he contacted Paul. Paul was pleased. He would supply his own questions to Rupert to give to the Real IRA-supporting journalist. It was the first time that MI5 would be able to ask questions to McKevitt.

*****

On the following Tuesday night, Maureen and David prepared themselves for their dinner with the McKevitts at the Ballymascanlon House Hotel. Rupert told Maureen: "Remember, this is just for you to get a feel of the controls. Just relax into it."

Maureen was to bond with Bernadette as much as possible but the conversation should be between the four of them.

When they got there, there was an electrical outage in the area and they moved the dinner to the other restaurant in Dundalk where McKevitt met contacts.

Rupert is still convinced that MI5 had something to do with the electrical outage at the hotel.

My MI5 source is adamant that would never happen. "Cause an electrical outage in the Republic of Ireland? Risk destroying relations with the Republic, carefully built up over years by both sides? Again, it's the goblin stuff that people think we do, but we don't."

The restaurant was on a single floor, close to the Dublin Road. As soon as they sat down, Maureen and Bernadette spoke of family and children. Maureen was impressed by Bernadette as a mother – she was very protective and determined that her children would have a better life.

She mentioned the Omagh bombing and that her children were being ostracised and picked on at school, because their parents' names were linked to it in the papers.

Maureen's eyes widened. "Really? Oh my God, that's just awful, that's terrible, to have to go through that."

Bernadette was glad she understood what her children were suffering.

"Awful for the kids," said Maureen.

Rupert: "I thought, 'Why is Maureen so concerned about Bernadette's kids after Omagh?' Then I realised, that was acting."

Maureen: "I was a spy too, after all. I was living in the same world as David. I liked Bernadette very much but at the same time you are thinking of why we are really here."

Maureen's post-Omagh sympathy for the McKevitts led her to the question, "Do you think you can ever get your business back again?"

The McKevitts had been kicked out of their shop in Dundalk in the days after the Omagh bombing.

Bernadette no longer wanted it back, she said. She had now moved on to a communications and computer course and was on a new path in life.

Bernadette seemed confident and upbeat. The Ruperts were due to fly out the next day and both expressed their delight in seeing the McKevitts.

Mickey and Bernie both said that they looked forward to the Ruperts coming back to see them in the Spring.

A garda on surveillance outside saw all four of them leave the hotel together and walk to their cars. Rupert gave a last wave and he and McKevitt wished each other good luck.

It was the last time they would ever speak.

CHAPTER 19

"Don't tell me what to do! Don't tell me what to do!"

Rupert's face was pushed up against the agent. They were pointing at each other angrily. One of the Chicago group had to break them apart.

Rupert's lifelong hatred of what he called "federal arrogance" had exploded, just as Smyth was about to come to the Holiday Inn in Worcester.

"We're just fucking asking you do your job!" said the agent.

"I'm doing my job, you're not," shouted Rupert.

As they wired up the hotel room with bugging devices and a hidden camera, the agent was urging Rupert to draw Smyth into incriminating conversations.

Being condescended to by authority was Rupert's greatest hatred.

"It was the worst argument I ever had with the FBI. I don't know what I called this guy. I've always had my own way of doing things. I never ask too many questions, I never draw people out and this jerk is trying to lecture me on what I should say into the microphone. He didn't know the first thing about the operation. Smyth was a very dangerous guy, I'm trying to get into my usual relaxed head space and this FBI guy is in my face. I shouted back, it was bad."

The Chicago field office asked to speak to the agent outside the hotel room. When he came back in he stayed in the background and didn't talk to Rupert.

Chicago had handled Rupert for years and they had seen him blow up on them before.

When the microphones and video cameras were set up, the agents retreated. Rupert called Smyth, who was leaving his house on Epworth Street, a short drive from the hotel.

Smyth walked into the hotel room carrying two large holdalls.

"Alright big man?"

He put the bags on the bed.

Inside were two dozen disassembled Uzis, several hundred rounds of ammunition and the army council's shopping list of bomb parts – plastic explosives, timers for Intertec sports radar guns, Apogee RockSim 4.0 game consoles, scanning devices and infrared detectors.

Agents from the Boston and Chicago field office were watching from video cameras on either side of the hotel room.

Smyth explained that he had taken the guns apart and erased all their serial numbers.

"He says, 'You want me to show you how to put them together?' I said: 'No, I already know, thanks.'"

Rupert had no idea how to reassemble the guns but was concerned for his safety if Smyth had two dozen functioning Uzis in the hotel room.

"In the rooms either side of us are heavily armed FBI guys and I'm in this room with this trained assassin who has all these Uzis and hundreds of rounds. I really didn't want this situation to escalate."

Smyth suggested that Rupert should make absolutely sure McKevitt approved of the plan to get the guns and bomb parts to Ireland.

He wished Rupert good luck and left. Out on the street, Boston FBI agents photographed Smyth walking to his car.

Rupert looked around the room. "Alright, we're done," he said.

The Chicago agents were the first in. They leaned over one of the bags and looked inside. The Boston field office came in behind them and began photographing.

Rupert sat on the bed. Six years he had been spying, and this was his final day.

It was 20 December 2000, five days before Christmas.

After the FBI finished in the room, he flew that same day back to Maureen and her family.

Maureen mentioned over Christmas dinner that David was going back to Ireland in the new year. "As far as my family knew, David was gun-running for the IRA. That's what they assumed from the company he was keeping and the Irish republican mementos and all that. So my father and my brother would give me these looks whenever I said David was going to Ireland, as if to say, 'Come on, we know he's mixed up in something bad.'"

On 8 January, Rupert flew in to Dublin and booked into a hotel in the city centre. He knew little of the city: he usually only visited for the Republican Sinn Féin events.

He walked to Harcourt Street garda station. Martin Callinan, Diarmuid O'Sullivan and the Special Branch officers were waiting on the top floor. They had never met him before.

O'Sullivan, a wiry officer with 20 years' experience, immediately sized up Rupert: "The first thing I noticed was the enormity of his size and his personality. He was quite opinionated about himself and the subject."

Rupert held a long grudge against the gardaí for the way he was treated when he was at the Drowes, for which the gardaí felt no responsibility as they never had an agreement with him.

O'Sullivan bristled. "As far as he was concerned, we were not at the races. We were unprofessional and he was going to tell us that."

Over the day, as the information poured out, he saw another side to Rupert.

"As we discovered, he had very good reason to have an opinion on the subject because he had huge knowledge. He had very detailed knowledge of the organisations, of their workings in Ireland, their connections in the US and how those connections came about and how the funding operated and the main players in the States. It made sense to us because the detail he was talking about could only have been had by meeting these people."

Rupert remembers blasting the gardaí about the Drowes, and then getting down to business.

"It was all top-secret stuff, nobody outside this small group was supposed to know," said Rupert. "They sat me down and explained the process. Then for three full days, I told them everything."

*****

At a hotel near where Rupert was making his statement, a journalist called Bakr stirred his tea as he waited.

Michael McDonald walked up the foyer steps and looked around. "Are you...?"

McDonald had spoken to Bakr on the phone, in coded language, as had McKevitt and Campbell. This was their first face-to-face meeting. From the phone calls, MI5 knew that McKevitt was keen to travel to Baghdad soon.

Bakr came with a notebook and pen and was dressed smart-casual, like a serious journalist hoping to understand the Irish conflict.

McDonald was enjoying the subterfuge.

Bakr had presented himself over fax and email as a Lebanese journalist, until both sides understood that journalism was a front for his real work as an Iraqi agent.

McDonald gave Bakr a rundown of IRA history, and how its campaign had been heavily armed by Colonel Gaddafi in Libya.

Gaddafi had gifted the IRA over 100 tons of weapons and plastic explosives and three million pounds sterling. His supplies had been enough to keep the IRA bombing and shooting for 20 years. If they got that level of cooperation from Saddam, it would rip the peace process apart.

Bakr slid his notebook to McDonald, who began to write from a coded list he kept in his pocket.

"£1.5m, 500kg of explosives, 500 handguns, 2,000 detonators, 200 rocket-propelled grenades and a wire-guided missile."

He slid it back to Bakr, who ripped the page from his notebook and slid it into his wallet.

McKevitt had pulled off the IRA's biggest coup with the Gaddafi shipments. Now McDonald was in his place and was on the verge of pulling off an even bigger shipment, one that would include wire-guided missiles that could accurately take out British helicopters. In the IRA-controlled border areas, the dream of destroying the British air capability had been a long one.

He, McKevitt, Campbell and the entire army council had missed some vital clues about Bakr.

McKevitt had failed to get Saddam's attention until he told Rupert about his frustration, and then suddenly an Iraqi agent appeared.

Also, McKevitt told Rupert that he wanted the Iraqis to make contact with him directly in Dundalk, and then one day he received a fax from an Arab journalist seeking an "interview", but clearly with bigger intentions.

Two British intelligence officers sat in a car, watching the meeting between Bakr and McDonald.

According to Rupert, Bakr had been "recycled" from British intelligence's Iraqi operations for use on "the Ireland problem".

"Operation Samnite", as it was now known, was hidden from the Irish government. If MI5 were caught operating within the independent Republic of Ireland, it could create a diplomatic problem in a country with a deep mistrust of British spies. MI5 chiefs believed that the potential prize of putting away the entire Real IRA army council was worth the risk.

Before they parted, McDonald and Bakr, a British spy posing as an Iraqi spy who was posing as a journalist, had agreed to set up several more phone calls with McKevitt on a secure phone line.

At that exact time, David Rupert was a short distance away on Harcourt Street, completing the third and final day of his statement to the gardaí.

It was already 40 pages long.

He told them of every meeting with McKevitt, the American weapon shipments, the army council meetings, how the Real IRA's structure worked, how Bobby Sands' sister was third in command, every IRA shooting and bombing he knew about, going right back to the killing of Prince Charles's great uncle he heard about in Murray's pub.

Rupert talked and talked and a police officer wrote it down. Callinan had selected a fourth officer to type up the written notes. It was so sensitive that only one officer could be trusted as a typist.

"It amazed me that the top guys in the gardaí only trusted one typist," said Rupert. "They had told me about two Northern Ireland police officers who were murdered coming from Dundalk station because a garda had tipped off the IRA. So, hey, I got the secrecy."

Once Rupert had finished his statement, the entire three days of notes were read back to him and he signed it.

He was not allowed outside in case he was identified.

"It was funny, I was up in the part of the garda station where the upper echelon had their offices.

"I went through a doorway to go to the bathroom and couldn't get back in. It didn't occur to the gardaí that it was a one-way door. I'm locked out in the corridor and I had a flock of people around me, wondering who I was. I had no ID, I had a US accent and everybody was nervous about what I was doing there.

"They asked who I was there to see. I couldn't remember the names of the gardaí. I said I'm with the FBI/Department of Justice.

"They said, 'Well, do you have ID?'

"I said, 'Actually no. It's kinda unofficial.'"

Finally, an anti-terrorism officer opened the door and said, "It's ok, he's with us."

Rupert walked past the crowd, wordless.

He stayed with the gardaí all evening, talking and eating. They were killing time, waiting for nightfall, so that they could sneak him up to the border and into IRA homeland.

As they were eating, Michael McDonald arrived back from Dublin and pulled up at McKevitt's house in Blackrock to tell him the good news – that Saddam Hussein was on board for tons of weapons.

Back at police HQ in Dublin, it was explained to Rupert that his entire credibility rested on his ability to identify the places in his statement. So that the police could use his evidence in court, he would have to lead them to Mickey McKevitt's house, the army council and bomb-making houses, all without any prompting from the detectives.

Two car-loads of gardaí set off from Dublin at 1am. Rupert was in one car with three Special Branch detectives.

The car behind had four armed gardaí.

It was 2am, now 12 January 2001, when they reached Blackrock village, just south of Dundalk.

At the centre of the village, they turned left and left again into the comfortable middle-class estate and past McKevitt's two-storey house.

"If you are coming around to McKevitt's street at 2am you are either gardaí or Provisional IRA coming to shoot him.

"He had a lot of cameras in his house, linked up to TV," says Rupert. "There were two cars and one of them was all armed gardaí. We could have had a shoot-out because now Mickey had a lot to lose."

They approached McKevitt's house. "That one, with the low gate, on the corner," said Rupert pointing to the house on the left.

"Are you identifying the house here on the left at the corner after the greenway?"

"Yes."

Mickey and Bernie McKevitt were asleep as David Rupert came within feet of their house. The two dark-coloured cars turned at the end of the street and drove past the house again. "That's it for sure," said Rupert.

The car returned to Blackrock village and turned left for Dundalk.

There were roadworks in the town, which confused Rupert. The gardaí were getting nervous. It took him more than half an hour to find his way.

"We went up and back, up and back, I just couldn't place it. The police weren't allowed to help me. Eventually, I found the right turn and we went up into the housing estate."

Rupert pointed out the house at Oakland Park where the bomb team had their meetings.

Next, they drove out on Greenore Road to the countryside, and to the cottage where the Real IRA army council held its meetings.

"There at the top of the hill, up the driveway." Rupert pointed up at the remote house.

They drove back to Dublin. Rupert was very relieved to be out of Dundalk.

It was past 4am when the car dropped him off at the hotel in Dublin and disappeared around the corner. He entered the hotel room, kicked off his shoes and fell asleep in his clothes. At 6.30 the next morning, he called Maureen.

They both laughed with excitement. After six years on the road, he had completed his final mission.

"I was just so happy because I was really worried all week," said Maureen. "Most of all, I was dying to reveal the truth to my family. David is not the man you think he is, after all."

CHAPTER 20

Maureen went out for lunch with her friends, Judy and Sue, and told them that David had been a spy within the IRA and that she would have to go away with him. She didn't know when she could come back. Judy and Sue were two women from mid-America, with no concept of the world Maureen was living in, except that it was foreign and terrorist-related and scary.

They put their hands on hers and wished her well and said if there was anything they could do, they would be there.

Maureen went on a tour of the area, talking to relatives, friends and neighbours.

On 13 January, the day David arrived home from making his statement in Dublin, they drove over to Dorie's house for a last goodbye.

She and Dorie hugged each other and cried.

Two days later, David and Maureen got into an FBI-hired mini-van and headed for the freeway. They had no idea where they were going. They only knew that the FBI would help them sell their house, and pay for any losses on the property, and that they should stay on the road for as long as possible.

They agreed only to head south, to avoid the snow and bitter cold of Illinois. David drove from early morning all day, stopping for the night in Russellville, Arkansas.

Maureen felt a burst of freedom. The good weather, the southern charm, the food – it felt like a different country from Chicago. The next day, they drove to Florida.

When they got to Tallahassee, Mark called. It sounded urgent.

Martin Callinan and Diarmuid O'Sullivan, two of the most senior anti-terrorist gardaí in Ireland, urgently wanted to see Rupert again, as soon as possible. They would fly to Chicago and needed more information and more statements. He should bring his passport for formal identification.

The Irish government was taking the case extremely seriously. Rupert was its only real hope of destroying the Real IRA.

Maureen and David were too exhausted that day to head to Chicago. They rested for the night and the next day got in the mini-van and headed north.

Maureen was disappointed to be back up north in the cold and snow and misery again.

In her diary, she was recording the trip, but also the number of calories she burnt. That day, she walked 3.5 miles and burnt 375 calories.

Even on the run, it meant a lot to her to lose the weight she had gained over the Ireland adventure.

The next day, as Maureen walked another 3.5 miles to lose 225 calories, Mickey McKevitt was on the phone for what he thought would be the biggest weapons deal in IRA history.

With a throwaway burner phone and using the pseudonym "Karl", he took a call from someone he thought was an Iraqi government agent in Baghdad.

In reality, it was another Iraqi MI5 agent calling from London, and Scotland Yard officers were in the room recording the conversation.

"Karl" didn't want to get into too many details, only that he was willing to travel to see the equipment and had been to the Middle East before. MI5 knew from Rupert that McKevitt loved to travel to see weapons, that it triggered memories of his Libya arms shipment. The agent held out the prospect that they would invite him to Baghdad. McKevitt said he would like that very much but said he had to be cautious.

It was the first of 19 phone calls between McKevitt and Michael McDonald on one side and three MI5 agents posing as Iraqi government spies on the other. McKevitt was adamant on one point – they needed a million euros in cash to begin with, and Saddam would be well rewarded with a series of attacks on the British establishment in London.

Once off the phone, McKevitt moved quickly to put a link on the 32CSM webpage, extoling the virtues of Saddam Hussein's government, and how it had been wronged by an illegal invasion after the Kuwait war.

The link became a source of great amusement for Paul and the other members of the MI5 team.

On 20 January 2001, the day after the first phone call between "Karl" and Iraqi intelligence, David and Maureen drove in to Chicago to meet Diarmuid O'Sullivan and Martin Callinan, along with Mark Lundgren.

As they sat around a conference room, O'Sullivan explained what they had come for – they wanted Rupert to testify against McKevitt directly in a courtroom in Dublin.

Rupert was adamant that his FBI contract was very clear – he was an undercover agent who provided evidence that could help them reach a prosecution. He was not, under any circumstances, going to take the stand.

Lundgren countered that the FBI was working on a new contract for Rupert that would be extremely generous on monthly payments for whatever security he and Maureen needed.

All sides agreed to think about their positions. Lundgren called Maureen, who said she would try to convince David to testify.

"Thank you, thank you, thank you," her diaries recorded Lundgren as saying.

Rupert was stressed.

He and Maureen took to the road again. After weeks of travelling all over America, they finally found a house to rent in Coral Gables, Florida. The FBI was delighted. It would pay the rent for however long it took.

That week, an event occurred in London that almost derailed the investigation. Dermot Jennings, the Special Branch garda who had the first contact with Rupert, went to London to meet MI5. It had potentially damaging memos – the first from when Rupert met Jennings in the back of a bread van in Boyle, when Jennings is supposed to have said that he didn't care what happened in Northern Ireland, he wanted information on what was happening in the south. It also had a memo of a conversation with the FBI, in which Jennings had described Rupert as "a bullshitter".

Jennings suggested to the MI5 agent that the references should be removed from the record before being disclosed in any trial. Jennings didn't know it at the time, but the MI5 agent was secretly recording him.

A very senior garda source said it was the worst time in the investigation. "We could not believe that MI5 would record a police officer without his knowledge when we were supposed to be working together," he said. "We were furious when it emerged, and so were the FBI, who felt it was a betrayal of a case they had worked so hard on. Old habits die hard with MI5, I guess."

On 15 February, Maureen and David moved into the new house. Maureen was delighted. Her diary entries are overcome with a sense of excitement at finding stability.

Two days later, as Maureen unpacked their belongings, David, who was feeling restless, drove up to Chicago to see Dorie's new house. Dorie later drove him to his old house to pick up some personal possessions. Just as he arrived, he got a call from Liam Clarke, the *Sunday Times* journalist. He said he was looking for David.

Rupert stayed on the line for a few seconds, not knowing what to do. Then he hung up.

The *Sunday Times* had got a leak from the gardaí – Rupert was a spy for the FBI on the Real IRA army council. It was an unbeatable story. After a few days, they contacted Joe Lori, a *Boston Globe* reporter, offering to share the story with him and pay him if he could find out about Rupert's life in Madrid.

The following Wednesday, while David was still in Chicago, a woman with an English accent called David's phone, looking for "Dave Rupert". It was a very bad connection. She called back a few minutes later.

Then Joe Lori called Maureen. "I understand you know a Dave Rupert," he said. She hung up.

The next day, Liam Clarke called David again.

Maureen's diary records the conversation:

"Mr Rupert?"

"No."

"Well, I'm calling you from Ireland."

"You got the wrong number."

Click.

Mark Lundgren called the following day. The *Sunday Times* had hired a private detective to find David and Maureen. They thought it was disgusting. They had done nothing wrong and it was putting a police operation, and their lives, at risk.

They went to see the film *The House of Mirth* to relax. Maureen couldn't understand any of it. "AWFUL!" she wrote.

The next day, 21 February, a 14-year-old old army cadet named Stephen Menary spotted a flashlight lying on the ground at the gates of a Territorial Army barracks in Stepherd's Bush, London. He picked it up. It exploded in his hand, sending packed shrapnel in every direction. Menary lost his left hand and left eye, and suffered severe stomach and chest injuries. He almost died.

The attack was exactly as McKevitt had described to Rupert several months earlier – he came up with the idea of a bomb in a flashlight that had blown a soldier's arm off at a checkpoint and he thought it could be used again. It was a device of which he was very proud.

It showed an intelligence failure. MI5 was moving towards prosecution, but it had failed to inform the army of this most basic of tip-offs – that McKevitt was very proud of his flashlight bomb and that the army should be aware that it might reappear.

Two days later, on 23 February, Liam Clarke called again. Rupert told him he had the wrong number. Clarke: "I know it's the number for David Rupert because I checked it." He put Rupert under pressure, saying he was running an article on Sunday and wanted Rupert's comments.

In reality, Clarke was under pressure from the newspaper lawyers – he had to get Rupert to confirm the details of the article or they wouldn't let him run it. It was a trap that many people fall into with reporters – explaining themselves when the entire purpose of the call is for the reporter not to hear their side of the story, but to trick them into confirming facts.

Rupert knew what Clarke was trying to do. He hung up and decided to change their phone numbers that day.

Everything was starting to move faster and faster. Mark Lundgren called within the hour – he was in Washington, just after a meeting with the heads of the FBI. They reviewed Rupert's emails and wanted him to stop using the word "deployment" about his travels to Ireland – it sounded too FBI, too coached. When testifying, he should say "trip" to Ireland.

Rupert demanded, "What do you mean, 'testify'? I'm not testifying."

Mark stumbled, trying to find a way out, and said it all depended on the circumstances.

The next day, David travelled to Chicago for a meeting with the FBI. He was furious.

His first visit was to Maureen's dad to give him their new mobile numbers.

When he got there, Mr Brennan was in a fury, demanding to know where his daughter was.

Rupert said that she was in Florida.

Mr Brennan went into a rage, calling Rupert a selfish bastard and accusing him of deliberately holding his daughter hostage in Florida.

He said that this IRA stuff had destroyed the family, forcing Maureen to divorce her own family and abandon her own daughter.

Rupert shouted back that he was lying.

It was the nastiest conversation between them.

"You don't even know what a close family is," said Mr Brennan. That hurt Rupert. There were divisions within the Rupert family, Mr Brennan knew it. Now he was being accused of trying to keep Maureen from her own family for his own selfish reasons.

Mr Brennan was up close against him. He was so mad he was about to punch Rupert.

Rupert screamed back at him that he had no right to talk like that, that it was an FBI operation.

He stormed out of the house, enraged.

Maureen: "Both of them called me, shouting about the other one. I thought, 'What a pair of assholes.' I didn't say that back to my dad but I sure as hell said it to David. I couldn't believe it. Like we didn't have enough problems, the two of them acting like little boys."

Maureen was so angry with both of them that she couldn't sleep that night.

She woke up the next morning still upset with her dad. How could he say that she had abandoned her own daughter? Didn't he know that she had to be away from Dorie to protect her? That people who would kill 29 civilians and not even care wouldn't think twice about torturing and killing her and David?

Her father called to apologise, but said he would not be coming to visit her in Florida, as planned, as he had a sinus problem and couldn't fly. It made her even madder. Did he really expect her to believe that?

Dan, a banker who had been Rupert and Maureen's next-door neighbour in Indiana, called the same day. Liam Clarke and Joe Lori were both at the old house outside Chicago. He could see them peering in the windows and sitting in a car down the street, waiting for Rupert.

David had a meeting with the FBI's logistics officer the following day. It was the first time they met. The man was small and tough and looked like Joe Pesci, the nickname Rupert gave to him from then on, even to his face.

Rupert complained that the money still hadn't come through for paying off the mortgage on their old house, which the FBI had agreed to do.

"Hold on a second, here," said the logistics officer. "We are not under any obligation to pay your mortgage."

"You'd better."

He had been warned about Rupert.

"Really," he said. "And what are you gonna do if we don't?"

"I fucking quit is what I do," said Rupert. He grabbed the leather satchel he brought to the meeting and was leaving the office.

"No, no, wait," said the officer. "Wait." He didn't want to be blamed for the collapse of the case. "Wait, let's talk it through. I didn't say we wouldn't."

Rupert: "It was like that all the time. It was this constant battle with the FBI, as I saw it. I was always bringing things to the brink because that was the only way I could get anything done."

After the meeting, Rupert drove back to Maureen's father, at her insistence. She threatened to never speak to Rupert or her father if they didn't talk it through.

Mr Brennan stretched out his hand. His voice was faltering and he was almost crying as he apologised. It was a huge strain on him and all the family to lose their daughter. "She's gone," he said, "and we don't know if she can ever come back."

Mr Brennan called Maureen and said that they had made up. He had also called his doctor, he said. It wasn't sinuses after all, it was a just a cold and he would be coming to Florida to see her. Maureen was overjoyed.

The very next day, David bought a Harley-Davidson motorbike, after Mark wired them $17,902.

"David, why didn't you tell me you were buying a Harley-Davidson?" said Maureen.

Rupert said he travelled to relax and needed it.

Maureen said that his James Bond lifestyle had gone to his head and it was feeding into his midlife crisis. She was worried sick because he could be killed if he was thrown from the bike, or end up injured just as the McKevitt case was coming to a climax.

They argued and argued but he wouldn't listen.

She told him that if he didn't sell the motorbike, she would tell the FBI. "Go right ahead," he said.

The next day, 8 March, Maureen's friend, Sue, emailed her. She had got a call from Joe, the reporter for both the *Sunday Times* and the *Boston Globe*. Did she or anyone in the area know Maureen and David Rupert? What were they like? He had a private message for them, and would she have a number for them?

Sue emailed Maureen straightaway. "I've been contacted. What to do?" she wrote.

Maureen called Sue, reassuring her that it would be ok.

It added to Maureen's lingering anxiety and depression. She realised that they would always be on the run. She lay in bed, unable to move. "I think the reality of it all hit me. David did all the unpacking today," she wrote in her diary.

As she struggled with her mood, David surprised her by suggesting that she try his supply of St John's Wort, the natural anti-depressant. He had been hiding it from her.

The stress of not having a connection with Ireland anymore and of no longer having the adrenaline rush of being a spy had caught up with him. He hid the depression from her, because his generation just didn't talk about it.

They went to a boat show in Fort Myers to relax, then a car show at the local Elks club. When they came back, David called his brother, Dale. Dale said that a reporter had called their brother Bud and sister Bonnie.

The reporter had asked Bud for a picture of David and said he'd pay for it. Then he asked Bud, "Would you consider David a violent man?"

The next day, David called his friend Christina in Massena. A reporter had called her grandmother, asking about David.

Mark at the FBI called. Everyone was now very concerned that the media would break the story before McKevitt was arrested.

Mark and his FBI partner, Doug, flew down to Florida the next day and David picked them up at the airport.

Mark went into the rental office and booked a large storage space in his own name, expensed to an FBI bank account, to be used by the Ruperts.

They picked up Maureen and all four of them decided to drive down to Miami for a chat. Along the way, they reviewed the situation. The FBI were denying all knowledge of David Rupert to the press, even putting out a statement to the *Sunday Times* to that effect, but it was only a matter of time before the story broke. Mark wanted them to consider completely new identities. It would involve new names, new family members and new life experiences.

Maureen was completely against it. She could not deny who she was. If she met other parents, how could she deny the existence of Dorie, who was the greatest joy in her life? When they got back home, there was a two-word email from David's sister Betty. "Call Me!" it said.

David called her. Joe Lori had called the local high school that David had attended and spoke to the principal and to Marsha, the secretary.

Marsha told him that David had organised the school's first sit-in, which was a demand for more food. She also told him that the caption on David's yearbook picture was "The Rebel Kid" and that Betty worked at the school. Now Betty was worried that he would turn up at the school and harass her.

In the middle of all this tension, Maureen called her father to wish him a happy St Patrick's Day. His grandson, Maureen's nephew, had sent him a hand-drawn card. It was a reminder of that other Ireland. That gentle one of Irish Americans who exchange cards on St Patrick's Day and toasted the old country. The Brennans had hated David's IRA connections. Now, they hoped, he would soon be back to being one of them again. The peaceful silent majority.

Still the calls flooded in from Joe Lori and Liam Clarke all week – to friends and family in Chicago and Madrid and Massena. Everyone was asking them what was going on. The circle of the informed had to be widened. No, they weren't in any kind of trouble with the law, they had been doing their duty for America. No, they weren't in danger, everything would work its way out.

On 20 March, it reached its lowest point. A woman with an American accent first emailed Betty with the original *Sunday Times* article about David funding the Real IRA. She then called Betty at the school. The woman explained that she was part native American and had been adopted. She needed help to reach a man who had attended the high school many years ago and may be the man in the article. Her long-lost brother, David Rupert, she said.

Betty paused. "That cannot be the case. I'm David Rupert's sister," she said.

The woman immediately hung up the phone.

Mark called from Ireland. The FBI had a meeting in Dublin and insisted on arrests as soon as possible because Rupert was about to be exposed by the media.

There were frantic last-minute calls between Ireland and America. All the arrests, from Jim Smyth in Massachusetts, to Mickey McKevitt in Blackrock, would have to happen simultaneously, so nobody destroyed evidence.

On 26 March, David drove back to Florida alone, listening to an audiobook of World War II history.

Maureen went back to her father's house and met her friend Julie for dinner at a crab restaurant. She hadn't seen her since she went on the run.

On the evening of 28 March, Mickey McKevitt made a call to the Iraqi agent he now knew as Khalid, who was in the advanced stages of preparing weapons the Real IRA needed. McKevitt was in a very insistent mood. He wanted to travel to Baghdad as soon as possible. No money had yet arrived and they were promised a million euros. Gaddafi had given two million immediately, without being asked, he said.

Khaled promised it would be coming very soon, but there were bureaucratic considerations in Baghdad.

McKevitt hung up the phone and went to bed annoyed. At 6.45am the next morning, there was a thunderous knock on his door.

CHAPTER 21

McKevitt opened the door. It was Diarmuid O'Sullivan and William Hanrahan of the Irish Special Branch, flashing badges and a search warrant. Behind them were over 30 gardaí, some from forensics, some masked and heavily armed Emergency Response Unit officers.

The gardaí rushed into the house and up the stairs. They knew from Rupert that Bernie kept the sensitive information on an external drive that could be easily removed. The children were asleep in their rooms upstairs.

In the home office, as Rupert had predicted, there were guidebooks to Yugoslavia, where McKevitt had set up arms deals, and a detailed map of Belle-Isle-en-Terre, the Breton village that McKevitt loved.

The forensics team removed McKevitt's Compaq computer, a gift from Rupert, the external drive and Bernadette's home computer. Rupert had installed all the programs on both computers, and his description matched what the gardaí found.

Mickey was read his rights and taken from the house. Bernie just had time to call a friend and tell her to come and look after the children, that she was being taken away.

They were both driven in a long convoy to Balbriggan garda station in north County Dublin for questioning. Senior gardaí made the decision to stay clear of Dundalk for security reasons.

In three jurisdictions, Real IRA members named by Rupert were being arrested.

The owner of the house where the army council meetings took place was also arrested, along with Eoin Quigley, whose home was used by the engineering department.

In Massachusetts, James Smyth was roused from his bedroom to his girlfriend's protests and taken away by the FBI.

Never before in Irish history had simultaneous arrests taken place across such a wide area.

Eleven arrests in Ireland, one in America and more to come.

Rupert had made the gardai and the FBI promise him that Frank and Joe O'Neill would not be arrested, becasue they were old men and would not survive prison. Besides, they were old friends who brought him into the republican scene in the US and Ireland. The gardaí and the FBI kept their word to Rupert – they were not arrested, despite extensive evidence of their role in funding terrorism and, in Joe O'Neill's case, planning attacks.

In Boston, James Smyth picked a spot on the wall and stared at it, refusing to say anything except his name and address.

All of the other arrestees answered only to deny IRA membership.

In Balbriggan, there were frantic last-minute preparations before the formal questioning of McKevitt. Special Branch officer Peter Maguire had put a team together to prepare over 700 questions for McKevitt. They knew he wouldn't answer them, but his silence would be used as an inference.

At 4.40pm, Diarmuid O'Sullivan was ready. The questioning of McKevitt began.

McKevitt looked very relaxed. He had been arrested many times since the early 1970s and had never done any time in prison.

He was not a member of the IRA, he said flatly.

The questions continued, all about IRA membership, each time O'Sullivan warning him that an inference could be drawn from silence or a failure to give a material answer.

"I am not a member of the IRA," he repeated.

The gardaí then came to the main point.

"Michael, do you know David Rupert from the USA?"

There was a pause.

"I don't know him by name," said McKevitt.

O'Sullivan was surprised. He expected McKevitt would deny IRA membership and nothing further. He sensed unease.

"Down through the years, McKevitt had the normal approach to An Garda Síochána from Provos [Provisional IRA members] – don't communicate, don't talk, don't tell them anything," Diarmuid O'Sullivan later told me. "He did answer a lot of questions during interview when Rupert's name was brought up, which was surprising enough."

Was he surprised to be linked to Rupert?

"He let on he was surprised. His answers were that he didn't know David Rupert, which, to me, was a big mistake."

The gardaí wanted to pin him down on accepting their description of the very distinctive looking American, someone whose appearance he would surely know.

"Michael, do you know a person by the name of David Rupert who is about 6 feet 7 inches in height and is from the USA?"

Again, a pause.

"I know nobody of that name," he said. His response was a little more curt this time.

He gave rote answers, knowing he had to answer them. "I don't know a David Rupert," he repeated over and over.

In another interview room, Bernadette gave similar answers. She knew nothing of a David Rupert, she was not a member of the IRA, or the Real IRA, or Óglaigh na hÉireann.

They were taken to holding cells for the night.

The next morning, gardaí met in the station again and reviewed progress. Bernadette was released – leaving the children without both parents would be heavily criticised by human rights groups and they could always interview her again.

Just after 2.30pm, an interview with Mickey McKevitt began. It was time to focus solely on his relationship with Rupert – now they would produce real evidence.

"Do you know David Rupert?"

"I don't know a David Rupert," he said again, "I can't recall any meeting with David Rupert."

Then they hit him with it – receipts, in McKevitt's handwriting for money he received from the IFC in Chicago for war expenses, all of which Rupert had saved and given to the FBI.

One said, "Received from IFC the sum of $6,500". It was signed Pat O'Hagan but it was McKevitt's writing and his fingerprints.

They had another piece of paper with the name and address of James Smyth in Massachusetts, again with McKevitt's fingerprints.

McKevitt sat back.

"I don't know a David Rupert," he said.

O'Sullivan could see that, through the mask, he was starting to look concerned.

The gardaí were in a difficult situation. Despite a major operation mounted outside the bomb-makers' meetings, and watching Rupert and McKevitt outside the house talking, they had no photos of Rupert and McKevitt together.

After the second session ended, he was taken back to his holding cell. He had guessed by now that Rupert had turned. Every single thing, every secret of the Real IRA, he had shared with Rupert – from the valet business where the weapons were shipped, to the entire structure and names of the army council. The engineering department meetings, and every piece of bomb-making equipment they were looking for. A disaster.

There was also the ship on Carlingford Lough. No sooner had McKevitt said to Rupert he wanted marine magnets to blow it up than the ship was moved out to sea.

Every email was running through computers Rupert gave him, everything on the 32CSM website was coming through the system he set up. Even the engineering team's encryption software had come through Rupert.

But he didn't know about the Iraqis. McKevitt never had time to tell him that Saddam's people were in touch. Saddam would save the day.

That evening, he was allowed a meeting with Bernadette. He told her about Rupert. Bernadette was furious that Rupert had been in their home, had spoken at 32CSM meetings at her insistence and had set up their computers.

She went home and immediately called some of the tech team to help her dismantle the 32CSM website.

It was being taken down because of "a sinister element" that had infiltrated the webpage and would be back up at a later date, the website said.

At 8.10pm, McKevitt was released when the legally permitted time was up. As soon as he left the garda station, surrounded by gardaí, he was immediately rearrested and told he was to be taken to the Special Criminal Court in Dublin, a three-judge, non-jury court that handled only terrorist and organised crime cases.

Sometimes the court sat at midnight, sometimes on Sunday mornings, but the person had to be taken there directly under emergency anti-terrorist legislation created in the 1970s.

The motorcade of cars and motorcycle escorts with sirens blazing rushed down the motorway to Dublin, arriving at the court at 9.15pm. It was ink-dark outside.

It was the first time that any of the media present had seen McKevitt when he wasn't wearing a jacket with the collar pulled up past his chin and hat pulled down low over his face.

He was remanded in custody until the following Tuesday. He was driven under heavy escort to Portlaoise Prison. The prison housed the south's IRA prisoners, who were kept in the E-wing. They were given special privileges – they could order in food from wherever they wanted and didn't have to do prison work. McKevitt was greeted by his men as a hero and immediately took command of the dozens of Real IRA prisoners.

The next day, the case was front-page news.

Bernadette, known as the head of the 32CSM, was already a national hate figure. She had been on TV and radio many times, denying that she or the 32CSM had any connection to the Real IRA and saying that they were simply concerned about Irish sovereignty. Now the truth was emerging. She didn't just know about the leadership of the Real IRA, she was married to it – a cottage industry of death and its justification.

Every newspaper in the country was calling around to any Special Branch contact they had, desperate to find out if the gardaí had any big information that led to the arrest.

That night, Maureen went out to dinner with her father and her brother. Her father was in a reflective mood: he could now accept that his daughter had meant the best, that she had not abandoned her family and that David was on the right side. Still, she wrote in her diary, he looked sad.

Back at the house, Maureen's friend Sue came over. She peered in the door and pretended to be looking for an assassin. It began a series of jokes that lasted the night. Maureen was falling sideways laughing – it was a relief.

On Monday morning, Maureen hugged her family and flew back to Florida to be with David.

It felt good, she wrote, to be back with him and in the warmth of Florida. Mark called from Chicago. The Chicago newspapers were asking questions; it was only a matter of days before something very big broke.

"Could be national news by the end of week," he said. In other diary news, coming straight after Mark's warning, Maureen wrote, "Didn't fill the salt and pepper shakers!"

On Thursday, eager to see family before the media descended, they flew from Florida to Massena, then drove to Madrid to see Rupert's siblings, Dale, Bob and Betty.

David sat them down and explained everything and told them not to be alarmed. The media would surely break the story soon and then journalists will swamp the town.

Betty was the most concerned. "I had no idea of any of this," she said. "We knew David was going to Ireland and there had been some article about him in the papers over this, but FBI and all that – I didn't know what the heck was going on."

David and Maureen came back to the hotel and checked the 32CSM website. David read for the first time about the "sinister element" that had infiltrated the group and that the website had to be shut down.

Most people wouldn't take insults from a terrorist website all that seriously, but he did. He became extremely angry, pacing up and down. He was inordinately sensitive to personal slights, a trait that he'd carried with him since high school. How could Bernie? And on the internet.

That evening, Bernie called a member of the Real IRA army council and demanded a meeting.

The army council member remembers it well. "She was surprised, yeah, for sure. But mostly she was very, very angry. She couldn't believe David did this to her, after they invited him into their house."

Across Ireland, there was a frantic series of calls.

Vincent Murray, the now peace-loving republican bar owner in Sligo, who had been David Rupert's first step into Irish republicanism, got a call from Joe O'Neill.

Murray: "Joe said, 'Did you hear about David Rupert? I can't believe it. I don't know what's going to happen now. He must have got himself in some mess, he's messed up with the FBI.'"

"I wasn't concerned for myself, not in the slightest. I had no interest in armed struggle, I didn't see the point, so Rupert lost interest in me. But people like Joe O'Neill were getting worried."

Joe took it worse than almost anyone. It was a personal wound. He clung for the next year to the hope, and the often-expressed belief, that Rupert had got himself into trouble in the trucking world in America and was forced by the FBI to turn on the republican movement.

Michael Donnelly was very worried but said it was fortunate that he had fallen out with McKevitt. "To be honest, I was really panicked for the first week. I thought, 'What is he saying about me?' But I also felt vindicated – I knew he was a spy. I knew it."

According to a republican source close to Liam Campbell, he was far more relaxed. He was already facing IRA membership charges. They already had their evidence against him. Would they really risk bringing Rupert back for his case?

David and Maureen flew from Massena back down to Florida. When they got home, they checked the *Irish Independent* online. There were two articles about the operation but no names. It said that the Real IRA had been compromised by a major US donor following an FBI operation. The public was fascinated. It made the top of the news bulletins on Irish state radio that night. But who was this spy?

A few hours later, Mark called from Chicago. The early edition of the *Sunday Times* in Britain and Ireland, already in the news stands by 10pm on Saturday night, had a massive front-page story with a picture of David Rupert. The photo, soon to become iconic, was from an IFC fundraiser in Chicago.

There were pages about the case on the inside of the paper.

The article said that David Rupert, from upstate New York, was an MI5 and FBI agent who had penetrated the Real IRA army council and had brought on the arrest of its alleged leader Mickey McKevitt.

All the digging in Madrid had paid off – the article said that Rupert was a trucker with a "shady past" who had been married four times.

Mark said security was now key – if David and Maureen wanted to leave their Florida home right away and move into a motel somewhere else, the FBI would pay for it.

He called back the next morning. His boss in the Chicago office, Kathleen McChesney, had rung around to the Syracuse, New York office (the closest to Madrid and Massena), warning officers not to talk to the media.

Friends and family started to email. David Rupert, international spy, was becoming a global story.

I was living in Ballsbridge, Dublin, at the time. I walked down to my local Spar shop. People were lifting up the *Sunday Times* and staring at Rupert, then turning the page. It was less than three years after Omagh and here was an American who had infiltrated the Real IRA and knew everything about the organisation. Who was he? Why did he come to Ireland? I bought a copy of the paper. It seemed nobody else was buying any other paper. His name was all over the radio all day. So was McKevitt's. More and more newspapers piled in over the next few days. Rupert was part native American, they said, from a reservation in upstate New York.

They all repeated the same lines – he had been married four times and been bankrupt three times. In Ireland, where divorce had been legal for four years, and where there were some of Europe's tightest bankruptcy laws, Rupert was a bizarre and exotic character. His personality fuelled more and more thirst for information. Interest was also fuelled by something else, a John le Carré/John Grisham fusion of international spying and terrorism, with a mysterious central character.

The FBI was calling every day to check in on them. Maureen's diary notes expressed her frustration. "'They' want us to leave ASAP," she wrote. "'They' want us to get new identities. 'They' want us to have surveillance."

In the following days, it was like the caverns of David Rupert's mind were falling inwards. His mood darkened, his thoughts became paranoid and suspicious. He was a blue-collar man who ran a trucking company and now every detail of his embarrassments and failures was international news. And the headlines: Rat. Informer. FBI. M15. Trucker. Divorced. Bankrupt. Sinister Element. Shady Past.

He became convinced the FBI would abandon him. It became an obsession. He was screaming with them on the phone and ranting about it to Maureen every day. "The FBI are going to screw us," became his mantra. His financial mistakes came back to him. It would be the Drowes all over again, it would be his bankruptcies all over again, but now with added foreign terrorists. He was losing it.

Maureen: "I honestly don't know if I would go through it again. I was very worried because he was so stressed."

She told the FBI about her fears. Mark called back – they had an idea. They would book a big group into a fantastic resort in Wisconsin. The FBI bosses would come, and the gardaí bosses would fly in from Ireland and they would relax, just chill out and discuss what happens from here.

When David heard it, he screamed at Mark down the phone. What did they mean?

Maureen was with him in the car at the time.

"So I'm sitting there, listening to this on speaker phone and David says, 'I know why you want to bring me in – so one of you can pin me down while the other one fucks me in the ass.'"

David: "Yeah, that happened."

Maureen: "I couldn't believe some of the things he was saying to them. I'm trying to keep the peace between them."

For David's increasingly paranoid mind, the Wisconsin trip was a kidnap with smiles. The FBI and gardaí would keep him there until they got him to agree to testify. They were just trying to scare him with talk of the Real IRA searching for him so they could trap him.

Rupert: "Just when Wisconsin came up, the FBI said they had some 'overhear' from the Real IRA that they were really worried about. It was National Security Agency-type information. Nowadays you'd call it 'chatter'."

Both Maureen and Mark tried to convince him to come to Wisconsin. The following day he relented, but warned them he was going to leave whenever he wanted.

David didn't sleep that night. He got up at 3am and was pacing up and down their room and pacing in the kitchen. The FBI was going to screw them out of money. The FBI would always be around, watching them, judging them. The Real IRA would get them. After testifying, wouldn't it suit the FBI to have him bumped off? No awkward questions about its methods.

On Thursday 12 April, 2001, they left Cape Coral at 9am.

They drove across the country, spending the night in Knoxville, Tennessee. Again, David didn't sleep.

Early the next morning, he called Mark. The FBI was to call off its surveillance. He didn't want the FBI anywhere near him or his family. He didn't want to be under surveillance. Mark could see there were big problems with David's mental health. "OK," he said. "OK, David. That's not a problem."

David and Maureen drove from Knoxville to Dorie's house, arriving at 3pm. Just because David loved dogs, Maureen suggested they take Dorie's puppy for a walk in the park.

They stayed for four and a half hours, talking to Dorie and her boyfriend, Mike. By the time they left, Maureen was very worried about David. He looked exhausted, on the verge of collapse. He hadn't slept in days.

They decided to visit their old house outside Chicago. Along the way, they called on Dan from the bank, who greeted them as homecoming heroes.

"Well, I'm so proud of you," he said. "Now I know somebody who saved many lives."

They were both warmed by the visit. It gave David some perspective. Hero. A word he hadn't heard since the papers outed him.

While he collected some possessions from the old house, Maureen went to Sheer Designs, the hair salon she used to attend. Her hairdresser, Mary, hugged her as soon as she came in. The whole town was talking about nothing but Rupert, Rupert, Rupert. It was all over the Chicago papers.

Mary sat her down for a haircut. A woman with an Irish accent had called three weeks ago, pretending to make an appointment but then asked, casually, if she could have Maureen Rupert's number because she didn't have it with her. Mary hung up the phone. The story made Maureen laugh. David picked her up and they drove to meet Mark at the Chicago office. The meeting with Dan had been the best possible tonic before Mark, tentatively, introduced the head of the FBI protection unit. He wasn't there for surveillance, only protection. Maureen gripped David's hand.

"I understand," David said.

Mark went with them to her father's house. He knew her father had been distraught that his daughter was in hiding, away from her family.

Mark presented Mr Brennan with an FBI cap and mug. Everyone laughed. It was a little conspicuous to have family members wearing FBI caps when they were supposed to be in hiding.

That night, David and Maureen went out to dinner with her father and Mark.

FBI agents sat at tables near them and in a car outside. It was their first taste of this new world of close FBI protection.

Mark was relieved to see that David was a little more relaxed, but he was getting very sick. All the stress and sleepless nights were showing. Maureen was concerned about him.

They walked out of the restaurant and said goodbye to her father. They followed Mark's FBI car, with another car behind them, to the Lake Lawn, Wisconsin's most relaxing resort. Armed FBI agents were already at the resort, waiting for their arrival.

CHAPTER 22

A concierge led David and Maureen to their rooms. It was an entire suite, with a living room and a balcony overlooking the resort, with its long walks through the forests and a massage room and a swimming pool.

Even Rupert, still sceptical and not sure if he was being kidnapped, was very impressed. "I thought it was just going to be a room, like everywhere else we stayed. This was more like a home. And the FBI were in apartments either side of us."

The FBI also reserved apartments for the two senior gardaí, Martin Callinan and Diarmuid O'Sullivan, who would be coming from Ireland in a few days.

David and Maureen woke up to the sound of children playing outside. It was Easter Sunday and Chicago's rich had booked into the resort for the weekend.

Maureen was very excited. She went swimming in the pool.

Later, she called her father and Dorie to wish them a happy Easter and to tell them excitedly about the resort and how much the FBI loved it too.

Mark's wife arrived with their three children, to make the best use of the resort while they had it. Maureen was struck by how beautiful they all were. She looked like the perfect glamour wife and the children were extremely well behaved. They even brought their dog, Suzie Q.

David heard there was a bit of tension. Mark's wife's parents were upset with Mark for bringing the children to meet David Rupert. What if there was a terrorist attack? Had he thought about that?

David and Maureen were getting a hint of what was coming for the rest of their lives.

People would not call for family events, friends would make up excuses rather than let them into their homes. What if there was a terrorist attack? Weren't the IRA known for making mistakes?

As they talked in Mark's room, David perceived a very big personality change in his friend. Mark was once the wild man, regaling David with his tales of excess. How he was changing. Now it was about God, and family, and American values. Mostly God. Mark had come in from his spiritual wilderness. He was blessed. David was bored.

Mark said the FBI really wanted Rupert to testify. David was about to start on his rant about not getting paid when Mark came up with an offer – $12,000 a month, plus $9,000 a month for personal security, as David did not want the FBI around him. That was $21,000 a month, indefinitely, however he wanted to spend it. But that kind of money would only come if it was needed. He would hardly need $9,000 a month on security if he was simply passing on background information, rather than testifying, would he? There would also be a big bonus payment from M15 at the end of it.

Just about $250,000 a year, indefinitely, "until the threat went away", plus a settlement from MI5. He said he'd think it over, but that it was generous.

Over dinner, Mark had some big news. He wasn't sure how it would go down.

James Smyth was no longer in an American prison. He had been deported back to Ireland.

That was bad news.

Rupert had betrayed the Real IRA's best assassin, and he was back in Ireland, armed.

Rupert couldn't believe it.

Smyth was not charged with terrorism, despite being video-taped bringing weapons and bomb components to Rupert's room, because the Boston field office wanted nothing to do with IRA cases. One of their Irish American officers, John Connolly, was already in jail for acting as a double agent for IRA gun-runner and organised crime chief James "Whitey" Bulger. In a city as Irish as Boston, it was possible that someone with Smyth's Irish and military background knew law enforcement officers. The Boston FBI was already drowning in internal and justice department investigations in the wake of the Connolly/Bulger scandal.

Smyth, now barred from the US and his beloved girlfriend, was very, very angry. To Rupert, it was just more evidence that he couldn't trust the FBI.

The next day, Kathleen McChesney, the Special Agent in Charge at the Chicago office, and Pat Daly, another senior FBI officer, arrived at the resort.

To other holidaymakers, they were just another group gathering to celebrate Easter week with facials, saunas and walks in the woods.

If Maureen had a platonic crush on Mark, David had one on Kathleen. He was different around her. Less surly, more eager to please. She was pretty, Irish, intelligent and a redhead, just like

Linda Vaughan. Maureen could pick up David's sudden change in tone and wondered if she could use it to her advantage.

Maureen had already emailed Kathleen about David's Harley Davidson – she thought this would be a perfect time to raise it. Wouldn't Kathleen agree that riding around on a motorbike was bad for security and could also lead to an accident, right when David was trying to decide whether he wanted the $21,000 a month to testify?

Kathleen was primed. She told David that it was a very, very bad idea. He had very distinctive features and had lived in Florida before and he could be spotted. Kathleen said that the FBI would pay the difference between what he paid for the Harley and what he sold it for. She knew how to work him.

David agreed to get rid of it.

Maureen: "I couldn't believe it. I'm after him to get rid of that thing and one word from Kathleen and it's, 'Oh yes, yes, yes, ma'am. Right away, ma'am.'"

Kathleen had some other news and asked them not to be alarmed.

Bernadette Sands McKevitt had asked Martin Galvin, the Real IRA-supporting New York lawyer, to start digging up dirt on David and Galvin had already hired a private detective.

Rupert: "I had told stuff to McKevitt about the trucking world and all that and he was telling it to Bernie and his lawyer to get moving against me."

That evening, after dinner, they did a newspaper search on LexisNexis to see the press coverage for David Rupert – it brought up newspaper articles in nine countries just that day.

David's obsessive reading on the case continued. That day he checked online and found an article in the *Irish Echo* in New York. "FBI Denies Involvement in Informer Case," it read.

He was furious. It was more proof that the FBI was going to cut him loose, that the new contract wouldn't materalise. It was 11pm. Mark was in his apartment next door with his family, asleep. He called Mark's phone and left a message, demanding to know what was going on. David was still upset about it the next day, even as everyone else was enjoying themselves by the pool. He insisted Mark come over and read the article on his computer.

Mark called Kathleen McChesney. She had a way of calming David that nobody else had. Kathleen called over to the room and explained, as patiently as she could, that the FBI never made a statement confirming it had an informer. It was better to say nothing, to keep the Real IRA guessing.

They needed David in a good mood that day. Martin Callinan and Diarmuid O'Sullivan, the two senior anti-terrorism gardaí, were coming to the resort.

They arrived two hours later. Callinan gave Maureen a kiss on the cheek. O'Sullivan, the more formal country man, shook her hand. "Martin is the kisser!" she recorded in her diary.

O'Sullivan was very impressed by the resort.

"I remember it very well. It was very salubrious to say the least. It was great comfort – I could have stayed there for a while but, unfortunately, we had a lot of work to do."

If Rupert was to testify, they had to convince him of all the security he could expect in Dublin and what he could expect from the court experience.

O'Sullivan could sense that there was tension between Rupert and the FBI but was determined to stay out of it.

"There was always an underlying fear in Rupert. I never delved into that much," he said. "I certainly wasn't going to get involved between him and FBI. The last thing I wanted was to add to the confusion."

Despite his heavy cold, Rupert spoke pointedly in his suite about how the gardaí had treated him.

"He felt we weren't serious about him. The fact that he had been positioned up in Leitrim in [the Drowes pub] and we hadn't fulfilled our commitment to him."

This was by far the largest terrorist case in their lives. They couldn't afford to fail, or to fall out with Rupert. They listened and tried to explain the importance of testifying.

His meeting with the two Irish detectives began at 2pm. Below them, during the day, they could hear children splashing around in the pool and the chatter of families playing tennis and going for walks.

Kathleen and Maureen sat by the pool with drinks and talked about life. Maureen liked her immediately. She asked her how many children she had. David always wanted to talk money and terrorism, Maureen always wanted to talk family. Kathleen said she had 800 children – all the FBI agents who worked for her. Maureen laughed. It led to a discussion about managing men – they had both managed dozens of them: Maureen in the truck plaza, Kathleen in the FBI.

Maureen said they were as bad, if not worse, than women with workplace gossip and that women sometimes didn't realise that. Kathleen complained about how needy her male agents were, constantly coming to her, looking for approval. "They're exhausting in that respect," she said.

David didn't finish with the Irish detectives until 2am and they needed him to start again early in the morning.

He was sick and feverish but wanted to continue.

By 8am the next morning, he was back in talks with them again, while Maureen went for breakfast.

They finally finished at noon.

David was feeling happier about the protection he would get in Ireland if he did testify. It was time to check out.

The FBI was still trying to do all it could to placate him. Doug and Mark took David and Maureen's bags and loaded them into the mini-van. "Well, end of lockdown," said Mark.

Maureen got a kiss goodbye from Martin and a handshake from Diarmuid. Mark told her to "take good care of the big guy". "Only strained food for him, we don't need him choking," he said. "And no motorcycle," said Maureen. They left on good terms and drove off.

Mark called a few days later with a new media strategy. John McDonagh, the Radio Free Eireann host in New York, was denouncing Rupert on air as a "rat bastard". The silence on the FBI/Rupert side would have to be filled. He had called Rupert's friend, Dan the banker, and urged him to talk up "David the American hero" next time a reporter called. Galvin, John McDonagh, and Bernadette Sands McKevitt were spreading as many negative stories as they could. The FBI and the Ruperts would have to urge friends and family to spread a positive message when contacted.

The stress of keeping David together was starting to show on Maureen. She went completely off her careful diet that day. She went to a Chinese buffet with her family and then to the fast food chain White Castle.

The next day, Tuesday 24 April, Mark called again. John McDonagh had said on Radio Free Eireann that a major British TV current affairs show was in the US to do a big feature on David Rupert. McDonagh had probably already spoken to them.

David went to his old doctor, who diagnosed him with high blood pressure and depression. He prescribed tranquilisers and said that he'd try him out on antidepressants.

Rupert: "I started taking Paxil and anti-anxiety medicine. I still take antidepressants. It works. Life would be a bitch without it. I had an uncle and an uncle by marriage both commit suicide. Basically, I went overnight from being a spy to doing nothing. It was more stressful than anyone trying to shoot me."

The next day, another article about David appeared in the *Chicago Sun-Times*. He was stressed again and got in the car and headed west, just to drive somewhere.

Yvonne, Maureen's former hairdresser outside Chicago, told her that a woman with an Irish accent had called, looking for a number for Maureen Rupert. Then the woman asked what services the salon provided and if they did butt lifts. "She was a reporter, just looking for smut," said Yvonne.

Maureen could imagine the hoped-for article: "Maureen Rupert got hundreds of thousands of dollars from the FBI – then spent it on getting her buttocks shaped."

The media hunt never seemed to abate. The following Sunday, 29 April, David got a call from Suki, a former neighbour in Madrid. Five strangers were in town and had been in the coffee shop. They were wearing fishermen's clothes and waders and she caught them taking photos of her house. Their back-story was that they were passing through on a fishing expedition and just wanted to see the town, but nobody believed them.

The following day, Chris Fogarty, IFC member and Real IRA supporter, called another old friend of theirs in Wheatfield, Indiana, Jack, asking where they were and for details about Maureen's father.

David replied to Jack saying not to worry, that the FBI had the situation under control. Jack thanked him but said he was still checking under his car for bombs.

That week, David and Maureen decided to stay ahead of the media and Real IRA hunt for them and go on a road trip to Canada. Maureen knew it would calm David's nerves. They drove to Cornwall, Ontario.

At the Best Western Hotel, Maureen spotted the actress Shirley MacLaine. She had never seen a celebrity before and was really excited because MacLaine was in town to shoot a film with Kirstie Alley, one of Maureen's favourites.

She had to go find her: Shirley MacLaine would lead her to Kirstie.

David tried to stop her.

David: "Reporters from America, Ireland and the UK are on our tail every day, there is nothing they won't do to find us and the Real IRA wouldn't be far behind them.

"My wife is trailing all over the hotel trying to run into celebrities. I knew they wanted their privacy and I didn't want to draw attention to ourselves or let anyone know who were are, but Maureen was that determined."

Maureen drove to the Ramada Inn after dinner, looking for Kirstie Alley, but couldn't find her.

Then she insisted that they book out of the Comfort Inn and into the Best Western, where Shirley MacLaine was staying.

Maureen hung out in the bar, hoping for a celebrity sighting. Shirley MacLaine and her dog, Teri, came into the bar. Shirley told Teri that it was "too early to be drinking". Maureen followed her out to the corridor and was allowed to pet Teri. She was thrilled.

The rest of her diary entry for the day is worth repeating in full, because it's instructive about how their life was at that time:

"Bud went to see Sheriff in Canton, NY about security factor. Betty called. Someone sent her raffle tickets for Friends of Irish Freedom [event] for 13 May. People's Republic of China website article 'American Infiltrates IRA'. Went to Ramada looking for Kirstie Alley. Saw male star. Don't know his name."

Chris Fogarty was calling David's friends and family, trying to find as much information as he could.

On 8 May, Betty called. Fogarty called Joe, the school principal in New York, wanting information on Dale's conviction and imprisonment for transporting cannabis.

Then their friend Jack called and said he believed someone was following him.

David was extremely annoyed. He called Mark, who was in Ireland planning the case. He wanted an FBI statement distancing him from his brother's conviction. Mark pleaded with him to let it lie. "Someone needs to make a statement or we will," said Rupert.

The next day, there was a positive article in *Time* magazine about David. Maureen loved it, but David was still edgy and combative. He was convinced that the FBI was out to get him.

An Irish Special Branch detective very familiar with David's case told me, "David was a great agent in the field but we were starting to realise that he was a bit mad, and that opinion was definitely coming from colleagues in America. That was becoming a concern, for sure."

And through it all, the Real IRA's fanaticism continued, even harder now, to show that they could survive without McKevitt.

On Thursday, 7 June 2001, a gunman opened up with an AK-47 at a polling booth, in their attempt to stop Northern Ireland's elections for its new parliament in Stormont. He shot a voter and two police officers before fleeing to a waiting car. Noel Abernethy, the man who had flown to Chicago to win over US supporters for Rupert, was arrested in a speeding car 20 minutes later. He had thrown his top off as they sped from the direction of the polling booth. He was put on trial and acquitted for lack of evidence, although the judge made it clear that suspicion or likelihood was not enough – he had to be absolutely sure.

A week later, David and Maureen drove to Bloomington, Illinois, to pick up their Armed Forces IDs. They would both be members of the military on official documents. It would give them a good cover story and help explain David's movements abroad. They didn't want new identities. They would still be Maureen and David, but on official documents, they would be two other people serving in the military.

Mark had booked them a hotel room for the day, if they wanted to unwind. At 11am they met Mark, Doug Lindsey and "Joe Pesci", at a TGI Fridays in downtown Bloomington. After lunch, they took them to the state building to a woman who had a portable driving licence machine. She issued two licences for David in his new name, and one for Maureen. They then went back to the hotel with the group for an instruction on how to use their military driving licences and standard warnings on not using, for example, their real names on car rental documents and then booking the car with their new licences.

Over the following weeks, as members of the armed forces, they were learning the language and the tone of the military and creating a background story.

*****

Bud Rupert ran at Chris Fogarty's car with a gun in his hand.

He had another six guns inside.

"I'm going to blow your head off," he said.

Fogarty, would-be jeans supplier to Irish republicanism, stopped the car.

What was said between them is disputed. Fogarty denies threatening that the Real IRA would come after David Rupert. He said he was simply taking photographs of Bud's house and the houses of Rupert's two sisters as part of an information collection exercise to discredit Rupert's upcoming evidence against McKevitt.

Chris Fogarty: "We took photographs of his house. It was a tar-roofed shack with firewood stacked outside. We were having a last look. We never got out of the car. We were driving by and he jumped out and stopped us with a gun in his hand and said he'd blow my head off."

He said he'd blow your head off if you didn't leave?

Chris: "No, he just said he'd blow my head off."

Fogarty and his wife, Mary, had flown to Burlington, Vermont, then driven to Madrid and Massena, looking for information about Rupert that would help McKevitt's case.

Chris: "We went to the local cop, the garage and the police station."

Mary: "We went to Charlie's Tavern, that place Rupert had. Every business he had there, he ran into the ground."

They drove to all the local towns: Wallington, Madrid, Roosevelt, Massena, wherever Rupert had lived or worked, looking for negative information – divorces, bankruptcies, the unpaid loans to his two fathers-in-law, broken hearts, closed restaurants, brother's drug bust, they got it all.

Mary: "We spoke to the post-mistress there. We got information from a lot of people. We went to an Indian reservation where he was meant to have been sending cigarettes across the border, tax free. At a hotel, one man said to us, 'We heard the IRA is after him and I hope they get him.'"

Chris laughs and asks his wife, "Who said that?"

Mary: "A man who worked at a hotel. I forget his name."

Chris: "Was it a hotel where we stayed?"

Mary: "No dear, another hotel. That's what he told us, anyway. I have it in my notes some place."

I wonder what they think of the Rupert family's contention that driving up and down past their home slowly, as known dissident republicans, was deliberately intimidating.

Chris: "We took photographs at a distance. We didn't take photographs up close to the house, we took them at a distance, specifically not to be obtrusive."

They also called to the school, asking if anyone had information about Dale Rupert's drug bust and if it was related to David Rupert.

As a pair of amateur sleuths, they did astoundingly well, even applying for Rupert's bankruptcy documents from the federal government. Then they drove to Indiana, to the Ruperts' vacated new home, calling around to every business in the area, and calling on Rupert family members.

The pair flew to Dundalk and met Bernadette Sands McKevitt and McKevitt's lawyer and passed on everything they had. It was the beginning of a long process of disclosure of Rupert's past life.

*****

Dorie was working as an attorney at a civil law firm outside Chicago.

One day that week, the receptionist paged through a work call. "Hello, Dorie?"

The man, who had an Irish accent, said he was a journalist from the *Guardian* newspaper and that he wanted to know when David would testify.

Dorie said she didn't know.

"Where is he now?" he man asked.

Dorie said she didn't know and had to work.

The man's tone suddenly changed. "If he testifies, we will kill you and your family," he said. He hung up.

She looked around the office. Workers were busy with files, in their own world.

She called the FBI. Two agents were sent immediately.

She told the partners of the firm and said that the FBI were coming over. They looked alarmed.

The FBI came, and brought the bomb squad with them.

They checked around the office, in front of all her workmates, then checked under her car for explosives.

"I thought it was completely over the top," said Dorie. "It was more for show – 'Oh look, we're going to do something' – and it was not actually for security. If someone wanted to get me on my way to the supermarket, they could still do it."

The FBI insisted on bringing her to work and collecting her in the evening, every day for three months.

"I was really afraid of getting fired," said Dorie. "I was trying not to attract attention or look like a danger. Every time someone at work asked me about some guy dropping me off at the office, I would say, 'Oh my car is in getting serviced.' I had to invent a lot of car problems for those three months."

David's family in Massena began to see Real IRA everywhere.

Betty: "One day, we saw a boat come up the river. Nobody came up there that time of year. So we called the FBI. We thought there might be explosives on the boat. Turns out it was just some guy fishing."

The following week, Mark called David. He sounded very excited. He had big, big news, he said, but he couldn't say what it was on the phone.

"Is it from Ireland?" said David.

"No," said Mark. "It's from western Slovakia."

CHAPTER 23

On 2 July, three Real IRA army council members, Fintan O'Farrell, Declan Rafferty and their leader, Michael McDonald, sat at an Arab restaurant in the Slovakian spa town of Piest'any.

The Iraqi agents greeted them warmly and invited them to try Arab food.

McDonald had already promised the Iraqis that they would mount a blaze of attacks on London and "put a smile on your face" if given the right equipment.

Rafferty told them that the rocket attack on MI6 would be repeated many times over with Iraqi help, but with far greater destruction.

Over dinner, McDonald wrote a detailed shopping list on a piece of tissue paper. He wanted hundreds of tons of handguns, explosives, rocket-propelled grenades and detonators.

He didn't want the Iraqis to take the note, so it was left on the table. As they were talking, one of the Iraqis picked it up, blew his nose on it and put it in his pocket. His friend kept talking about how much the men would get, and very soon.

When the three left the restaurant after the meeting, they were immediately arrested and finally learned that their Iraqi friends were in fact MI5 agents.

The Rupert case had completely changed MI5's way of dealing with terrorism. Never in the agency's history had it mounted a foreign sting operation, but now it knew what it wanted – legally accepted evidence. It even brought its lawyers to the towns where the Iraqi meetings were taking place. Capturing a shopping list from the Real IRA members was also learned from the Rupert experience.

In Chicago, Mark told Rupert that he was crucial to the case against McKevitt and also against what was now known in the UK and Irish media as the Slovak Three. It was Rupert who had told MI5 that the Real IRA wanted Saddam Hussein or some other foreign dictator to come forward and sponsor them. Also, he would be needed to identify McKevitt's voice in the 19 phone calls he and McDonald had with the Iraqi agents.

Just to secure Rupert's cooperation, the FBI would work on getting his ever-rising tax bill down to the level it was in 1994, when he officially became a spy. From $750,000 it would be reduced to about $30,000. In return, Rupert would give evidence in England against the Slovak Three, who had been extradited, and Mickey McKevitt in Dublin.

It gave him the financial freedom to say goodbye, finally, to the rented house in Florida and move into a home on a large plot of land in the Midwest, free of the cities, where he could ride a tractor and enjoy the easy life. He also wanted somewhere so quiet that if any strangers came into the local town, or just drove around, they would be immediately noticed.

Maureen was as excited as he was to be buying a house and starting a new life. They contacted the local sheriff in the area, along with the FBI, and told him their story.

Rupert: "He was a real nice guy, even said he'd check on our place when I had to be away in Ireland. To be honest, when you're a rural sheriff, having someone like us move in adds a bit of spice."

They were to settle the deal with the FBI at a meeting in Charlotte, North Carolina. The gardaí would also be there.

On 9 July 2001, they flew to North Carolina and Maureen booked in at the Hilton Hotel as Mark Lundgren's sister-in-law, as instructed. They both loved the room and the view over Charlotte. That evening, Mark took them out to dinner. Maureen had too much wine, and she was in an excited mood.

The next day, David met Martin Callinan and Dermot Jennings. They had come all the way from Ireland to confirm, face-to-face, that he would give evidence in Dublin. Maureen went downstairs with Mark to give them some privacy. For Maureen, time with Mark was always well spent and time to share their mutual fears about David's stress.

In the room, David reassured the gardaí that he would give evidence, that his tax affairs were being settled and that he had nothing whatsoever to do with his brother's cannabis conviction. No matter what McKevitt's defence threw at him, he could take it.

Maureen saw them come out of the room.

Jennings was wearing a huge grin. He was "100 per cent sure" they would get a conviction against McKevitt, he said. He knew that the Irish prime minister, or Taoiseach, Bertie Ahern, had been leaning on the Irish justice department to make sure everything would be ready before the world's media arrived in Ireland for the trial.

The next few weeks were given to planning – if Rupert was to testify against the Slovak Three and against McKevitt, he would need some suits.

Rupert: "I said, 'You're the FBI, you sort out the suits. I've barely ever worn a suit in my life. You can pay for them 'cos I'll never wear them again.'"

Because of his height and size, nothing fitted, so "Joe Pesci" organised for the FBI to sneak Rupert to an upscale tailor in Chicago. He got three new suits fitted, with tailor-made shirts, in different colours. Mark, getting exasperated, sighed. They would pay for it.

When it was time to testify in the UK against the Slovak Three, Rupert was taken under escort to the US Attorney General's Gulfstream jet, which was to take him and the FBI team to an undisclosed location in England.

Rupert loved the plane. So did the agents. They lined up outside it for a photo. Everyone involved in the case was going: Mark Lundgren; Doug Lindsey; the Chicago field office lawyer, Jim Krupowski; Ed Buckley and several other agents who had worked on his case. The mood was light-hearted: they were all excited to have their own private jet. "Bet you wish you had one of these in the trucking business," said one of the agents. As they were flying across the Atlantic, one of the agents held up a copy of the *Irish Voice* newspaper. It was a big, double-page spread showing Rupert and Joe O'Neill at an IFC fundraiser in Chicago.

The pilot looked back at David. "Is this another Sammy Gravano?" he asked. The testimony of mafia member Sammy Gravano against his former boss, John Gotti, was still huge news in the US at the time.

The remark stung Rupert. He had been hurt when people thought he must be an organised crime figure, rather than an ordinary Joe who had successfully infiltrated one of the world's most dangerous terrorist groups. Any suggestion that he was a "snitch", rather than a professional spy, really hurt him. "I'm no Gravano," he shouted back.

It was now five months after the 9/11 terrorist attacks. America was infused with a rage against the abstract noun "terrorism", of which the Real IRA was a part.

The Real IRA was placed on the US list of foreign terrorist groups, as was Republican Sinn Féin, a legal political party in Ireland, and the Irish Republican Prisoners Welfare Association, based on Rupert's evidence of their close association with and cover for terrorist groups.

Rupert was the centre of the FBI's attention now. Anything to do with fighting terrorism was far above any other priority. That the IRA had longstanding ties with Arab terrorism just made the importance of destroying them all the more urgent.

Rupert looked out the window. They were flying in military airspace at 50,000ft – it was the highest he had ever been in his life.

They flew directly into Mildenhall, an RAF base in Suffolk. There was a US military base within the British base, so it was doubly protected. Rupert would stay there throughout the Slovak Three case, his FBI handlers told him, and, when giving evidence against McKevitt in Dublin, he would stay there on the American base at weekends and fly to Dublin during the week.

He was led in to the barracks, past American fighter pilots.

The accommodation was basic military, a long way down from his stays in Paris. He could expect to be living here for months, if not a year. He unpacked in his room and called Maureen. "You're not missing much here," he said.

The FBI agents bunked into rooms all the way down the corridor.

They had their own kitchen and ate together. Everyone was relaxed and in a good mood.

The FBI insisted on following Rupert everywhere within their compound. It had to be addressed. It was his old fear of FBI "surveillance" – he worried that he was their captive.

Rupert: "I told them that if I walk around the airbase and you want to follow me and stay in the shadows, that's ok, but I'm not asking for permission."

He soon discovered that there was a big American shopping centre on the base. It had a Wendy's and a Pizza Hut, a barber, souvenir shop and a store with very generous discounts on American goods. The FBI agents, and Rupert, weren't allowed into the shopping centre because they didn't have military ID.

Rupert discovered one day that he could go to the store and buy a newspaper just by putting his hands behind his back and looking like a pompous general in civilian clothes. He simply nodded his head at the military police, as if they should know him.

"I was playing the big guy with the big attitude," he said.

"I was coming back every day with a newspaper and American stuff and my guys, who had FBI IDs, couldn't buy a candy bar. They would say, 'Where the fuck are you getting that? You can't buy anything there unless you have military ID.' I said, 'Or unless you look like you belong there.' Nobody ever questioned me after that."

MI5 showed up. They hired a consultant on courtroom etiquette to talk to David on how to address the court in the Slovak Three case.

"It was just how to address the judges as 'my lords' instead of 'your honour' and stuff like that. He showed me that in the US you are technically supposed to address your answers to the jury, but in the UK, you speak to the judge."

The consultant left him a booklet on how the UK courts worked.

While there, Paul brought him the tapes of "Karl" setting up the arms shipments with the Iraqis. Rupert listened intently. It was definitely McKevitt. Paul looked very relieved.

Rupert hadn't heard McKevitt's voice since their last dinner together with the spouses. "On the tape, Mickey was getting pissy with the Iraqis because they hadn't sent the million euros that they promised and he wanted it as soon as possible to escalate things."

M15 was now very confident they would get a conviction.

Rupert and the MI5 agents waited around the base for three weeks. Scotland Yard showed up and took Rupert and the FBI agents for day trips, under very tight security. He remembers it felt like a school field trip.

"On days out, there'd be two car loads of Scotland Yard and some of the FBI guys came too. Once we went to a military museum. Another time, we went over to the east coast of England and I went walking out on the beach by myself. I had Scotland Yard agents armed to the teeth up there on the wall watching me as I walked. I think that was the only time I had to myself off the base."

Another week, they visited Windsor Castle and Blenheim Palace.

"At Windsor, there was a long queue to get in. So the Scotland Yard guys just got out of the car and took us to the exit. They showed their ID and we went in that way, past everyone else. Blenheim I remember very well, it has the bedroom where Churchill was born and we toured around the rooms. That was pretty neat. I was getting to know the Scotland Yard guys too, they were enjoying the days out as much as the FBI."

After three weeks of waiting around at the base, news came through that the Queen Mother had died. Britain was in mourning and there was a delay in the case. MI5 said it could take some time and that the barrister for the defendants was in talks with his clients about what to do. The FBI decided it would fly Rupert back to America and wait.

They flew back again on the Attorney General's plane. It was a boys' club outing that had come to an end. Back home in their new farm house, Maureen greeted him with a big hug.

When Rupert was out on his tractor one day, Lundgren called him. The Slovak Three were going to plead guilty, highly unusual in an IRA case. Rupert would not have to go back to the UK.

The three men expected to get six or seven years for conspiracy to commit terrorist acts. At their sentence hearing, the judge lambasted them for being "at the centre, or close to the centre" of the organisation that caused the Omagh bomb, and they were conspiring with an enemy of the UK, the Iraqi government, to cause more Omaghs and more destruction to ordinary families. He jailed them for 30 years each, a record in the UK for a guilty plea on a charge of terrorist conspiracy.

The three left the courtroom stunned.

Over time, they became angry with McKevitt. He had promised them it would only be a light sentence if they were caught. Their lives were ruined. They were transferred to Ireland to serve their sentence. According to a security source, O'Farrell in particular was angry at McKevitt for trusting Rupert, and for assuring them that they would not get heavy sentences if caught.

MI5 was elated. It was a highly risky, even outrageous, mission. The agency was changing. It was showing that it could come out of the Cold War still relevant. It could get convictions.

Now the media's attention turned towards Dublin. Mickey McKevitt, Real IRA leader, would never plead guilty. It was time for him to sit in court and see his old friend, face to face.

CHAPTER 24

The royal jet dropped down into the US airbase in Suffolk.

Rupert was back at the US military base, awaiting transport to Dublin.

The plane normally used to ferry the Queen and her family on royal appointments was now David Rupert's private jet.

One of the agents took a photograph of the royal air hostess as she offered chocolates to Rupert, while he held a drink in his other hand. The royal crest is visible on the headrest behind him.

Within an hour, they were in Baldonnel military airport outside Dublin and were taken by an army and garda escort to a townhouse on the north side of the city.

The original plan, made weeks earlier, was to fly him by garda helicopter, but he refused to sit in one.

"I've seen those garda helicopters, those old Alouettes. I'm not interested in that," said Rupert.

The entourage gradually broke away. He got out of the car and switched to another. The houses either side of the safehouse were reserved for garda protection and there were plain-clothes gardaí walking up and down the cul de sac, which was not viewable from the road or any nearby housing estates.

Why give him accommodation in Dublin? Wasn't that a risk?

Diarmuid O'Sullivan: "People expected him to be locked in a castle an hour from the city. I can't get into it, even now, because the devil is in the detail in these things, but you wanted to keep certain people guessing."

The gardaí were excited and tense. Rupert wasn't allowed to leave the house, or go near the windows, but they would get anything he wanted from the shop. The kitchen already had orange juice, coffee, tea and bread. They decided to order in pizza. The gardaí didn't want anyone coming near the house so they went out to collect it. Martin Callinan called over to wish Rupert well and to ask if there was anything else he needed.

At the courthouse in the city centre, at the request of the prosecution barristers, gardaí measured the witness box. It had been used for 200 years and was very small. They were concerned that Rupert's large frame wouldn't fit in it.

Liz Walsh, a journalist who covered all the trial, remembers a garda telling her: "We'll get Rupert into the witness box, getting him out's going to be the fucking problem."

Journalists were gathering from all over the UK, the US and Ireland. This, the leader of the Real IRA up against a 6ft 7 New York trucker, was a sensational story and one of the most discussed criminal cases in Irish legal history. Would it hold up? The fact that Rupert was being paid – how could his evidence be admissible? Would MI5 give evidence for the first time in Irish history?

Back at the townhouse in Dublin, Rupert called home to Maureen to tell her he was OK and that the security was very tight.

The gardaí and the FBI had explained to Maureen that she should stay in the US and she agreed.

Diarmuid O'Sullivan: "Nobody knew how long the trial would last and what direction it would go. She probably would have been a help to David Rupert but it was decided between the FBI and gardaí that it would require extra security. There were an awful lot of unknowns at the time and she was going to be sitting in a hotel room, she's not going to be in the court. What's that going to do to someone, sitting in a hotel room waiting to see her husband every day?"

The trial opened on a warm day in late June.

TV crews had to set up their cameras further down the street. The back entrance to the Green Street courtroom was completely shut off. Army snipers sat on the roof of the court building.

At the townhouse, Rupert got up, got ready and put on his suit.

The FBI agents hurried around him and the gardaí got him quickly into a bomb-proof car. There were garda cars and motorbikes waiting for them further down the road, so that they wouldn't draw attention to the house. Soon there was a large entourage heading into the city centre. Gardaí motorbike riders went ahead, blocking rush-hour traffic at junctions so that the entourage were the only cars on the road. Hundreds of cars were blocked in. People came out onto the street to have a look.

Rupert snapped a photo from the back of the car at the street ahead of him.

To his left and right he heard the police sirens and radio signals. In the car around him were armed gardaí carrying Uzi machine guns.

"I could see all the people out on the street looking at all of us go by, and then this helicopter flying over the courthouse, waiting for us."

The barricades opened up at the back of the courthouse and they drove into a yard at the back of the court. The army snipers watched carefully as Rupert was led into the courthouse.

As they waited, he posed for a photo at the entrance to the court cells. Further down that corridor, McKevitt was pacing up and down. The photo was like a hunter and his catch.

Then Rupert and the gardaí sat in the courthouse kitchen, made tea, and waited.

Everyone who entered the Special Criminal Court went through a metal detector and had to sign their name. By 9.30am, there was already an overflow of people. Journalists complained that they were being placed in the public gallery, in a 200-year-old courtroom with bad acoustics.

Ruairí Ó Brádaigh, the Continuity IRA and Republican Sinn Féin leader, arrived, eager to hear what would be said about his group, and what McKevitt had said about him. Bernadette Sands McKevitt arrived with her supporters, reiterating to pet reporters that her husband was being framed by the British.

Ordinary members of the public squeezed past the media, curious to see the American spy and the spectacle that would follow. By 10.30, the survivors of the Omagh bomb had arrived, on a rented bus. Like Sands McKevitt and Ó Brádaigh, they too would come every day of the trial. With them in the public gallery were Real IRA members, MI5 agents and the FBI.

Never in the history of the court, which had heard hundreds of terrorism cases, had victim and perpetrator, British and Irish, nationalist and royalist come into such close proximity.

Several of the Omagh victims spotted Bernadette Sands McKevitt when they came in. They had lost babies, grandparents, children, mothers, fathers, sons and daughters and the woman primarily responsible for glibly justifying their deaths was right beside them. The commotion started almost immediately.

"You fucking murderer," said one woman. "I hope you're proud of yourself, you fucking murdering bitch," said another.

One of Bernadette's supporters told her to ignore them and told them to sit down.

Until now, Bernadette had lived in a bubble, surrounded by Real IRA supporters in Dundalk and South Armagh. For the first time, she was being confronted with the truth of what her group represented, what they had done. She stared ahead and said nothing.

Michael Gallagher, leader of the then-titled Omagh Victims Group, lost his 21-year-old son, Aiden, in the bombing. He remembers the confrontations. "It had nothing to do with me. Some of the female members of our group confronted her. I didn't want anything to do with her, but yes, there was some disturbance – how couldn't there be?"

McKevitt was led by prison officers from his cell and up into the courtroom. It was an old-fashioned courtroom, with a dock for the accused that had to be climbed into, with a little door that shut behind it. McKevitt refused to get in. As a republican, he would not be treated as a criminal. He would sit beside the box, but not in it.

It was the first time that the general public saw McKevitt, except for photos of him with a cap low over his face and his collar cut up over his chin. He was wearing a suit and gold-rimmed glasses and was now balding. He took out a notebook and pen. Every word would be studiously noted and dissected. "He wrote angrily," one journalist noted at the time.

Barrister George Birmingham was leading the case against McKevitt.

Birmingham, a quick-witted and affable veteran of the criminal courts, had a habit of putting his foot up on the seat in front of him and resting his arm on it. He spoke softly and methodically. There was no jury to impress, only the three judges.

"I now call David Rupert," he said.

Rupert was brought out from downstairs and walked up into the witness stand, which was as awkward to get into as the dock. He squeezed in. The wigs and the gowns of the barrister, the old wooden, creaking furniture – it added an air of gravitas, of history, not seen in American courtrooms.

This was where some of the biggest names in Irish rebel history had been tried – Robert Emmet, Wolfe Tone. Some of the senior garda in the country wanted to move out of the building – too much history, too much historical legacy to which the Real IRA should not be laying claim.

The gardaí had instructed Rupert on courtroom behaviour in Ireland. No matter who was asking the questions, he must only answer to the three judges and say, "Yes, your honour," and, "No, your honour."

Rupert: "From the beginning, I was determined not to look around the courtroom, because I knew Mickey was there and I knew he'd be staring at me. And I knew there would be a lot of people and I'd get real nervous because I'm not good at public speaking. I tried not to look, but at the corner of my eye, I was taking it all in."

Birmingham looked around the courtroom. "And, for the court, could you identify Michael McKevitt?" Rupert was forced to look through the mass of people. His eyes met with McKevitt's cold stare. McKevitt's barrister had told him not to react to this moment, so he just looked. Rupert pointed. "That's him there, in the body of the courtroom, between the two garda."

"For the record, Mr Rupert is pointing at the accused, Mr McKevitt."

Rupert lingered a second longer and looked away.

"And, Mr Rupert," can you outline to the court where you are from?"

He began to detail his life story, the trucking years and how he met Linda Vaughan in the Harp and Thistle and how she introduced him to the Murrays in Sligo and Joe O'Neill in Bundoran. The media, and McKevitt, wrote non-stop as he described Ed Buckley walking into the truck plaza in Chicago.

At 1pm, the court broke for lunch. TV and radio journalists hurried from the courtroom to do outside broadcasts. The BBC, Ulster Television, RTE, Channel 4. It was the first time that the public came to hear about David Rupert's life story and his unlikely meeting with Linda Vaughan. The tale wasn't just a court case formula, it was the FBI and MI5 and intrigue and deception. It made for a great news story. Rupert's giant frame and 300 pounds added to the fascination.

Over lunch, Rupert ate in the dingy kitchen with the FBI agents and his heavily armed garda minders, oblivious to the news outside.

One of the married FBI agents had already spotted a beautiful, petite MI5 agent in court. He had met her at one of the trial planning meetings in London and he was besotted by her upper-class accent and big, bright eyes. He wanted to find some way to talk to her during the trial. The fact that she was a spy added to the intrigue.

"Jesus," said Rupert. "Anything else going on in here?"

In the afternoon, Hugh Hartnett, the senior defence counsel, was arguing about how Rupert's huge volume of emails to the FBI and MI5 should be introduced to the court. He also wanted MI5 agents to give evidence and be cross-examined. The prosecution objected. The gardaí had taken statements from Paul and the other MI5 agents and the British ambassador to Ireland would give evidence that they were genuinely MI5 agents. It was the first time in Irish legal history that the British ambassador would take the stand in a criminal case.

Hartnett, tall and bearded and sharp, was known as a furious battler in court and one of the best legal minds working the Special Criminal Court.

Rupert watched him intensely as he spoke.

"I could see this guy was going to be tough. He was good at his job. I just tried not to be nervous," Rupert said.

Hartnett had discovered that Rupert had planned to write a book with Abdon Pallasch, a journalist with the *Chicago Sun-Times* who had a keen interest in Irish affairs. He was seeking disclosure of all of Pallasch's interview notes and tapes, to see if Rupert's version of events were different on tape to his official statement in court or to the gardaí.

It had opened a separate legal battle in Chicago, with Pallasch and the *Sun-Times* arguing their First Amendment right to free speech, free from government interference. They lost and were forced to hand over the tapes and notes.

Hartnett told the court he would be introducing the interview notes to test contradictions in Rupert's evidence.

When court broke at 4pm, Rupert was exhausted from all the legal argument. The convoy drove out again at speed, breaking into smaller and smaller groups until one unmarked, bullet-proof car reached the safehouse.

Rupert watched the 6 O'Clock News with the FBI agents and the gardaí. They were the first item on the news. "There you are!" said Mark of the entourage of cars and motorbikes driving towards court.

Early the next morning, one of the gardaí brought the newspapers over to the house.

The *Irish Times* headline ran, "All Eyes On the Spy from the FBI", about how the courtroom was transfixed by David Rupert's tale of spying.

Again, the roads were blocked off all the way to court. He looked out of the window to the hundreds of people watching the entourage drive by. When they got to the court, there were barriers blocking the back entrance. A junior garda was at the gate. He refused to move the barrier because he had been told not to let anyone through. One of the Emergency Response Unit gardaí shouted at him to "move that fucking gate now". He refused. In front of the media, the car sped forward, smashing the barrier out of the way. "We all thought it was hilarious," said Rupert. "This garda telling us, 'But I've been told that nobody gets in.' A little too eager in his job."

After three days of the entourage going back and forth to the court, with ever-increasing crowds packed into the public gallery, David Rupert had finished giving direct evidence.

Now the cross-examination would begin. It was already shaping up to be the longest cross-examination in Irish legal history. There was a lot for Hartnett to discuss – seven years of spying, four wives, two bankruptcies. Volumes of statements – Rupert's 40-page written statement to the gardaí versus his direct evidence to George Birmingham, all measured against everything dug up by private detectives and what he said to the book's author.

Rupert is adamant that he supplied most of the material for cross-examination himself. "The media think that the defence dug up all this negative stuff about me. They didn't. I had to write a disclosure statement and I had to include every bad thing I'd done – anything that would damage my reputation, any illegal act, anything that would make me look bad. I included everything about my marriages, about the bankruptcies, nothing was left out. I wanted to make sure that there were no surprises."

For the cross-examination, there were more reporters than usual. Everyone wanted to hear what dirt the defence had on Rupert.

Hartnett knew this was the biggest moment of his career.

"Mr Rupert," he began. He had a habit of looking sideways, as if addressing some incredulous, invisible jury.

A stack of documents lay on the table in front of Hartnett – Rupert's garda statement, his company records, hours of transcripts of his interviews with Abdon Pallasch, Rupert's disclosure statement.

Hartnett's greatest asset, which he was determined to keep, was that nobody had any photographic evidence that Rupert and McKevitt had ever met.

He looked at the judges as he spoke. How come a full team of gardaí sat outside the bomb-makers' meeting in Dundalk, supposedly saw McKevitt and Rupert together, yet mysteriously never took any photographs?

The defence was determined to concede no ground. They stuck rigidly to the story that Rupert and McKevitt had never met, that Rupert was a dishonest person who would do anything for money and had fed fanciful spy stories to the FBI and MI5.

Every aspect of Rupert's life was to be turned over, analysed, dissected, reviewed and held up to the court as evidence of dishonesty.

It began with his childhood.

He grew up in a "Christian Protestant New York household" where he learned the importance of honesty, Rupert said.

When Hartnett snapped back that Rupert didn't learn the Ten Commandments very well, judging from his business record, Rupert kept in his anger. He looked towards McKevitt and said that the Ten Commandments clearly forbade murder.

"Hartnett dropped that line of questioning immediately. He knew if he went down the religious route, I'd bring McKevitt along with us," Rupert recalled.

As he had hoped, Hartnett suggested Rupert must be a smuggler across the Canadian border.

Rupert was waiting. The only thing he'd ever smuggled from Canada were fireworks, when his father asked him to stuff them in his pockets when he was a kid.

Hartnett soon jumped on to Rupert's four marriages.

In a country where divorce had been legal for just seven years, Rupert's wives were a source of great public fascination.

At one point, Rupert was talking about one of his exes.

"And which particular wife was that?" asked Hartnett.

"Number Two," said Rupert. Some in the public gallery erupted into giggles. One of the judges smiled broadly and tried to keep in the laughter.

Diarmuid O'Sullivan felt that the defence was making a major mistake by denying that Rupert and McKevitt had ever met.

"It was very silly of the defence to go down that road," he said. "Far be it from me to make judgment calls on how the defence run their case but I don't think you should be disagreeing with the obvious."

Much of what Hartnett threw at Rupert was minor, or was different in an American context, such as bankruptcy filings.

Some of what the defence had on him, and which Rupert had disclosed, required serious explanation. How come, in the 1970s, his co-driver was in the company of a 16-year-old girl?

Rupert explained that he had told the driver that giving a lift to a runaway hitchhiker was a bad idea but the guy didn't listen.

Hartnett wouldn't let it go.

"It really had nothing to do with me," said Rupert, who was able to show that the police had no problem with him, only his driving companion.

Days and days went by, accusation after accusation. Two bounced cheques. No charges. Didn't pay his father-in-law back. Didn't have the money at the time. His driver was involved in a fatal accident. It wasn't the driver's fault. What was he doing in the Cayman Islands, a well-known tax haven? On holiday with Linda Vaughan.

How come the Drowes burned down just after he owned it?

Rupert thought that one was ridiculous. "I said to Hartnett, 'Listen, if a business owner is going to burn down some place, it's for insurance. I didn't have a penny insurance on the place so I would gain nothing from its destruction and I wasn't even renting it at the time.'"

At the end of the first day of cross-examination, Rupert was depressed. He didn't expect the process to be so searing, for Hartnett to be so aggressive.

He ate in silence in the safe house. So did the FBI.

"I don't like to be in front of people. I don't like being in the spotlight and there is nothing as public as being in the witness box.

"I was shook up that night. One of the garda said that Hartnett was always going to throw everything he had at me on the first day, anything he thinks will get to me.

"By the second day, I'd found my sea legs and I was able to hold my nerve. By the third day, I was able to figure it all out."

As the days of cross-examination dragged on, Rupert noticed an American attorney on the defence benches. He jokingly called her the Wicked Witch of the East. The FBI agents were dismayed to see her. She specialised in FBI cases and had beaten them in the famous Wen Ho Lee case, in which a Taiwanese-American scientist working at a New Mexico nuclear installation had been cleared of espionage.

The FBI discovered that she had hired one of the private detectives, Paco Chavez, to dig up information on Rupert.

It was Rupert who was now trying to reassure the FBI.

"The FBI were real worried about her. I kept saying, 'There's nothing I'm gonna say that's not the truth.'"

He began to notice the size of the defence team.

"They had enough lawyers with them to choke a horse, it was unbelievable. There was one in the benches, I don't know what his role was but I used to call him the Dweeb. He would sit there pulling faces, with his eyes wide open and his mouth open, trying to throw me off, but I kept my eyes on Hartnett."

At the end of each day, journalists tried to get close to Rupert but they were blocked by gardaí. As the days went by, the journalists hoping for an interview with Rupert became more and more female, as his womanising days became a feature of the defence evidence.

"It was never going to work," said Rupert. "Even if I wanted to talk to them, the FBI and the prosecutors would never have allowed it."

Under Hartnett's increasingly testy cross-examination, he agreed that he once owned a maroon Rolls-Royce, which he drove around Massena. That was when he was going well in trucking and it wasn't new, he said. He also drove a DeLorean, but said it was too small for him. Again, it drew sniggers from some in the public gallery. Some of the press were smiling broadly at the image of 6ft 7 Rupert trying to impress the ladies in a tiny gull-winged DeLorean.

Hartnett went for it: "Isn't it true that people say the DeLorean was "built by a crook and driven by a crook?"

"I don't know," said Rupert.

He was pressed and pressed about his first wife – a decent, religious woman – and why they broke up.

Rupert said that their relationship wasn't easy at times and that she could be "a bit of a bitch".

The loan from his father-in-law drew one of the flintiest exchanges from Hartnett.

When Hartnett pressed him, Rupert retorted that non-payment of the loan was far short of murder.

He looked over at McKevitt, the only time he did so in cross-examination.

The private detectives had discovered that wife number two, Julie Smith, was now a masseuse. Hartnett pressed the point.

"Hartnett was trying to make out that Julie, a masseuse, must be involved in something more than massage. That was ridiculous. She's totally straight up. He was just throwing stones. Shots like that made me more comfortable because there was nothing to it."

Through it all, McKevitt wrote and wrote into notebooks, sharing his thoughts with the defence every day. Mickey McKevitt, Real IRA leader, was now replaced by Mickey McKevitt, legal analyst. With his legal pad, suit and gold-rimmed glasses, he had transformed himself into what he saw as a great legal mind.

As the cross-examination went on, one republican prisoner noted, Mickey's demeanor changed. He was hoping that Hartnett could make that big land and destroy Rupert's credibility, but nothing major had emerged.

A week into their exchanges, Rupert and Hartnett had broken the record for the longest cross-examination in Irish legal history and still there was no end in sight. The court was looking concerned. The judges began to ask, politely, how much longer the defence expected to keep Mr Rupert.

A strange Stockholm Syndrome began to envelope Rupert. The longer the cross-examination went on, the more he seemed to gain respect for Hartnett, like two heavyweight boxers hugging each other through a gruelling 12th round.

"The way I saw it," said Rupert, "Hartnett knew Mickey was guilty but had to go out there and do his best. I liked him. He was just doing his job and he was damn good at it."

When they moved on to his meetings with McKevitt, Rupert's recall of number plates and the exact position of people in a room appeared to throw the defence. He wasn't being coached, he said, it was the memory techniques he learned in school to overcome his reading problems.

"I was probably a whole lot smarter than they thought. They expected this dumb truck driver and they had no previous contact with me," said Rupert. "I had an excellent recall and I also tried to be likeable, which they also probably weren't expecting."

By the end of the first week, the media were reporting it as not so much as a cross-examination as a never-ending freak show. David Rupert, four times married, twice bankrupt, who didn't pay his dentist, attempted to be a professional wrestler, and tried to set up illegal gambling with the mafia.

David Rupert who was womanising in South Florida when he hit upon an IRA lobbyist, then became an FBI agent.

Some reporters, consciously or subconsciously, sided with McKevitt – because his sins were already well known, there was nothing to gain professionally from uncovering them.

Rupert, on the other hand, was a huge man in a tiny DeLorean, a blue-collar man with aspirations, stumbling through life trying to find the answer to some unknown question.

Outside of court, his affability was still winning people over. By the second week, he was good friends with the Emergency Response Unit who escorted him to court. On the way to trial one day, one of them mentioned that Bobby Sands was a good republican and an honourable man, whereas Bernadette Sands and her personal army were not good people.

The comment shocked Rupert. "Here I am with these guys, armed with Uzis, and one of them is telling me what a good guy Bernadette's brother was. I thought, 'Jeez, you generally don't hear that at anti-terrorism trials in the US.' There was this ambiguity in Ireland that worried me at times. I knew Mickey and James Smyth enough to know that if they could find a way to kill me, they would do it."

Hartnett asked Rupert how he reconciled moral teachings in school with his business dealings with a mafia lieutenant like Guy Scalzi. "I had no known association with mob lieutenants," he said.

He could see that Hartnett tended to back off if Rupert switched it from his own life to McKevitt's, so he tried to hit back with references to the IRA.

Asked if Scalzi looked like a mob lieutenant, he replied: "I have no idea. That would be like asking what a republican would look like, they come in all shapes and sizes." At one point, Hartnett managed to rile him. Rupert was very sensitive about the humiliating bankruptcy of his trucking company.

Hartnett asked him who paid for him to lie on a beach in Florida, sipping a cocktail and smoking a cigar after the bankruptcy. Rupert retorted that the question was "improper and wrong".

"When I was in Florida I would have had for all intents and purposes no money," he said sharply.

Feeling he might be admonished by the judges, Hartnett came as close to an apology to Rupert as he would ever go. "I withdraw the cigar," he said.

"By 11 or 12 days, it was getting old," said Rupert.

Hartnett wasn't able to get Rupert sufficiently annoyed but he did land some good comedy lines.

He challenged Rupert on whether he was going to make a movie about his life as a spy. Instead of Rupert the Bear titles like *Rupert and the Giant Sunflower* and *Rupert and the Snow Globe*, the next works of fiction could be "Rupert and the IRA" or "Rupert and the Mafia", he said.

Hartnett: "The Rupert the Bear comparison line was an obvious one to make – it seemed to go down well."

Liz Walsh, now herself a barrister, remembers hearing it with a group of other journalists. "It was the funniest line of the trial. We were falling sideways laughing. Hartnett was good at little asides like that."

Every weekend, Rupert would be brought to the Irish air force's base in Baldonnel under heavy escort and flown by royal plane to the American airbase in England. Most weekends, if he and the FBI men wanted, Scotland Yard would take them on day trips – more palaces and gardens – always with heavily armed detectives walking close by.

Every Sunday night, he was flown back again to Baldonnel and then taken again by escort to the safe house in Dublin.

Every Monday morning, he was back in court again. In the second week, Hartnett appeared to get more and more frustrated, and the witty asides disappeared.

One day, Hartnett was doing his characteristic head turn to the side while asking a question, as if addressing the imaginary jury of his mind.

Rupert complained to the judge. "I said, 'Look, the defence counsel doesn't have to look at me but I need to know what he is saying'. Hartnett got mad, he just sat down. The judge looked over at him and said, 'Are you finished?'

"Hartnett said he wasn't done yet. And he pops back up and the judge tells him that when a defence counsel sits down it usually means they are done. I liked that from the judge."

On the eleventh day of cross-examination, it was finally winding down.

Hartnett had closed his case. He talked with another barrister and a solicitor and then asked if he could have one more question. The chief judge asked Rupert if he accepted. "Sure, go ahead," said Rupert.

Hartnett stood up and said that he had to put it to Rupert that he had never met McKevitt and that all his evidence was a concocted lie.

Rupert, looking a little stunned, retorted, "That's foolishness."

That was the end of cross-examination. There was a palpable sense of relief in the courtroom, not least among the journalists, who had grown weary of the ordeal.

40 witnesses were lined up to confirm Rupert's story, including Martin Callinan and Diarmuid O'Sullivan, who testified that Rupert and McKevitt were seen together, and Breda McNulty, wife of the owner of the Drowes, who confirmed that Rupert did have the lease, as he had claimed.

Rupert didn't wait to hear their evidence. He was exhausted and eager to go home. MI5 signalled ahead. A Hercules transport plane, with SAS soldiers on board, flew to Cork, in the south of the country. The Irish air force did not want a British military plane on its runways and flying out of Cork would switch the routine.

While still in the court building, packing up to go, Rupert asked for a garda baseball cap as a souvenir for Dan, the former next-door neighbour and banker, who collected them.

There happened to be a uniformed garda standing near him. Callinan asked him for his peaked, formal garda hat and gave it to Rupert. "I'll get him another one," he said.

Rupert got into the bomb-proof car with the Uzi-carrying emergency response unit. A car led ahead of them and there were two cars behind and two garda motorbike escorts, blaring sirens as they drove from Dublin all the way to the very south of the country.

Rupert knew this was the last trip he was ever going to make in Ireland. He looked out at the green fields and the people stopping to watch the motorcade.

Along the way, there was a sudden emergency.

"We were on our way out of Dublin, with three or four cars in line. Suddenly there were two guys on a motorcycle, with dark helmets on. I didn't see them at first but the gardaí did. They were trying to come up beside us to pass us. So the garda escort car behind us pulled them up and blocked them." A garda jumped out, holding a gun and flashed his badge.

"I never knew if it was bad guys or just two guys on a motorcycle trying to check us out," said Rupert. "But they were very close to us, coming up on the inside."

At Cork Airport, they got out of the car.

There was a delay while the British turned the Hercules. On board would be three passengers – an MI5 agent, Rupert and Mark, the FBI agent.

"Everyone else on board were SAS who were deployed for us. They were worried about a potential rocket attack, so they told us the plane was loaded with chaff, which is big loads of distracting material that can be released if there is a missile coming our way."

It was time for Rupert to go home. He shook hands with the gardaí. "Fair play to you, boy," said one of them.

The ramp on the back of the Hercules was open and he walked up it, holding his garda hat and travel bag, never to return to Ireland. He turned around for a last wave and the ramp door lifted.

CHAPTER 25

Paxil. Valium. Prozac. Zoloft.

The drugs began to mount.

Post-trial was the worst time of Rupert's life. He, Maureen and Dorie were all taking prescription drugs to get over the fear and anxiety, and most of all for David, the ennui.

Dorie, the most stable and grounded of attorneys, found that she was physically dependent on Paxil.

"It was real hard to get off it. It was a struggle. Eventually, I got it down to liquid-form with smaller and smaller doses. It wasn't easy."

Rupert, who once had 50 trucks running for him and employed dozens of people, could never go back to trucking again. He was too much of a target for the Real IRA, too easy to find through the trucking networks. Even if Irish Americans didn't know which trucking company he was with, truckers could soon identify him by appearance.

"The FBI basically bought out the rest of my life. I got a lot of money, but I was bored and depressed."

By that point Rupert had made over $3m from his spying work, through direct payments, tax write-offs and expenses.

He spoke to Kathleen McChesney about it. She knew he needed adrenaline again. No matter how much he complained about the FBI, he needed them.

That summer, they were running an operation at the docks in Los Angeles to find huge drug routes coming from South America and to investigate a major fraud case.

The Chicago FBI office called the Los Angeles office – they had a man with more than 20 years' truck management experience, an excellent reputation as an on-the-ground agent and courtroom experience.

LA liked it straight away. They would set him up in a trucking office in the port. It would be far from the trucking networks of Chicago, New York or Boston, where he might be identified.

Rupert flew into Los Angeles and met Kathleen and another agent at a coffee shop.

They walked together to the FBI Los Angeles office and were led in. The office was set up in cubicles, and agents moved between them. As they stood in silence, Rupert overheard a conversation. One agent was talking to another about the port operations. "Yeah, we've a snitch coming in today about it," he said.

That old wound – being looked down on, being dismissed, compounded with the hurt that he would now be informing on his fellow truckers.

Rupert exploded. He started shouting. McChesney tried to calm him down. "How fucking dare he say that. I'm not a fucking snitch," he said. "If that's how professional they are, they can fuck it."

He stormed out of the building, leaving McChesney behind.

As the door slammed behind him, his nine years as an FBI agent ended.

Back in Ireland, McKevitt fired his defence team and withdrew from the trial. Until now, he had hoped that Hugh Hartnett would destroy Rupert, but it wasn't to be. McKevitt delivered a speech to the court, thanking Hartnett for his diligent work but said the odds were impossible, that MI5 and the FBI had set him up and there was no way he could get a fair trial.

It was clear that Rupert was being paid huge money and the trial made a mockery of justice.

He saw himself as a Nelson Mandela figure fighting the state.

"I withdraw with my dignity intact," he said. When he finished speaking, he handed his speech to a reporter. "For your records", he said, and left the court, back to the court cell with the prison officers.

For the rest of his trial, he was taken from the republican wing, to cheers, to the holding cell of the court, where he read books and newspapers, never to appear upstairs.

On 6 August 2003, the three-judge court delivered its 43-page ruling. McKevitt was brought to the court building but refused to come upstairs to listen, despite being ordered to do so. He sent up a written note denouncing Rupert, which was not read out in court.

Mr Justice Richard Johnson, presiding, said the court was satisfied that David Rupert was "a very truthful witness" with a considerable knowledge of republican groups. He had clearly identified McKevitt's house and other houses at Oakland Park, Dundalk, and Greenore Road, where he had attended Real IRA engineering and army council meetings.

"Overall he had very considerable knowledge of the facts to which he testified," Justice Johnson said.

The court was particularly struck by Rupert's ability to twice recall, 15 days apart in the trial, the exact seating arrangements in the Four Seasons Hotel in Monaghan the first time he met McKevitt along with Phil Kent, Michael Donnelly and Seamus McGrane.

The considerable sums he received from the FBI were as a paid agent and he was not an informer but someone employed to do a job.

The lengthy cross-examination had not in any way impugned the compelling evidence that Rupert presented to the court and he had not told any "deliberate untruths", the court said.

It was a resounding vindication for Rupert.

McKevitt became the first person in Ireland to be convicted of directing terrorism and was jailed for 20 years.

His sentencing was the main story on the news in Ireland that evening.

From his home and farm in the Midwest, Rupert got the news from Mark.

"I felt real happy after all that I went through with Hartnett. I told Maureen and she was thrilled too. Like I said at the time, if I had tax problems or went through three divorces, it didn't make McKevitt any less guilty of what he was doing."

In prison, McKevitt could see for the first time how hated the Real IRA were, and how small and irrelevant they were in the national political discussion.

Other imprisoned members of the army council, especially Liam Campbell, were adamant that the fight must go on.

A Real IRA member who was in prison at the time sums it up: "We couldn't believe it. As soon as McKevitt went to prison, he wanted to end the campaign immediately."

Was there an element of "my way or not at all"? "Absolutely, it was always like that with him. He couldn't handle not being in charge."

Tensions rose in the prison. There were now more than 150 dissident republicans inside.

Army council member: "I felt that prisoners had no right to tell the army leadership what to do. It was clear that the leadership wanted to keep fighting and he had no right to tell them what to do." A split occurred. Those loyal to McKevitt told those loyal to Campbell to get off their wing in Portlaoise.

Campbell was beaten with a snooker ball in a sock and taken to the prison hospital, then placed in solitary for his own protection.

McKevitt and his men blamed Campbell for disobeying orders, and for Omagh, from which the organisation had never fully recovered. Campbell blamed McKevitt for Rupert, whom he let in to the very centre of the organisation, despite everyone's misgivings.

McKevitt left the 32CSM, and so did Bernie, who had devoted the last six years to building it up.

Within a few months, McKevitt was allowed out to see his mother, who was dying.

For Americans, who didn't understand the nuances of Irish life, it was unthinkable.

Rupert: "I'm reading the Irish news sites online. McKevitt was close to his mother and she was dying. Over there, they just let you go home and see your mother. I got hold of the FBI and said, 'Hey, your man is out to see his mother.'"

It was just so funny to me, the difference in thinking. The FBI said, "That wouldn't be the case, that's not possible."

Then they called me back a few hours later and said, "Well, yeah. He went home to see his mother but he would have had guards with him and stuff."

They thought it would be like in the US with handcuffs and chains. I said, "No, he just went home to see his mother. That's the way they do it over there. There was so much the FBI didn't understand about how things operated in Ireland."

Rupert's name continued to make headlines in the Irish courts.

He was mentioned as the source of information for the arrest and conviction of Noel Abernethy for importing a huge haul of 15 million cigarettes seized by the Northern Ireland police.

Rupert was puzzled by this because he knew nothing about the day-to-day operations of the Real IRA's cigarette smuggling.

According to a very well-placed security source, Rupert's name was being used to cover for another mole deep within the Real IRA and who was well known to Abernethy's group.

Among those detained in this fresh wave of arrests was Gareth O'Connor, a Real IRA member from South Armagh. He was due to go on trial on Real IRA membership charges and had to sign on at Dundalk garda station every day.

One day in 2003, a group of men set up a checkpoint as he was returning from the garda station. He was never seen alive again. Two years later, O'Connor's badly decomposed body was found inside his car, which was dredged from the bottom of a canal in Newry. The Real IRA has since confirmed that it killed him as an informer and rolled his car into the canal.

"If I had been caught, that would have been me, but worse," said Rupert.

Very soon afterwards, and without McKevitt's strong personality to hold it together, the Real IRA began to disintegrate. McKevitt's faction called for peace.

The Real IRA itself split, with Seamus McGrane and several leaders carrying on as Óglaigh na hÉireann (Volunteers of Ireland). Until they finally called a ceasefire in 2018, they had killed nobody, but had blown the legs off an Irish-speaking, Catholic police officer to warn other Catholics not to join.

A separate group, the Real IRA, carried on, eventually coalescing with Republican Action Against Drugs and independent former Provisional IRA members in east Tyrone. A seemingly endless round of splits followed, and an endless round of new political fronts emerged, without popular support.

Things were getting worse for McKevitt.

The victims of the Omagh bombing sued him, Campbell, Colm Murphy and Seamus Daly, the Real IRA man who delivered the bomb.

Never, anywhere in history, had the victims of a terrorist outrage sued their bombers. The burden of proving that the defendants were members of the Real IRA and that they committed the Omagh bombing would be extremely difficult.

Murphy had been convicted of causing an explosion in Omagh but it was overturned on appeal because gardaí had falsified part of his confession.

The lawyers for the victims urgently needed Rupert to give evidence.

He, Mark Lundgren and Doug Lindsey flew to London for a meeting with MI5. The FBI's reaction to the conviction of McKevitt had been one of satisfaction; MI5's had been one of elation. Rupert was greeted as a hero by Paul and the other agents in the London office. Those who had worked on the case were eager to meet him.

"There was an older guy who had been covering Northern Ireland for MI5 for 25 years. He had been chasing McKevitt all that time. He was so excited to sit down with someone who was involved with McKevitt personally."

A dozen MI5 agents invited the visitors to the Buck's Club, made famous by PG Wodehouse and a favourite meeting place of the Tory establishment.

"One of the agents went up to the door. A little slot opened, like you see in the movies, and all 15 of us were let in. There was a picture of the Queen Mother on the wall. She had belonged to the club, I believe. It's a pretty uppity place."

One of the agents told David that MI5 was against him testifying in the Omagh case, because evidence might emerge that could give McKevitt grounds for appeal in the criminal case. Rupert: "He said, 'McKevitt is like a fish that has been caught and is mounted on the wall. We don't want to do anything that might make the fish come alive and jump off the wall.'

"It wasn't like I didn't want to give evidence, but both the FBI and M15 were really against it. But I worked very hard for the Omagh people to get the emails from M15 – I really insisted on it and that wasn't easy."

He met the Omagh lawyers in Chicago and swore an affidavit, confirming the emails as genuine and retelling what he knew about the Omagh bomb.

It was by far the most important piece of evidence in the lawsuit.

As Justice Declan Morgan, hearing the case, put it:

"By far the greatest volume of material upon which the plaintiffs rely is the hearsay evidence of David Rupert. David Rupert made an affidavit on 24 June 2004 in which he referred to various statements and emails generated by him and indicated his wish to give evidence in these proceedings."

Under public pressure, the Irish state allowed the Omagh lawyers to have a transcript of Rupert's evidence from the McKevitt trial in Dublin for free, saving them £40,000.

The court in Belfast accepted the transcript, and the emails, as evidence, to the many objections of the defendants' lawyers, who wanted Rupert in court for cross-examination.

The decision not to have Rupert give direct evidence was probably a wise one. The Belfast court accepted the 11 days of Rupert's cross-examination in the McKevitt criminal trial as evidence that his version of events had been adequately tested.

In 2009, Justice Morgan ruled in favour of the Omagh families, in a global precedent. Rupert's evidence was credible, he said, and he cited the many times that McKevitt, Campbell and Murphy had discussed the Omagh bomb with him.

"The suggestion by McKevitt that he could not remember meeting Rupert, which he made at interview after arrest, is plainly false, as is the case put at his criminal trial that he never met Rupert," he ruled.

He also said that Rupert's evidence that McKevitt was seeking a foreign sponsor showed that he was controlling the Real IRA and so was personally responsible for the Omagh bomb.

Rupert's emails about Murphy were "significant and cogent evidence" that Murphy was involved in the Omagh bomb, the court ruled, while the emails also showed that Campbell's involvement was beyond doubt.

McKevitt, Campbell, Murphy and Daly were collectively ordered to pay the Omagh victims £1.6m. Michael Gallagher and the other campaigners hugged each other outside the courtroom in Belfast. It became a global story.

Other good news came through. The FBI Chicago office had applied to the federal Rewards for Justice Fund, which gave money to civilians who helped the war on terror.

In the summer of 2005, it paid out $5m to David Rupert without declaring it publicly.

Still, he was waiting on a final lump sum from MI5.

Norman Baxter, a senior Northern Ireland police officer, came over to Las Vegas to meet Rupert, along with an M15 agent and an officer from Scotland Yard. Rupert helped as much as he could with the Omagh investigation and, over drinks, they discussed the final payment from MI5.

Rupert won't say how much it was. Baxter says it was "generous but dwarfed by what Rupert got from the FBI". It was about $750,000, an informed source said. To date, Rupert has received about $10 million in total from US and UK authorities.

Since then, he has lost some major sums of money on the stock market, mostly trading on oil futures.

"I came into the market and then oil shale came along and prices went south. I got burned but we're still comfortable," he said.

With the money, he was able to buy Dorie a house and his sister Wanda a car.

He also gave Maureen and Dorie weapons training out the back of the house, in case McKevitt's US supporters, or James Smyth, caught up with them.

Family photos of the target practice show Maureen, Dorie and David posing with their guns and firing at a cardboard man.

Only David has a gun today.

Dorie: "I do not want a gun under any circumstances, and my mom, no way. Outside of practice, the only time she fired a gun was twice, indoors, by accident. I don't want us having anything to do with it."

The threat is not idle. In 2008, according to a Northern Ireland police source, an Irish American republican visited a leading dissident paramilitary leader in prison and was asked to try to get David Rupert's social security number in preparation for an assassination.

The police passed on the information to the FBI, who contacted Rupert immediately.

They didn't tell him what it was about, only that there was a "credible threat" to his life and to be extra cautious.

He and Maureen did more target practice and continued their life of relaxation, marijuana, enjoying friends' company and holidays. Both found that marijuana helped reduce their anxiety since trial and its use became almost medicinal.

Maureen complains repeatedly that she cannot visit her grandson at his kindergarten. The other grandparents go and have lunch with their grandchildren, but not Maureen, because entering the school grounds would require a background check. David believes that a background request from the school would be flagged by the FBI which would then call the school and start asking questions about who was checking out Maureen Rupert.

Dorie sighs. She would love her son to spend his lunchtimes with her mother. "This is what I call a David Created Problem. I don't see any problem with it whatsoever. It's like with family events David doesn't want to go to, suddenly the security issue is a problem."

Despite friction over kindergarten and family events, David and Maureen seem still very much in love, and continue to make each other laugh. Writing this book brought back many memories of Ireland, and Maureen, in particular, would like to return some day, if incognito.

In 2013, Rupert was invited to FBI headquarters to receive an award for being one of their greatest civilian agents. He flew to Langley, Virginia, where he posed with Kathleen McChesney, Mark Lundgren and others while getting a certificate of appreciation. It was one of the happiest days of his life. He had what he craved all his life – official respectability and encouragement.

"It was kind of the end of everything. I know my family were real proud too. Not in a million years could you recreate the circumstances of how this all happened. But there I was."

On Easter Sunday 2016, while hundreds of thousands of people were marking the 100th anniversary of the 1916 Easter Rising with official parades in Dublin, Mickey McKevitt was released from prison, to much comment in the newspapers. He had no regrets, he told the newspapers. "Armed struggle is the only language the Brits understand," he said.

I called at his house in Blackrock to see if he would talk to me about David Rupert and the Omagh civil case. From his bellicose statement upon release from prison, I wondered if he was genuinely committed to peace, or just holding it in until he got a reduction in sentence for good behaviour.

His daughter answered the door. I could hear him talking in the back room.

"Absolutely no way," she said to an interview request, as he and Bernie were sitting down to dinner. Absolutely no way he would do it on another day, she said.

There was an awkward silence between us, so I shrugged my shoulders. "Well," I said. "I tried."

"Yeah, you tried," she said. "And let me tell you something – you're a brave man."

I thanked her and walked to the Blackrock mini market at the end of the street. A 19-year-old woman was serving behind the counter. I was hoping she could supply me with some information on the McKevitt family but she had never heard of them. She totted up my total for an orange juice and a newspaper. "Mickey McKevitt," I said. "Lives just up there. Just got out of prison. "Oh yeah," she said blankly. "I think my dad said something about that."

I felt disappointed and then an enormous sense of relief. Her generation knows nothing of political violence, nor should they. Rupert got his $10m and fame. McKevitt got what he deserves: anonymity.

*****

For me, this book was never about David Rupert. He is an anomaly, an alien, who by a strange set of circumstances fell through a portal into Ireland and who, more than anyone else, helped bring a final end to our centuries-long national nightmare.

This book, really, is about Ireland. There were invasions from England for 600 years, centuries of oppression and a famine when a million died. A rebellion freed the south but the north teetered on the edge of violence until it exploded in the late 1960s. Co-ordinated political violence came to an end with the imprisonment of McKevitt and Rupert's heavy infiltration of its army council and US fundraising wing.

What he has achieved should not be measured in FBI commendations, or MI5 medals, or in the financial rewards from the US government. It is measured, maybe, in the confidence and peace in the soul of Northern Ireland, long ravaged by sectarian violence that had gone on far longer than any possible political objective could have allowed. Ireland has been transformed since Rupert first visited with Linda Vaughan in 1992. Trendy coffee shops now line the fashionable new districts of Belfast, police patrol South Armagh, unionist ministers visit the south, unguarded. The country has peace and those who seek to destroy it have admitted defeat.

*****

I drive up to Tyrone to see Michael Gallagher, a mechanic who lost his son, Aiden, in the Omagh bombing.

Michael led the legal challenge to sue Real IRA leader Michael McKevitt.

Nobody in the world had ever successfully sued the perpetrators of a terrorist attack before and, at the time of writing, Michael and the other Omagh families are in the process of having McKevitt and the other three men declared bankrupt.

"David Rupert is the best agent there has been, it's that simple," Michael says. We are driving to Omagh Integrated Primary School to pick up Michael's two grandchildren, 11-year-old Finn and 8-year-old Fara. Unlike Michael, or me, the two children attend a co-religious Catholic/Protestant school, one of many that have sprung up on both sides of the Irish border.

We drive past Claire Gallagher's music school, where Fara and Finn had music classes. Claire was blinded for life in the Omagh bombing at age 15 and runs the largest music school in the town, teaching classical and traditional Irish music.

A Subway restaurant is just a few hundred feet up the street, and just beyond that is the memorial where the bomb exploded.

In the restaurant, over a sandwich and hot chocolate, Michael explains that the children recently met Prince Charles and his wife, Camilla.

"I met him before," he tells the kids. "Grandpa, are you famous?" says Fara. "Ammm... Infamous is probably the word," says Michael.

Fara breaks into an imitation of a posh British accent. "May I have some tea, please?" she says in Kensington English. Michael laughs. "That's very good. An actress, like your mother."

Finn says he wants to go home. They load up their clothes. Michael, one of 11 children, tells them that they had to share two rooms – one for all the boys, and one for all the girls, in a tiny house when he was growing up. "You should see their house," he says of his grandchildren. "Even a cinema room and a games room, isn't that right?"

"Tell David Rupert I said hello," he says, as they pile into the car. "Maybe I'll see him again, some day."

I watch them drive off, past the bomb memorial, take the next left and off home.

Back in the Subway, I take a call from an Omagh councilor, Sorcha McAnespy, who is all over the news on both sides of the border after politicians from the southern political party, Fianna Fail, came to Omagh to launch her as their first ever candidate north of the border. Party bosses were furious, and fired the two politicians from their frontbench positions. They didn't feel the north was ready yet for southern political parties.

I was hoping to meet Sorcha for coffee in the centre of Omagh but she is going up to Belfast for her daughter's birthday.

We talk local politics – Brexit, the move of southern political parties into the north, the collapsed northern parliament. "The north is so different for my daughter and her friends. They have no idea. When I think about…" She falters. "1998… the bomb… I lost my school friend, I lost… it was…" She breaks into loud, gasping sobs. The more she tries to stop crying, the worse it gets. She makes four or five attempts to finish the sentence and yet she can't. "We want to be known for more in this town than the bombing and yet you can't… young people have to know."

She is still trying to compose herself. I look around the Subway. Two women are serving teenagers from the integrated college. Shoppers walk up and down the street in front of us.

"I'm glad you are doing all of this," she says eventually, wiping her tears. "It's a lonely road you are following, covering all of this. Tell people what it's like, but also that we have changed. There are new shops now, new life in the town. It had to end somewhere. It had to end with someone."

*****

As I was finishing this book, I drove to meet David and Maureen in a small town in the American mid-west, a two-hour drive from their home.

I followed their car down a small country road past cornfields and the town's water tank to a restaurant.

David hulks over the other diners as he sits at a booth by the window.

Maureen is as lively as ever, peppering me with questions about Ireland. I tell her the book's fact-checker was very thorough. He wanted to know why she mentions in her diary that she lost 375 calories walking 3.5 miles as McKevitt was setting up the Iraqi arms deal, and only 225 calories walking the same distance the next day.

With glass of wine in hand, Maureen throws her head back laughing. "Jesus, I'm glad he didn't ask about my wine consumption!"

"Sounds like a math test," says David.

He has not contacted the FBI about our meeting – he prefers to keep them at a distance.

I look around the other booths in the diner. People come in and out – farmers, plumbers, and waitresses starting their shifts.

"I'd really love to come back to Ireland," says David, "but not in this lifetime."

I tell him that a senior Real IRA member asked me where he is living these days.

"Oh, I bet he did," he says. "But it's some Irish American, some guy trying to prove his worth to people in Belfast and Dundalk, that's who I've got to worry about."

I thank them for lunch. As they can never return to Ireland and I am rarely in the US, this is likely the last time we will ever meet.

David offers to lead me out onto the motorway, so I can find the way back to St Louis, Missouri, where I'm attending a funeral.

Their car pulls out and I follow them, one road leading into another, past more corn, farms and, over time, neon-lit box stores of American suburbia. David puts out his hand and signals for me to turn right onto the motorway to St Louis. I wave and turn, taking a last look as they drive down the motorway, their car blending in with hundreds of others. They pull left into the next lane and they are gone.

SUMMARY

Michael McKevitt, the Real IRA chief of staff, was jailed for 20 years, as a result of David Rupert's evidence.

His evidence and proposed testament was vital in jailing three Real IRA army council members for 30 years each for attempting to co-opt Saddam Hussein as their chief sponsor.

His testimony against McKevitt went on to form the largest single piece of evidence in the Omagh victims' lawsuit against four Real IRA bombers, the first such case in world history. Through Rupert, the court was able to directly link the Real IRA and three of the bombers to the murder of 31 people in Omagh.

His testimony also led to the Real IRA, Republican Sinn Fein and the Irish Republican Prisoner Welfare Association being declared terrorist groups in the US, ending their fundraising routes.

He identified over 100 people linked to dissident republican groups, and identified the weapon and fundraising paths in the US on which they relied.

He lives in America with his wife, Maureen, and two large mastiffs.

ACKNOWLEDGEMENTS

My very special thanks to Sarah Hale, for her patience, dedication and advice, without which this book could not have been written.

Also a very special thank you to David, Maureen and Dorie for allowing me into their lives, to read hundreds of their emails, read their diaries and press them through dozens of hours of interviews.

A big thank you to my very genial agent, Peter Buckman.

Also a big thank you to Betty and Wanda Rupert and the people of Madrid and Massena, and Barbara DeVane and Sean Nordquist in Florida.

Thank you to Jo Sollis and everyone at Mirror Books.

Thanks also to Patricia Packer for writing 'Home Is Where The Harp Is', which offered great background to my interview with Sean Nordquist.

A major thank you to retired Chief Superintendent Diarmuid O'Sullivan and thank you to Vincent Murray, Michael Donnelly, John McDonagh, Chris and Mary Fogarty and Liz Walsh.

A huge thank you to senior sources in the PSNI, MI5, FBI and Real IRA who cannot be named. It is an odd thing to spend months chasing someone down the street and end up having a four-hour dinner with them, discovering that they are not how you imagined them. I came away with a better understanding.

Finally, a big thank you to Thomas Rice, who was very kind to me when I called to his house asking him if he was an international assassin. He is not – his identity was stolen, and he makes a very nice cup of tea.

Also by Mirror Books

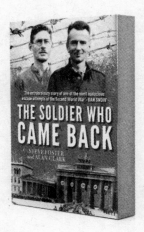

The Soldier Who Came Back

Steve Foster with Alan Clark

Northern Poland 1940. At the Nazi war camp Stalag XX-A, two men struck up an unlikely friendship that was to lead to one of the most daring and remarkable wartime escape stories ever told.

Antony Coulthard had a first-class honours degree from Oxford. Fred Foster, was the son of a Nottinghamshire bricklayer. This mismatched pair hatched a plan to disguise themselves as advertising executives working for Siemens. They would simply walk out of the camp, board a train - and head straight into the heart of Nazi Germany.

Their route into Germany was one that no one would think to search for escaped PoWs. This audacious plan involved 18 months of undercover work. They set off for the Swiss border taking notes of strategic interest while drinking beer with Nazi officers, just yards from Hitler's HQ.

But when they reached Lake Constance, with Switzerland within their reach, Antony crossed over into freedom, while Fred's luck ran out. What happened to them next is both heartbreaking and inspiring.

m
B

MIRROR BOOKS